fedora

Fedora 12

Virtualization Guide

The definitive guide for virtualization on Fedora

❖

Fultus™ *Books*

fedora

Fedora 12
Virtualization Guide

ISBN-10: 1-59682-183-3
ISBN-13: 978-1-59682-183-5

Copyright © 2009 Red Hat, Inc. and others. All rights reserved.

Cover design and book layout by Fultus Corporation

Published by Fultus Corporation

Publisher Web: *www.fultus.com*
Linbrary - Linux Library: *www.linbrary.com*
Online Bookstore: *store.fultus.com*
email: *production@fultus.com*

This material may only be distributed subject to the terms and conditions set forth in the Creative Commons ShareAlike 3.0 License (CC-BY-SA),
(the latest version is presently available at *http://creativecommons.org/licenses/by-sa/3.0/legalcode*).

Fedora and the Fedora Infinity Design logo are trademarks or registered trademarks of Red Hat, Inc., in the U.S. and other countries. Red Hat and the Red Hat "Shadow Man" logo are registered trademarks of Red Hat Inc. in the United States and other countries. All product names and services identified throughout this manual are trademarks or registered trademarks of their respective companies.

The author and publisher have made every effort in the preparation of this book to ensure the accuracy of the information. However, the information contained in this book is offered without warranty, either express or implied. Neither the author nor the publisher nor any dealer or distributor will be held liable for any damages caused or alleged to be caused either directly or indirectly by this book.

fedora

Fediora Release	Book Name	Edition
F12	Virtualization Guide	1
Authors		**Emails**
Christoph Curran		ccurran@redhat.com

Copyright © 2009 Red Hat, Inc.

Table of Contents

Legal Notice 8
Abstract 9
Preface 10
   1. About this book 10
   2. Document Conventions 10
      1.1. Typographic Conventions 10
      1.2. Pull-quote Conventions 12
      1.3. Notes and Warnings 13
   2. We Need Feedback! 13
Part I. Installation 14
Chapter 1. Installing the virtualization packages 15
   1.1. Installing KVM with a new Fedora installation 15
   1.2. Installing KVM packages on an existing Fedora system 19
Chapter 2. Virtualized guest installation overview 20
   2.1. Creating guests with virt-install 20
   2.2. Creating guests with virt-manager 21
   2.3. Installing guests with PXE 31
Chapter 3. Guest operating system installation procedures 36
   3.1. Installing Red Hat Enterprise Linux 5 as a para-virtualized guest 36
   3.2. Installing Red Hat Enterprise Linux as a fully virtualized guest 78
   3.3. Installing Windows XP as a fully virtualized guest 88
   3.4. Installing Windows Server 2003 as a fully virtualized guest 104
   3.5. Installing Windows Server 2008 as a fully virtualized guest 107
Part II. Configuration 119
Chapter 4. Virtualized block devices 120
   4.1. Creating a virtualized floppy disk controller 120
   4.2. Adding storage devices to guests 121
   4.3. Configuring persistent storage 124
   4.4. Add a virtualized CD-ROM or DVD device to a guest 126
Chapter 5. Shared storage and virtualization 128
   5.1. Using iSCSI for storing guests 128
   5.2. Using NFS for storing guests 128

Virtualization Guide

- 5.3. Using GFS2 for storing guests 128
- **Chapter 6. Server best practices** 129
- **Chapter 7. Security for virtualization** 130
  - 7.1. SELinux and virtualization 130
  - 7.2. SELinux considerations 132
- **Chapter 8. Network Configuration** 133
  - 8.1. Network address translation (NAT) with libvirt 133
  - 8.2. Bridged networking with libvirt 134
- **Chapter 9. KVM Para-virtualized Drivers** 137
  - 9.1. Installing the KVM Windows para-virtualized drivers 138
- **Part III. Administration** 146
- **Chapter 10. Managing guests with `xend`** 147
- **Chapter 11. KVM guest timing management** 149
- **Chapter 12. KVM live migration** 152
  - 12.1. Live migration requirements 153
  - 12.2. Share storage example: NFS for a simple migration 153
  - 12.3. Live KVM migration with virsh 154
  - 12.4. Migrating with virt-manager 156
- **Chapter 13. Remote management of virtualized guests** 167
  - 13.1. Remote management with SSH 167
  - 13.2. Remote management over TLS and SSL 168
  - 13.3. Transport modes 169
- **Part IV. Virtualization Reference Guide** 173
- **Chapter 14. Virtualization tools** 174
- **Chapter 15. Managing guests with virsh** 176
- **Chapter 16. Managing guests with the Virtual Machine Manager (virt-manager)** 185
  - 16.1. The open connection window 186
  - 16.2. The Virtual Machine Manager main window 187
  - 16.3. The Virtual Machine Manager details window 188
  - 16.4. Virtual Machine graphical console 189
  - 16.5. Starting virt-manager 190
  - 16.6. Restoring a saved machine 190
  - 16.7. Displaying guest details 192
  - 16.8. Status monitoring 198
  - 16.9. Displaying guest identifiers 200
  - 16.10. Displaying a guest's status 201
  - 16.11. Displaying virtual CPUs 202
  - 16.12. Displaying CPU usage 203

- 16.13. Displaying memory usage 204
- 16.14. Managing a virtual network 205
- 16.15. Creating a virtual network 207

Part V. Tips and Tricks 215
Chapter 17. Tips and tricks 216
- 17.1. Automatically starting guests 216
- 17.2. Changing between the KVM and Xen hypervisors...216
  - 17.2.1. Xen to KVM...216
  - 17.2.2. KVM to Xen...218
- 17.3. Using qemu-img...219
- 17.4. Overcommitting with KVM 221
- 17.5. Modifying /etc/grub.conf 223
- 17.6. Verifying virtualization extensions 224
- 17.7. Identifying guest type and implementation 225
- 17.8. Generating a new unique MAC address 225
- 17.9. Very Secure ftpd..226
- 17.10. Configuring LUN Persistence...227
- 17.11. Disable SMART disk monitoring for guests 228
- 17.12. Cloning guest configuration files 228
- 17.13. Duplicating an existing guest and its configuration file...229

Chapter 18. Creating custom libvirt scripts 231
- 18.1. Using XML configuration files with virsh..231

Part VI. Troubleshooting..232
Chapter 19. Troubleshooting...233
- 19.1. Loop device errors 233
- 19.2. Enabling Intel VT and AMD-V virtualization hardware extensions in BIOS 233

Appendix A. Additional resources 235
- A.1. Online resources...235
- A.2. Installed documentation..235

Appendix B. Revision History...237
Colophon 238
Glossary 240
Fedora 12 Official Documentation Collection...247

List of Tables

Table 10.1. xend configuration parameters 148
Table 13.1. Extra URI parameters 172
Table 15.1. Guest management commands 177
Table 15.2. Resource management options 177
Table 15.3. Miscellaneous options 177

Legal Notice

Copyright © 2009 Red Hat, Inc.

The text of and illustrations in this document are licensed by Red Hat under a Creative Commons Attribution–Share Alike 3.0 Unported license ("CC-BY-SA"). An explanation of CC-BY-SA is available at *http://creativecommons.org/licenses/by-sa/3.0/*. The original authors of this document, and Red Hat, designate the Fedora Project as the "Attribution Party" for purposes of CC-BY-SA. In accordance with CC-BY-SA, if you distribute this document or an adaptation of it, you must provide the URL for the original version.

Red Hat, as the licensor of this document, waives the right to enforce, and agrees not to assert, Section 4d of CC-BY-SA to the fullest extent permitted by applicable law.

Red Hat, Red Hat Enterprise Linux, the Shadowman logo, JBoss, MetaMatrix, Fedora, the Infinity Logo, and RHCE are trademarks of Red Hat, Inc., registered in the United States and other countries.

For guidelines on the permitted uses of the Fedora trademarks, refer to *https://fedoraproject.org/wiki/Legal:Trademark_guidelines*.

Linux® is the registered trademark of Linus Torvalds in the United States and other countries.

All other trademarks are the property of their respective owners.

Abstract

The Fedora 12 Virtualization Guide contains information on installation, configuring, administering, tips, tricks and troubleshooting virtualization technologies used in Fedora 12.

Preface

This book is the Fedora 12 Virtualization Guide. The Guide covers all aspects of using and managing virtualization on Fedora 12.

1. About this book

This book is divided into 7 parts:

- System Requirements
- Installation
- Configuration
- Administration
- Reference
- Tips and Tricks
- Troubleshooting

2. Document Conventions

This manual uses several conventions to highlight certain words and phrases and draw attention to specific pieces of information.

In PDF and paper editions, this manual uses typefaces drawn from the *Liberation Fonts*[1] set. The Liberation Fonts set is also used in HTML editions if the set is installed on your system. If not, alternative but equivalent typefaces are displayed. Note: Red Hat Enterprise Linux 5 and later includes the Liberation Fonts set by default.

1.1. Typographic Conventions

Four typographic conventions are used to call attention to specific words and phrases. These conventions, and the circumstances they apply to, are as follows.

`Mono-spaced Bold`

Used to highlight system input, including shell commands, file names and paths. Also used to highlight key caps and key-combinations. For example:

---

[1] *https://fedorahosted.org/liberation-fonts/*

> To see the contents of the file `my_next_bestselling_novel` in your current working directory, enter the `cat my_next_bestselling_novel` command at the shell prompt and press **Enter** to execute the command.

The above includes a file name, a shell command and a key cap, all presented in mono-spaced bold and all distinguishable thanks to context.

Key combinations can be distinguished from key caps by the hyphen connecting each part of a key combination. For example:

> Press **Enter** to execute the command.
>
> Press **Ctrl+Alt+F1** to switch to the first virtual terminal. Press **Ctrl+Alt+F7** to return to your X-Windows session.

The first paragraph highlights the particular keycap to press. The second highlights two key combinations (each a set of three keycaps with each set pressed simultaneously).

If source code is discussed, class names, methods, functions, variable names and returned values mentioned within a paragraph will be presented as above, in `mono-spaced bold`. For example:

> File-related classes include `filesystem` for file systems, `file` for files, and `dir` for directories. Each class has its own associated set of permissions.

Proportional Bold

This denotes words or phrases encountered on a system, including application names; dialog box text; labeled buttons; check-box and radio button labels; menu titles and sub-menu titles. For example:

> Choose **System > Preferences > Mouse** from the main menu bar to launch **Mouse Preferences**. In the **Buttons** tab, click the **Left-handed mouse** check box and click **Close** to switch the primary mouse button from the left to the right (making the mouse suitable for use in the left hand).
>
> To insert a special character into a **gedit** file, choose **Applications > Accessories > Character Map** from the main menu bar. Next, choose **Search > Find…** from the **Character Map** menu bar, type the name of the character in the **Search** field and click **Next**. The character you sought will be highlighted in the **Character Table**. Double-click this highlighted character to place it in the **Text to copy** field and then click the **Copy** button. Now switch back to your document and choose **Edit > Paste** from the **gedit** menu bar.

The above text includes application names; system-wide menu names and items; application-specific menu names; and buttons and text found within a GUI interface, all presented in proportional bold and all distinguishable by context.

Note the **>** shorthand used to indicate traversal through a menu and its sub-menus. This avoids difficult-to-follow phrasing such as 'Select **Mouse** from the **Preferences** sub-menu in the **System** menu of the main menu bar'.

`Mono-spaced Bold Italic` or ***Proportional Bold Italic***

Whether mono-spaced bold or proportional bold, the addition of italics indicates replaceable or variable text. Italics denotes text you do not input literally or displayed text that changes depending on circumstance. For example:

> To connect to a remote machine using ssh, type `ssh username@domain.name` at a shell prompt. If the remote machine is `example.com` and your username on that machine is john, type `ssh john@example.com`.
>
> The `mount -o remount file-system` command remounts the named file system. For example, to remount the `/home` file system, the command is `mount -o remount /home`.
>
> To see the version of a currently installed package, use the `rpm -q package` command. It will return a result as follows: `package-version-release`.

Note the words in bold italics above — username, domain.name, file-system, package, version and release. Each word is a placeholder, either for text you enter when issuing a command or for text displayed by the system.

Aside from standard usage for presenting the title of a work, italics denotes the first use of a new and important term. For example:

> When the Apache HTTP Server accepts requests, it dispatches child processes or threads to handle them. This group of child processes or threads is known as a *server-pool*. Under Apache HTTP Server 2.0, the responsibility for creating and maintaining these server-pools has been abstracted to a group of modules called *Multi-Processing Modules* (*MPMs*). Unlike other modules, only one module from the MPM group can be loaded by the Apache HTTP Server.

1.2. Pull-quote Conventions

Terminal output and source code listings are set off visually from the surrounding text.

Output sent to a terminal is set in `mono-spaced roman` and presented thus:

```
books         Desktop    documentation  drafts  mss     photos   stuff  svn
books_tests   Desktop1   downloads              images  notes    scripts  svgs
```

Source-code listings are also set in `mono-spaced roman` but add syntax highlighting as follows:

```java
package org.jboss.book.jca.ex1;

import javax.naming.InitialContext;
```

```
public class ExClient
{
   public static void main(String args[])
      throws Exception
   {
      InitialContext iniCtx = new InitialContext();
      Object          ref   = iniCtx.lookup("EchoBean");
      EchoHome        home  = (EchoHome) ref;
      Echo            echo  = home.create();

      System.out.println("Created Echo");

      System.out.println("Echo.echo('Hello') = " + echo.echo("Hello"));
   }
}
```

1.3. Notes and Warnings

Finally, we use three visual styles to draw attention to information that might otherwise be overlooked.

Note

Notes are tips, shortcuts or alternative approaches to the task at hand. Ignoring a note should have no negative consequences, but you might miss out on a trick that makes your life easier.

Important

Important boxes detail things that are easily missed: configuration changes that only apply to the current session, or services that need restarting before an update will apply. Ignoring a box labeled 'Important' won't cause data loss but may cause irritation and frustration.

Warning

Warnings should not be ignored. Ignoring warnings will most likely cause data loss.

2. We Need Feedback!

If you find a typographical error in this manual, or if you have thought of a way to make this manual better, we would love to hear from you! Please submit a report in Bugzilla: *http://bugzilla.redhat.com/bugzilla/* against the product **Fedora Documentation.**

When submitting a bug report, be sure to mention the manual's identifier: *Virtualization_Guide*

If you have a suggestion for improving the documentation, try to be as specific as possible when describing it. If you have found an error, please include the section number and some of the surrounding text so we can find it easily.

Part I.
Installation

Virtualization installation topics

These chapters describe setting up the host and installing virtualized guests with Fedora. It is recommended to read these chapters carefully to ensure successful installation of virtualized guest operating systems.

Chapter 1.
Installing the virtualization packages

1.1. Installing KVM with a new Fedora installation

This section covers installing virtualization tools and KVM package as part of a fresh Fedora 12 installation.

> **Need help installing?**
>
> The *Fedora 12 Installation Guide* (available from *http://docs.fedoraproject.org*) covers installing Fedora 12 in detail.

1. Start an interactive Fedora installation from the Fedora 12 Installation CD-ROM, DVD or PXE.

Fedora 12

2. Complete the other steps up to the package selection step.

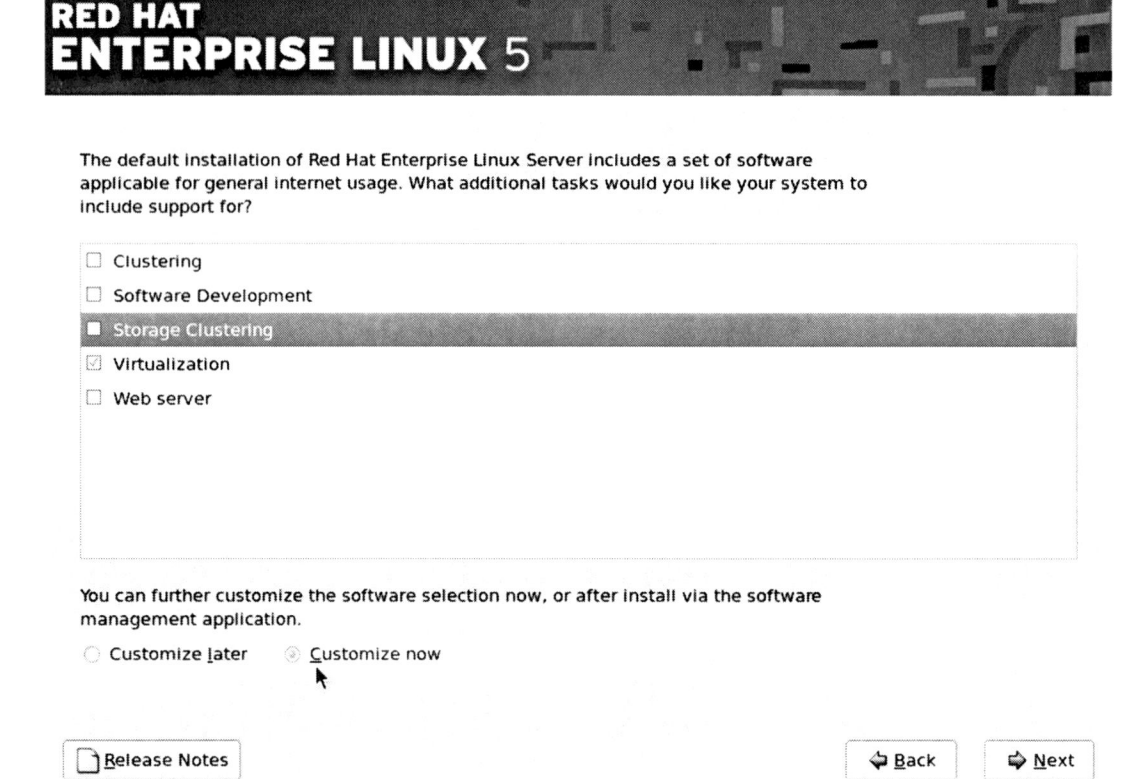

> **RED HAT ENTERPRISE LINUX 5**
>
> The default installation of Red Hat Enterprise Linux Server includes a set of software applicable for general internet usage. What additional tasks would you like your system to include support for?
>
> ☐ Clustering
> ☐ Software Development
> ■ Storage Clustering
> ☑ Virtualization
> ☐ Web server
>
> You can further customize the software selection now, or after install via the software management application.
>
> ○ Customize later   ◉ Customize now
>
> [Release Notes]   [Back]   [Next]

Select the **Virtualization** package group and the **Customize Now** radio button.

3. Select the **KVM** package group. Deselect the **Virtualization** package group. This selects the KVM hypervisor, `virt-manager`, `libvirt` and `virt-viewer` for installation.

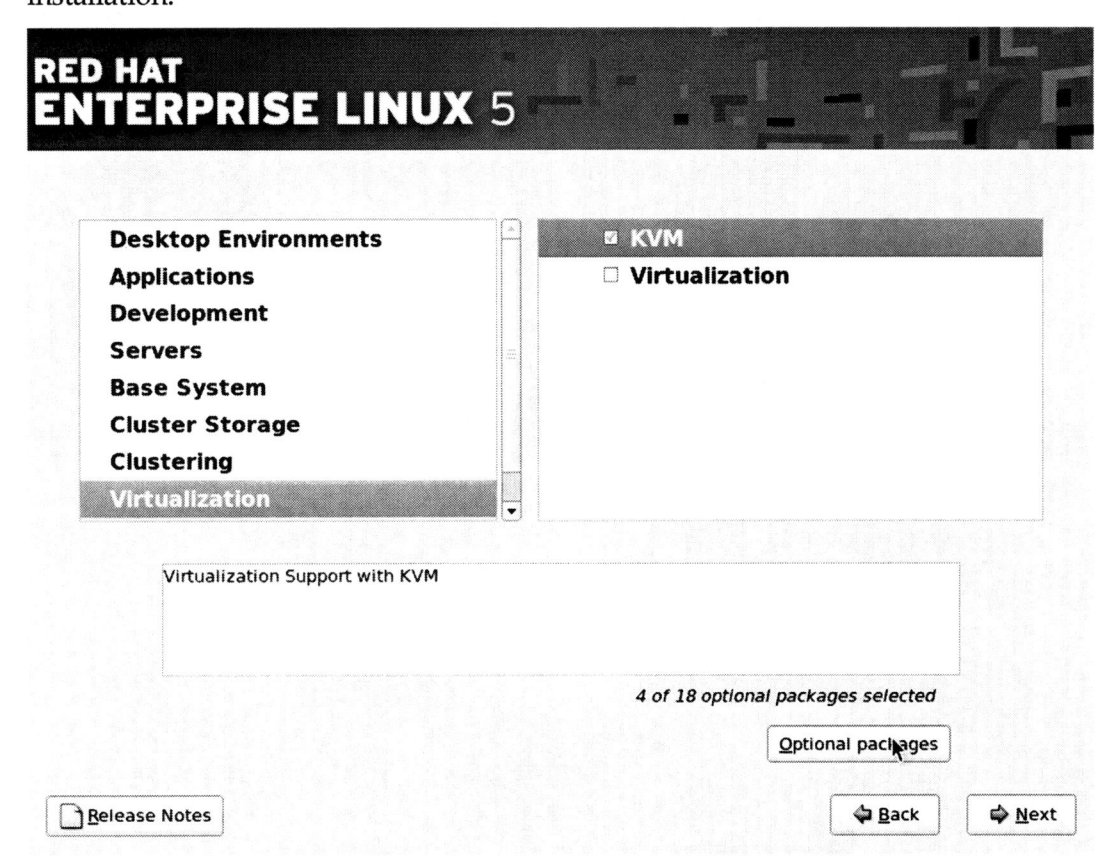

Fedora 12

4. Customize the packages (if required)

   Customize the **Virtualization** group if you require other virtualization packages.

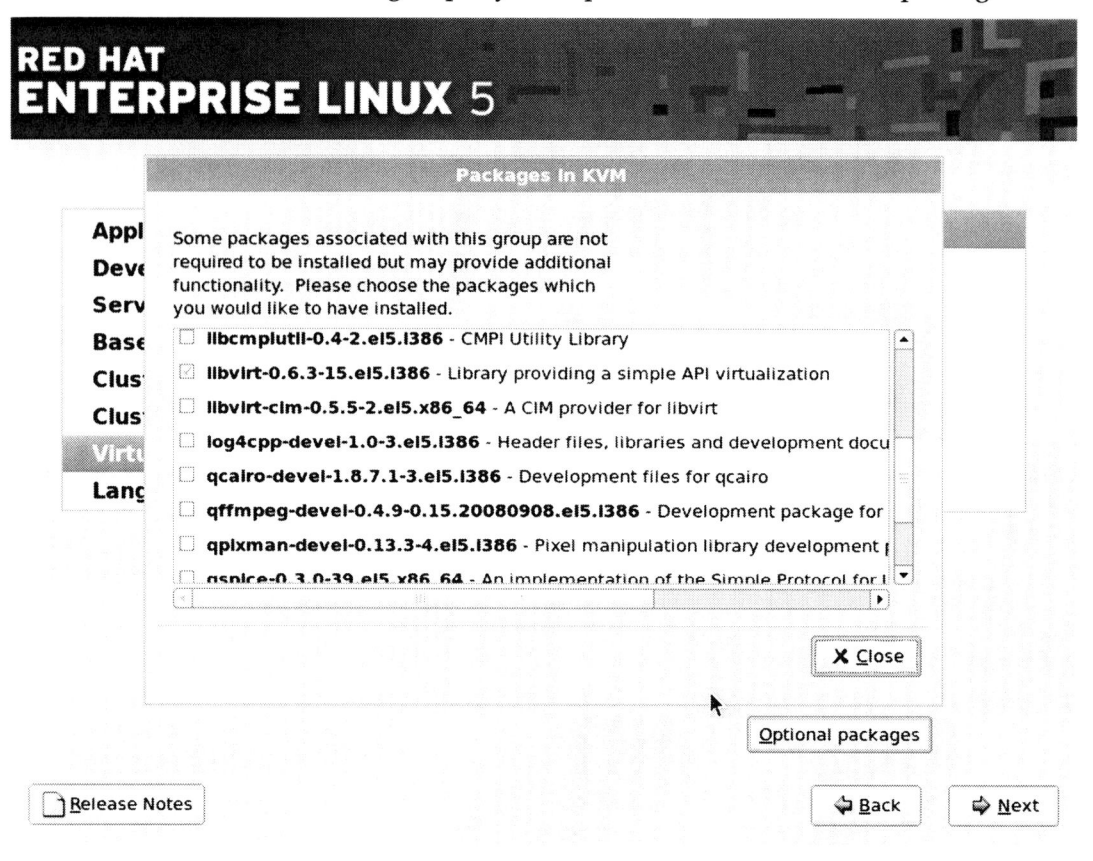

   Press **Close** followed by **Next** to continue the installation.

Installing KVM packages with Kickstart files

This section describes how to use a Kickstart file to install Fedora with the KVM hypervisor packages. Kickstart files allow for large, automated installations without a user manually installing each individual system. The steps in this section will assist you in creating and using a Kickstart file to install Fedora with the virtualization packages.

In the %packages section of your Kickstart file, append the following package group:

```
%packages
@kvm
```

More information on Kickstart files can be found on the Fedora Project website, *http://docs.fedoraproject.org*, in the *Fedora 12 Installation Guide*.

1.2. Installing KVM packages on an existing Fedora system

The section describes the steps for installing the KVM hypervisor on a working Fedora 12 or newer.

Installing the KVM hypervisor with yum

To use virtualization on Fedora you require the `kvm` package. The `kvm` package contains the KVM kernel module providing the KVM hypervisor on the default Linux kernel.

To install the `kvm` package, run:

```
# yum install kvm
```

Now, install additional virtualization management packages.

Recommended virtualization packages:

`python-virtinst`

> Provides the `virt-install` command for creating virtual machines.

`libvirt`

> `libvirt` is an API library for interacting with hypervisors. `libvirt` uses the xm virtualization framework and the `virsh` command line tool to manage and control virtual machines.

`libvirt-python`

> The libvirt-python package contains a module that permits applications written in the Python programming language to use the interface supplied by the `libvirt` API.

`virt-manager`

> `virt-manager`, also known as **Virtual Machine Manager**, provides a graphical tool for administering virtual machines. It uses `libvirt` library as the management API.

Install the other recommended virtualization packages:

```
# yum install virt-manager libvirt libvirt-python python-virtinst
```

Chapter 2.
Virtualized guest installation overview

After you have installed the virtualization packages on the host system you can create guest operating systems. This chapter describes the general processes for installing guest operating systems on virtual machines. You can create guests using the **New** button in **virt-manager** or use the command line interface `virt-install`. Both methods are covered by this chapter.

Detailed installation instructions are available for specific versions of Fedora, other Linux distributions, Solaris and Windows. Refer to *Chapter 3, Guest operating system installation procedures* for those procedures.

2.1. Creating guests with virt-install

You can use the `virt-install` command to create virtualized guests from the command line. `virt-install` is used either interactively or as part of a script to automate the creation of virtual machines. Using `virt-install` with Kickstart files allows for unattended installation of virtual machines.

The `virt-install` tool provides a number of options one can pass on the command line. To see a complete list of options run:

```
$ virt-install --help
```

The `virt-install` man page also documents each command option and important variables.

`qemu-img` is a related command which may be used before `virt-install` to configure storage options.

An important option is the `--vnc` option which opens a graphical window for the guest's installation.

This example creates a Red Hat Enterprise Linux 3 guest, named `rhel3support`, from a CD-ROM, with virtual networking and with a 5 GB file-based block device image. This example uses the KVM hypervisor.

```
# virt-install --accelerate --hvm --connect qemu:///system \
```

```
       --network network:default \
       --name rhel3support --ram=756\
       --file=/var/lib/libvirt/images/rhel3support.img \
       --file-size=6 --vnc --cdrom=/dev/sr0
```

Example 2.1. Using virt-install with KVM to create a Red Hat Enterprise Linux 3 guest

```
# virt-install --name Fedora11 --ram 512 --
file=/var/lib/libvirt/images/Fedora11.img \
       --file-size=3 --vnc --cdrom=/var/lib/libvirt/images/Fedora11.iso
```

Example 2.2. Using virt-install to create a Fedora 11 guest

2.2. Creating guests with virt-manager

`virt-manager`, also known as Virtual Machine Manager, is a graphical tool for creating and managing virtualized guests.

Procedure 2.1. Creating a virtualized guest with virt-manager

1. To start **virt-manager** run the following command as root:
   `# virt-manager &`

   The `virt-manager` command opens a graphical user interface window. Various functions are not available to users without root privileges or sudo configured, including the **New** button and you will not be able to create a new virtualized guest.

2. Open the **File -> Open Connection**. The dialog box below appears. . Select a hypervisor and click the **Connect** button:

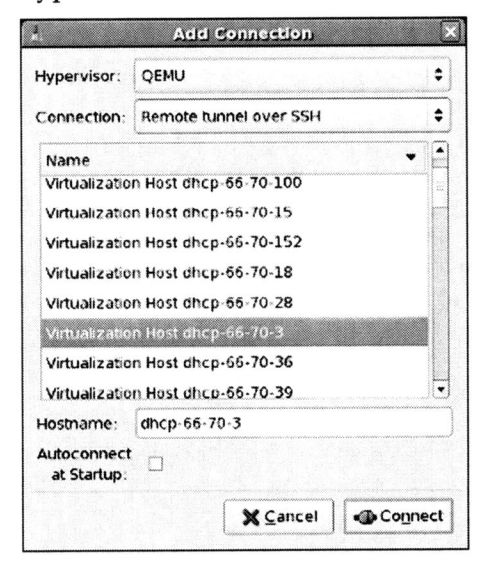

21

Fedora 12

3. The **virt-manager** window allows you to create a new virtual machine. Click the **New** button to create a new guest. This opens the wizard shown in the screenshot.

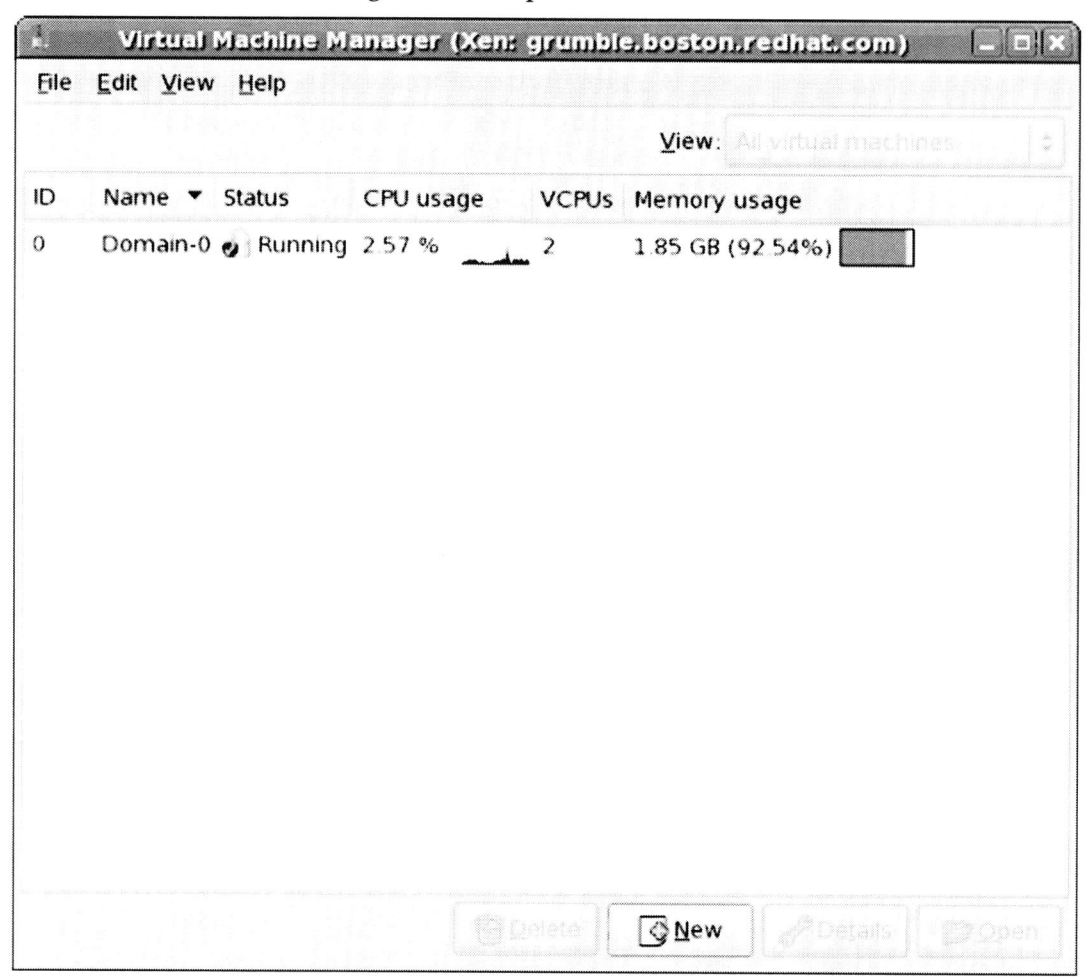

ID	Name ▼	Status	CPU usage	VCPUs	Memory usage
0	Domain-0	Running	2.57 %	2	1.85 GB (92.54%)

Virtualization Guide

4. The **Create a new virtual system** window provides a summary of the information you must provide in order to create a virtual machine:

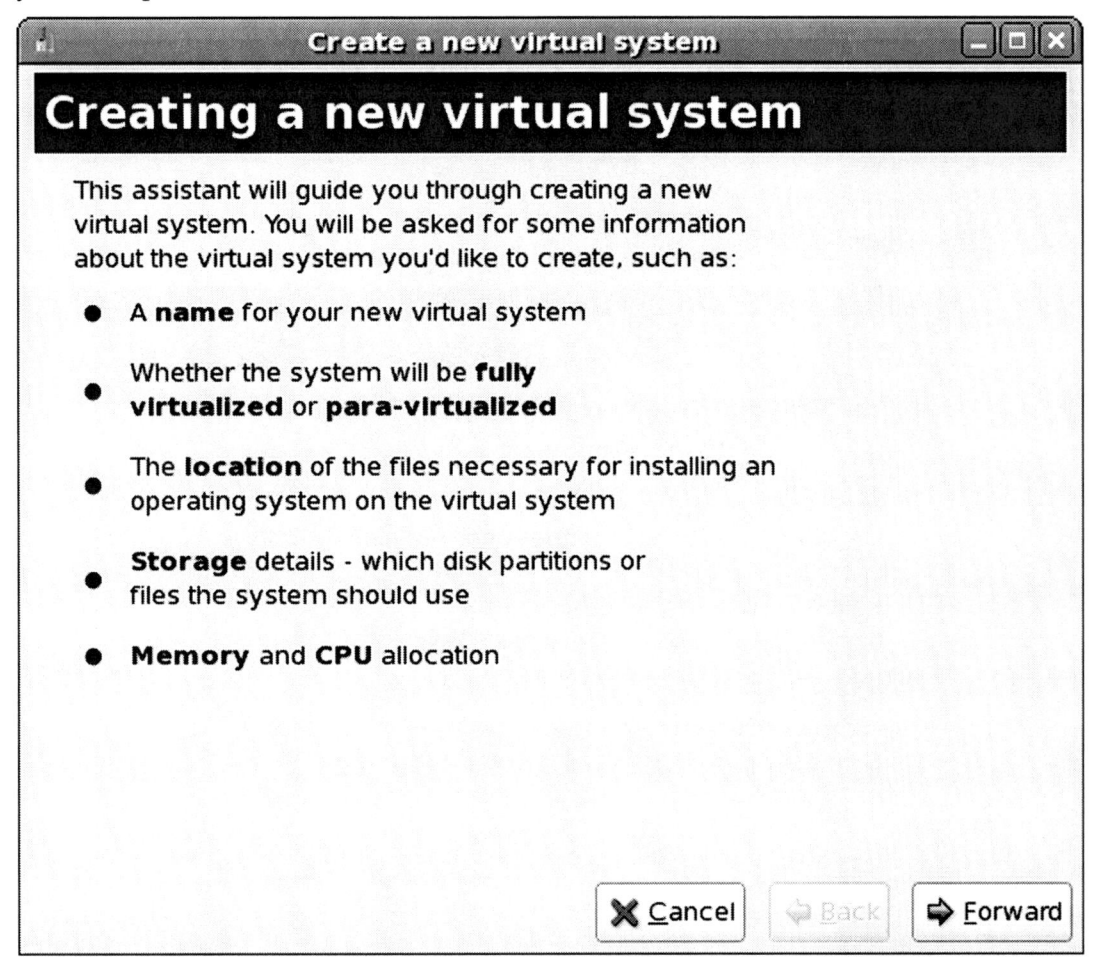

Creating a new virtual system

This assistant will guide you through creating a new virtual system. You will be asked for some information about the virtual system you'd like to create, such as:

- A **name** for your new virtual system

- Whether the system will be **fully virtualized** or **para-virtualized**

- The **location** of the files necessary for installing an operating system on the virtual system

- **Storage** details - which disk partitions or files the system should use

- **Memory** and **CPU** allocation

[**Cancel**]   [Back]   [**Forward**]

Review the information for your installation and click the **Forward** button.

Fedora 12

5. The **Choosing a virtualization method** window appears. Choose between **Para-virtualized** or **Fully virtualized**.

   Full virtualization requires a system with Intel® VT or AMD-V processor. If the virtualization extensions are not present the **fully virtualized** radio button or the **Enable kernel/hardware acceleration** will not be selectable. The **Para-virtualized** option will be grayed out if `kernel-xen` is not the kernel running presently.

   If you connected to a KVM hypervisor only full virtualization is available.

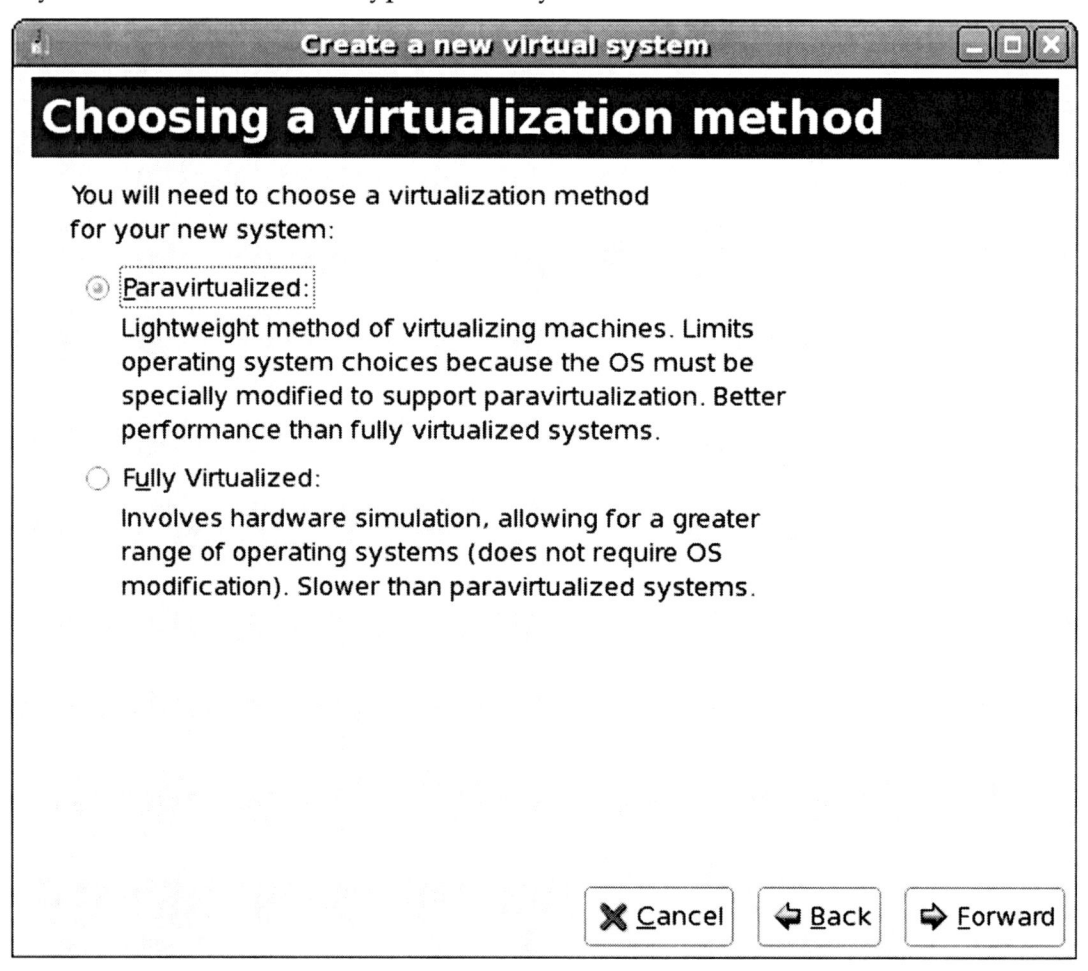

   ![Choosing a virtualization method dialog]

   Choosing a virtualization method

   You will need to choose a virtualization method for your new system:

   ● **Paravirtualized:**
   Lightweight method of virtualizing machines. Limits operating system choices because the OS must be specially modified to support paravirtualization. Better performance than fully virtualized systems.

   ○ **Fully Virtualized:**
   Involves hardware simulation, allowing for a greater range of operating systems (does not require OS modification). Slower than paravirtualized systems.

   [✘ Cancel] [⇐ Back] [⇒ Forward]

   Choose the virtualization type and click the **Next** button.

Virtualization Guide

6. The **Locating installation media** prompt asks for the installation media for the type of installation you selected. This screen is dependent on what was selected in the previous step.

    1. The para-virtualized installation requires an installation tree accessible using one of the following network protocols: HTTP, FTP or NFS. The installation media URL must contain a Fedora installation tree. This tree is hosted using NFS, FTP or HTTP. The network services and files can be hosted using network services on the host or another mirror.

        Using a CD-ROM or DVD image (tagged as an .iso file), mount the CD-ROM image and host the mounted files with one of the mentioned protocols.

        Alternatively, copy the installation tree from a Fedora mirror.

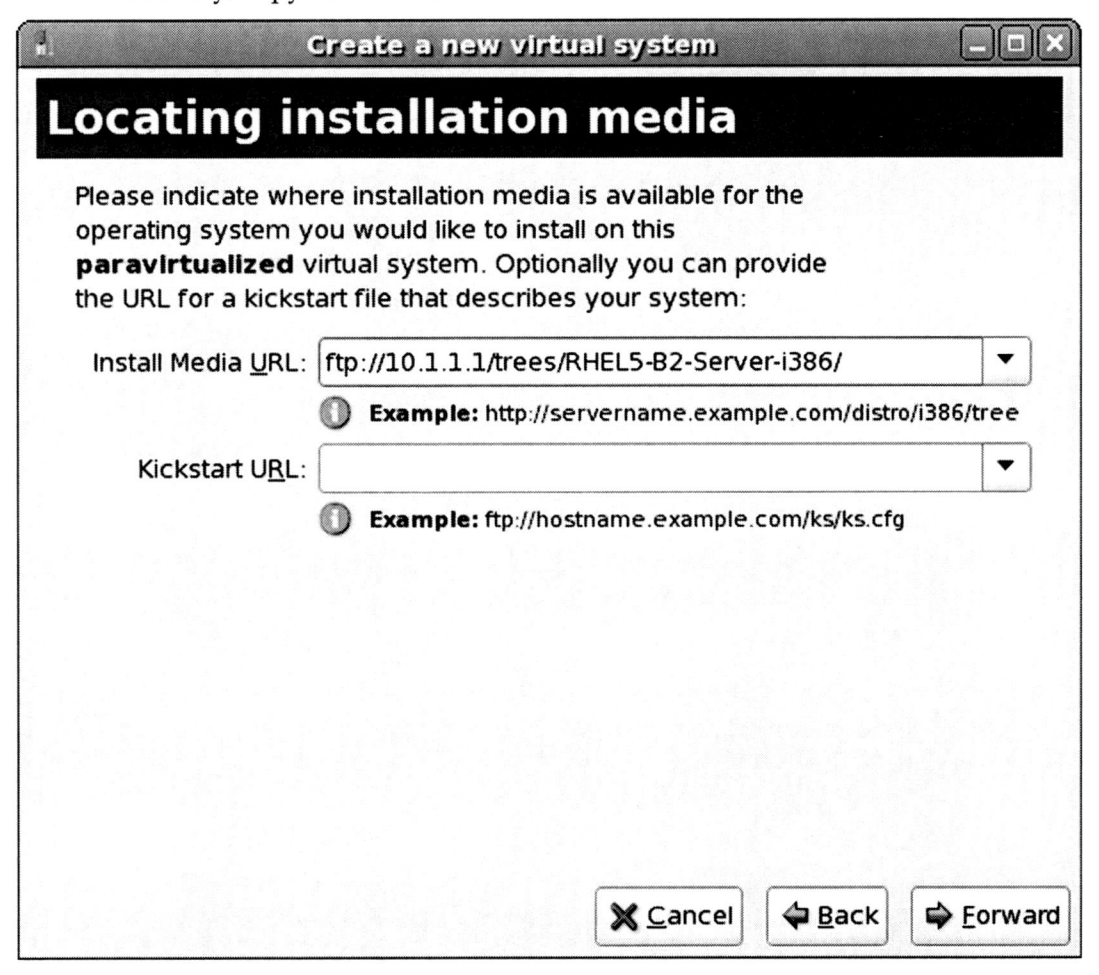

Fedora 12

2. A fully virtualized guest installation require bootable installation DVDs, CD-ROMs or images of bootable installation DVDs or CD-ROMs (with the .iso or .img file type) locally. Windows installations use DVD, CD-ROM or .iso file. Many Linux and UNIX-like operating systems use an .iso file to install a base system before finishing the installation with a network based installation tree.

Locating installation media

Please indicate where installation media is available for the operating system you would like to install on this **fully virtualized** virtual system:

○ ISO Image Location:

    ISO Location: /Server/images/boot.iso Browse...

○ CD-ROM or DVD:

    Path to install media:

✖ Cancel   ⬅ Back   ➡ Forward

After selecting the appropriate installation media, click the **Forward** button.

Virtualization Guide

7. The **Assigning storage space** window displays. Choose a disk partition, LUN or create a file based image for the guest storage.

    The convention for file based images in Fedora is that all file based guest images are in the /var/lib/xen/images/ directory. Other directory locations for file based images are prohibited by SELinux. If you run SELinux in enforcing mode, refer to *Section 7.1, "SELinux and virtualization"* for more information on installing guests.

    Your guest storage image should be larger than the size of the installation, any additional packages and applications, and the size of the guests swap file. The installation process will choose the size of the guest's swap file based on size of the RAM allocated to the guest.

    Allocate extra space if the guest needs additional space for applications or other data. For example, web servers require additional space for log files.

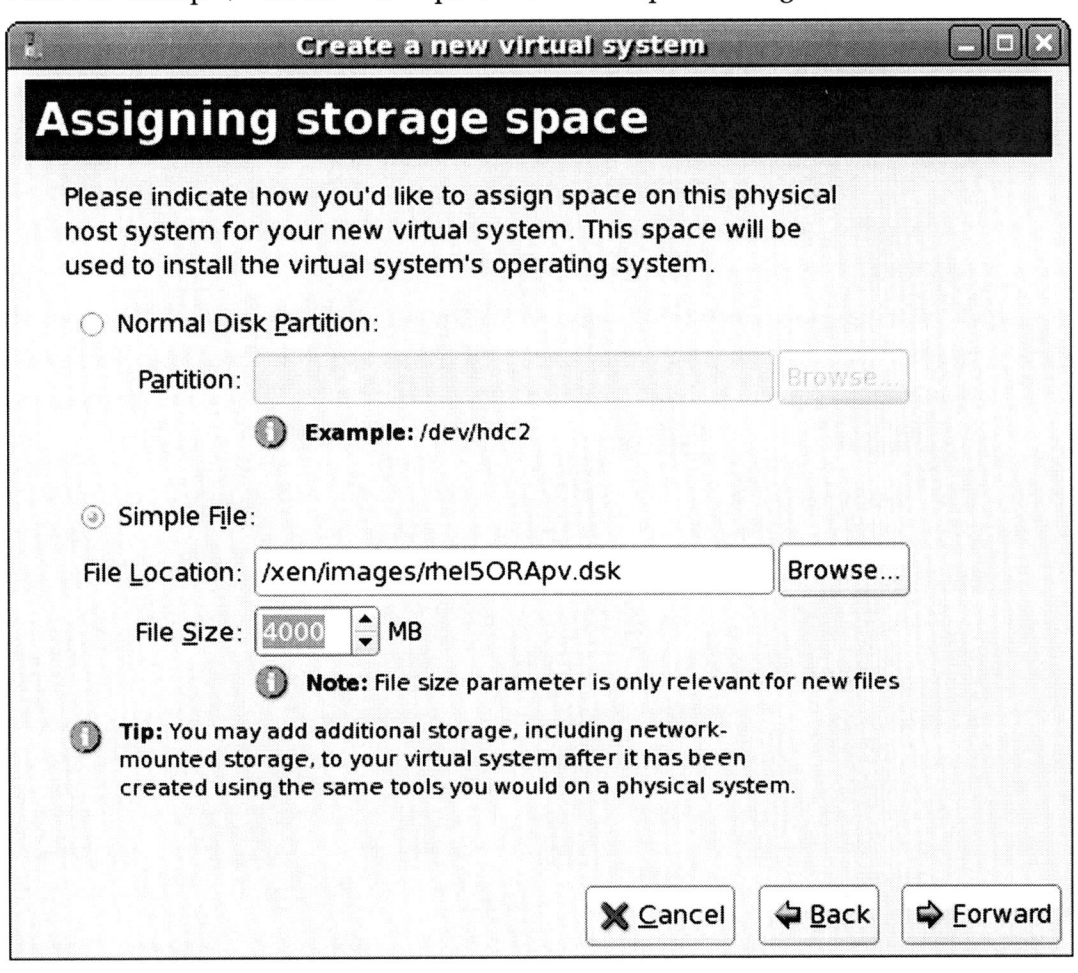

Fedora 12

Choose the appropriate size for the guest on your selected storage type and click the **Forward** button.

> **Note**
>
> It is recommend that you use the default directory for virtual machine images, /var/lib/xen/images/. If you are using a different location (such as /xen/images/ in this example) make sure it is added to your SELinux policy and relabeled before you continue with the installation (later in the document you will find information on how to modify your SELinux policy).

8. The Allocate memory and CPU window displays. Choose appropriate values for the virtualized CPUs and RAM allocation. These values affect the host's and guest's performance.

    Guests require sufficient physical memory (RAM) to run efficiently and effectively. Choose a memory value which suits your guest operating system and application requirements. Most operating system require at least 512MB of RAM to work responsively. Remember, guests use physical RAM. Running too many guests or leaving insufficient memory for the host system results in significant usage of virtual memory. Virtual memory is significantly slower causing degraded system performance and responsiveness. Ensure to allocate sufficient memory for all guests and the host to operate effectively.

    Assign sufficient virtual CPUs for the virtualized guest. If the guest runs a multithreaded application assign the number of virtualized CPUs it requires to run most efficiently. Do not assign more virtual CPUs than there are physical processors (or hyper-threads) available on the host system. It is possible to over allocate virtual processors, however, over allocating has a significant, negative affect on guest and host performance due to processor context switching overheads.

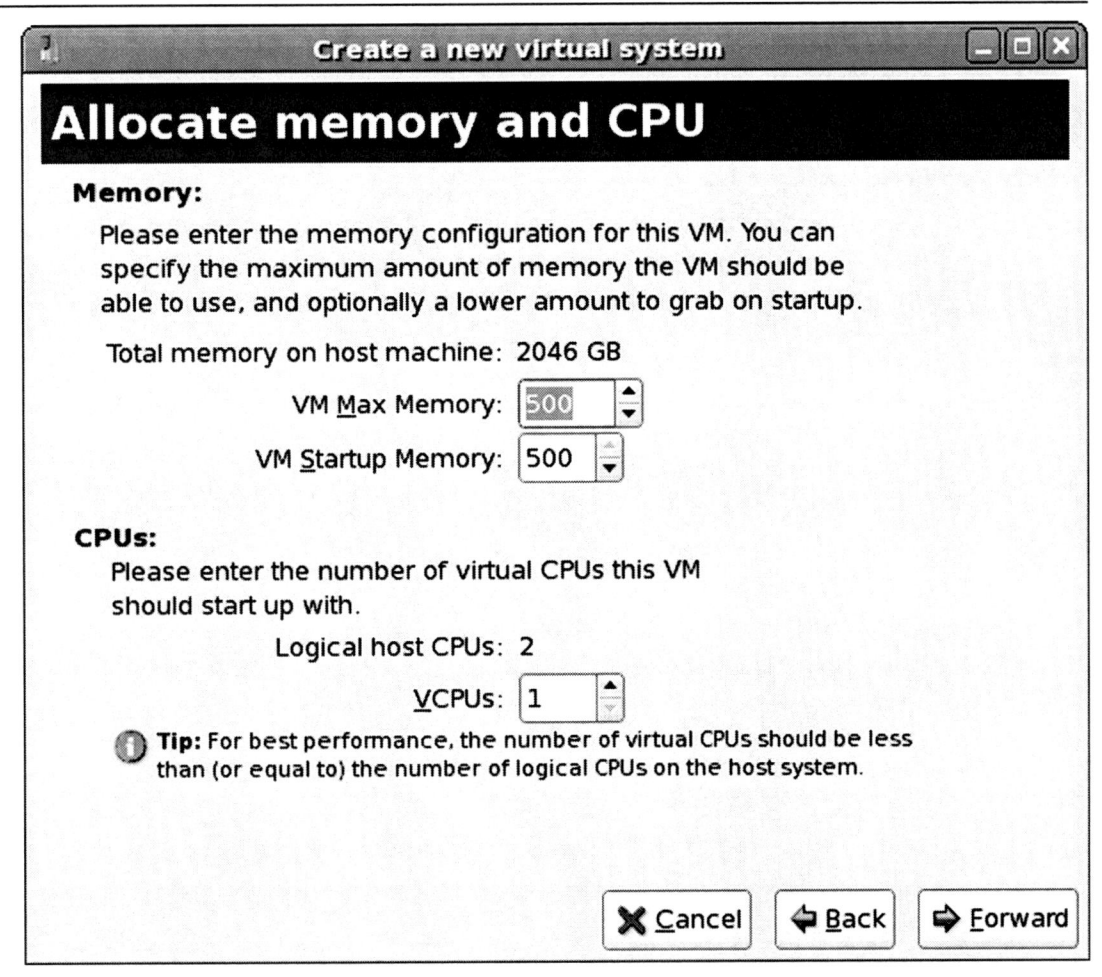

Virtualization Guide

Create a new virtual system

Allocate memory and CPU

Memory:

Please enter the memory configuration for this VM. You can specify the maximum amount of memory the VM should be able to use, and optionally a lower amount to grab on startup.

Total memory on host machine: 2046 GB

VM Max Memory: 500

VM Startup Memory: 500

CPUs:

Please enter the number of virtual CPUs this VM should start up with.

Logical host CPUs: 2

VCPUs: 1

Tip: For best performance, the number of virtual CPUs should be less than (or equal to) the number of logical CPUs on the host system.

✘ Cancel   ⬅ Back   ➡ Forward

Fedora 12

9. The ready to begin installation window presents a summary of all configuration information you entered. Review the information presented and use the **Back** button to make changes, if necessary. Once you are satisfied click the **Finish** button and to start the installation process.

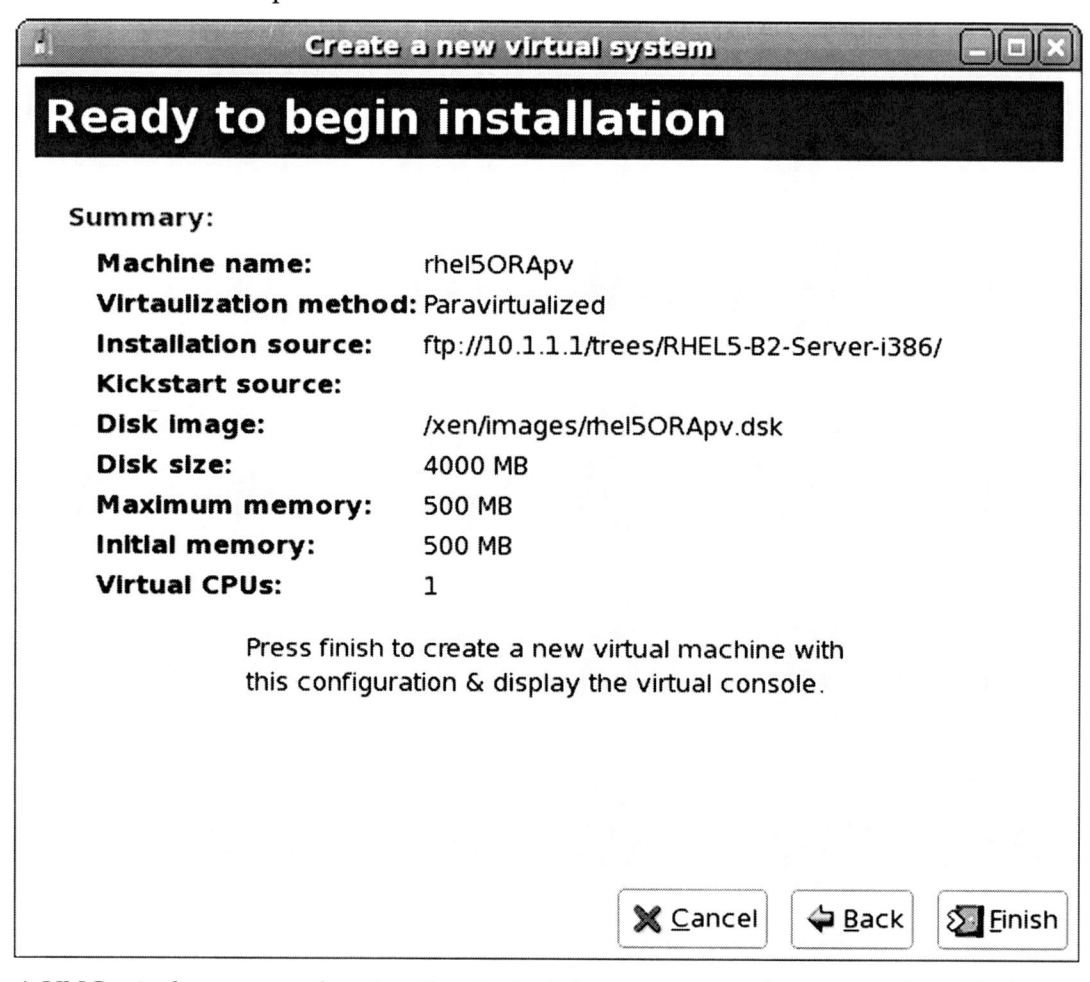

```
Create a new virtual system

Ready to begin installation

Summary:
    Machine name:          rhel5ORApv
    Virtaulization method: Paravirtualized
    Installation source:   ftp://10.1.1.1/trees/RHEL5-B2-Server-i386/
    Kickstart source:
    Disk image:            /xen/images/rhel5ORApv.dsk
    Disk size:             4000 MB
    Maximum memory:        500 MB
    Initial memory:        500 MB
    Virtual CPUs:          1

         Press finish to create a new virtual machine with
         this configuration & display the virtual console.

                              [Cancel]  [Back]  [Finish]
```

A VNC window opens showing the start of the guest operating system installation process.

This concludes the general process for creating guests with `virt-manager`. *Chapter 3, Guest operating system installation procedures* contains step-by-step instructions to installing a variety of common operating systems.

Virtualization Guide

2.3. Installing guests with PXE

This section covers the steps required to install guests with PXE. PXE guest installation requires a shared network device, also known as a network bridge. The procedures below cover creating a bridge and the steps required to utilize it the bridge for a PXE installation.

1. **Create a new bridge**

   1. Create a new network script file in the /etc/sysconfig/network-scripts/ directory. This example creates a file named ifcfg-installation which makes a bridge named *installation*

      ```
      # cd /etc/sysconfig/network-scripts/
      # vim ifcfg-installation
      DEVICE=installation
      TYPE=Bridge
      BOOTPROTO=dhcp
      ONBOOT=yes
      ```

      Warning

      The line, *TYPE=Bridge*, is case-sensitive. It must have uppercase 'B' and lower case 'ridge'.

   2.
      ```
      Start the new bridge.
      # ifup installation
      ```

   3. There are no interfaces added to the new bridge yet. Use the brctl show command to view details about network bridges on the system.

      ```
      # brctl show
      bridge name     bridge id               STP enabled     interfaces
      installation    8000.000000000000       no
      virbr0          8000.000000000000       yes
      ```

      The virbr0 bridge is the default bridge used by libvirt for Network Address Translation (NAT) on the default Ethernet device.

2. **Add an interface to the new bridge**

   Edit the configuration file for the interface. Add the BRIDGE parameter to the configuration file with the name of the bridge created in the previous steps.

   ```
   # Intel Corporation Gigabit Network Connection
   DEVICE=eth1
   BRIDGE=installation
   BOOTPROTO=dhcp
   HWADDR=00:13:20:F7:6E:8E
   ONBOOT=yes
   ```

Fedora 12

After editing the configuration file, restart networking or reboot.

```
# service network restart
```

Verify the interface is attached with the `brctl show` command:

```
# brctl show
bridge name     bridge id               STP enabled     interfaces
installation    8000.001320f76e8e       no              eth1
virbr0          8000.000000000000       yes
```

3. **Security configuration**

   Configure `iptables` to allow all traffic to be forwarded across the bridge.

   ```
   # iptables -I FORWARD -m physdev --physdev-is-bridged -j ACCEPT
   # service iptables save
   # service iptables restart
   ```

   > **Disable iptables on bridges**
   >
   > Alternatively, prevent bridged traffic from being processed by `iptables` rules. In /etc/sysctl.conf append the following lines:
   >
   > net.bridge.bridge-nf-call-ip6tables = 0
   > net.bridge.bridge-nf-call-iptables = 0
   > net.bridge.bridge-nf-call-arptables = 0
   >
   > Reload the kernel parameters configured with `sysctl`

   ```
   # sysctl -p /etc/sysctl.conf
   ```

4. **Restart libvirt before the installation**

   Restart the `libvirt` daemon.

   ```
   # service libvirtd reload
   ```

The bridge is configured, you can now begin an installation.

PXE installation with virt-install

For `virt-install` append the `--network=bridge:BRIDGENAME` installation parameter where installation is the name of your bridge. For PXE installations use the `--pxe` parameter.

```
# virt-install --accelerate --hvm --connect qemu:///system \
    --network=bridge:installation --pxe\
    --name EL10 --ram=756 \
    --vcpus=4
    --os-type=linux --os-variant=rhel5
    --file=/var/lib/libvirt/images/EL10.img \
```

Example 2.3. PXE installation with virt-install

PXE installation with virt-manager

The steps below are the steps that vary from the standard virt-manager installation procedures. For the standard installations refer to *Chapter 3, Guest operating system installation procedures*.

1. **Select PXE**

   Select PXE as the installation method.

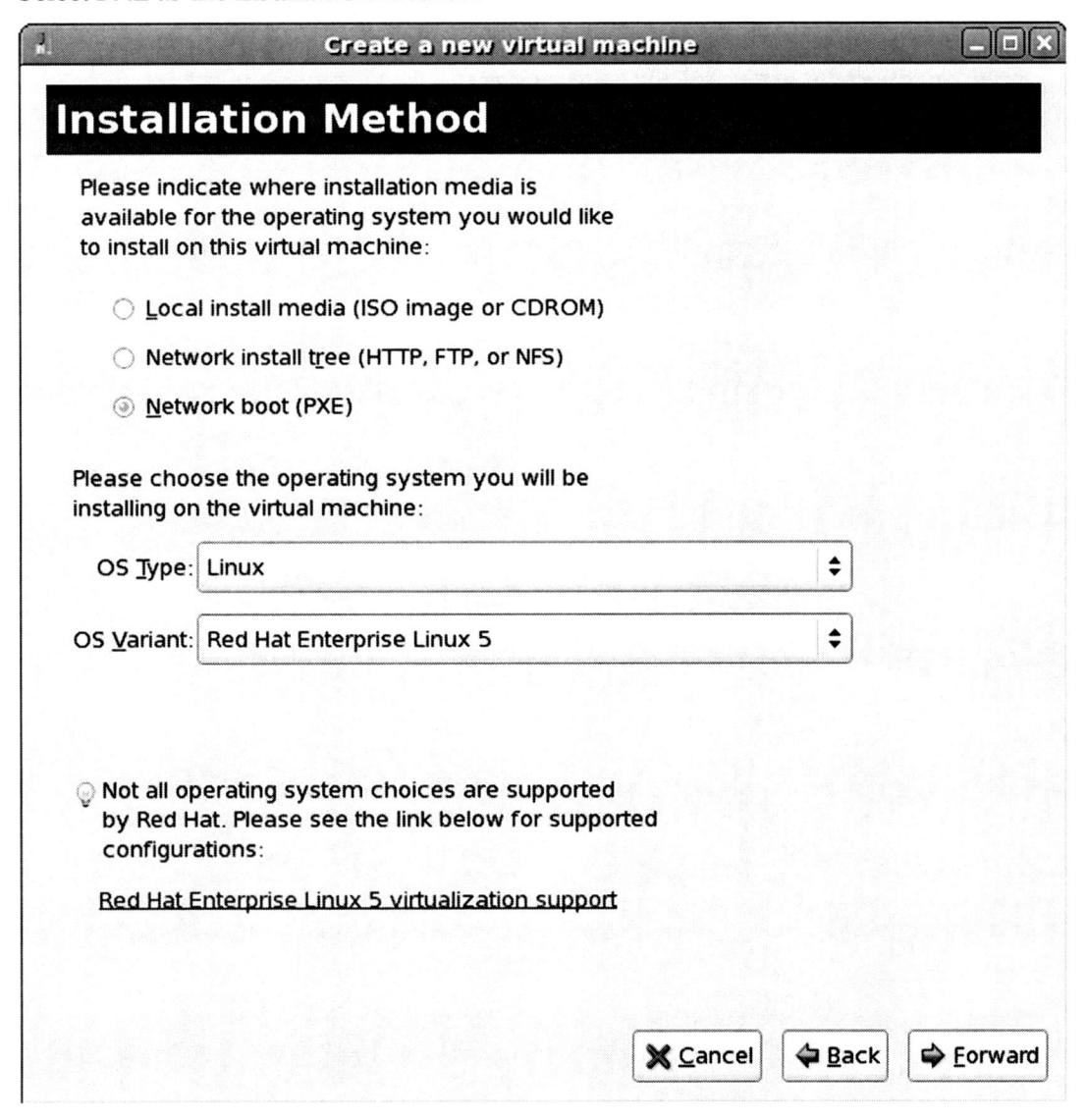

   ![Create a new virtual machine - Installation Method dialog with Network boot (PXE) selected, OS Type: Linux, OS Variant: Red Hat Enterprise Linux 5]

Fedora 12

2. **Select the bridge**

   Select **Shared physical device** and select the bridge created in the previous procedure.

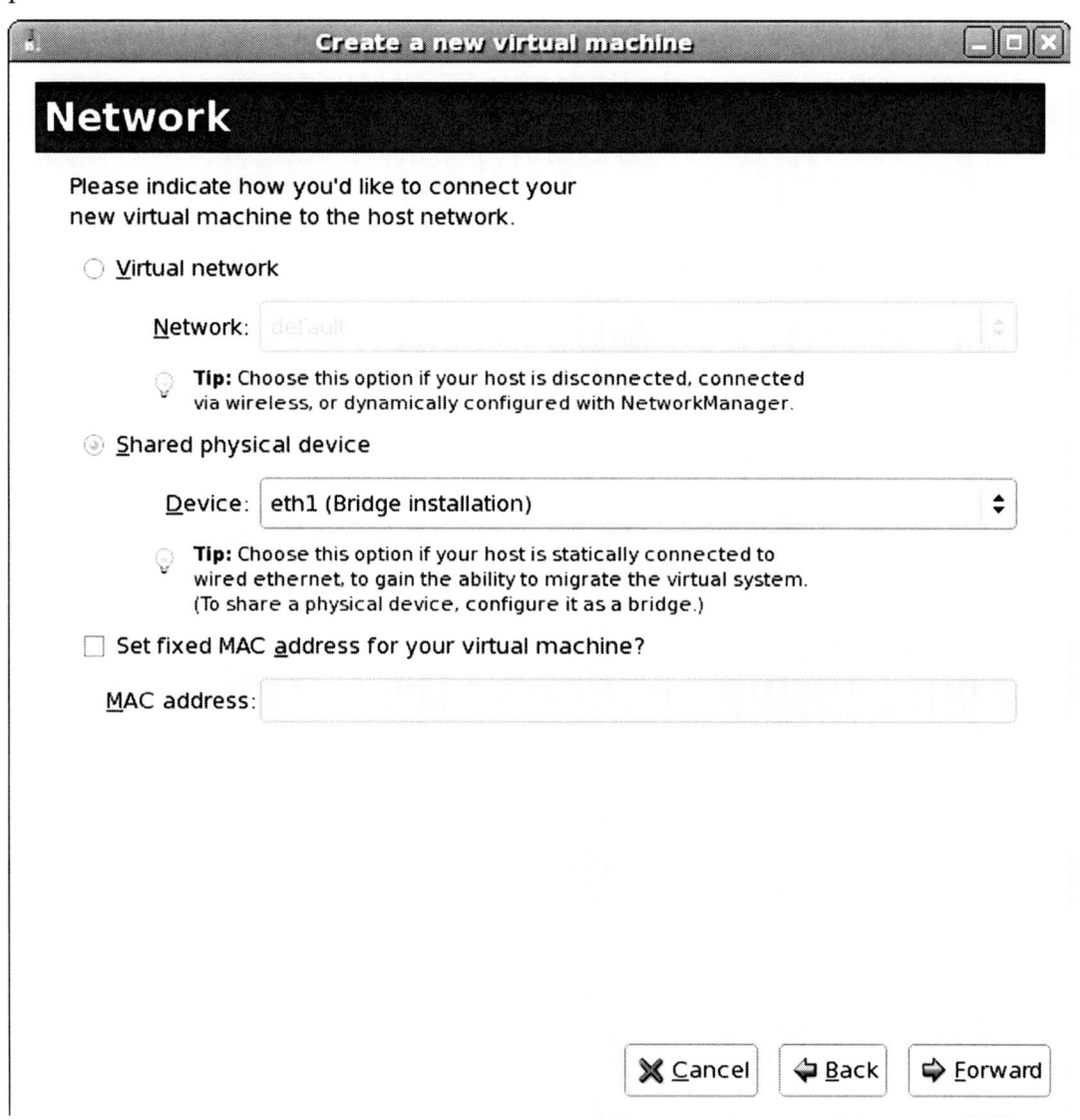

Virtualization Guide

3. **Start the installation**

   The installation is ready to start.

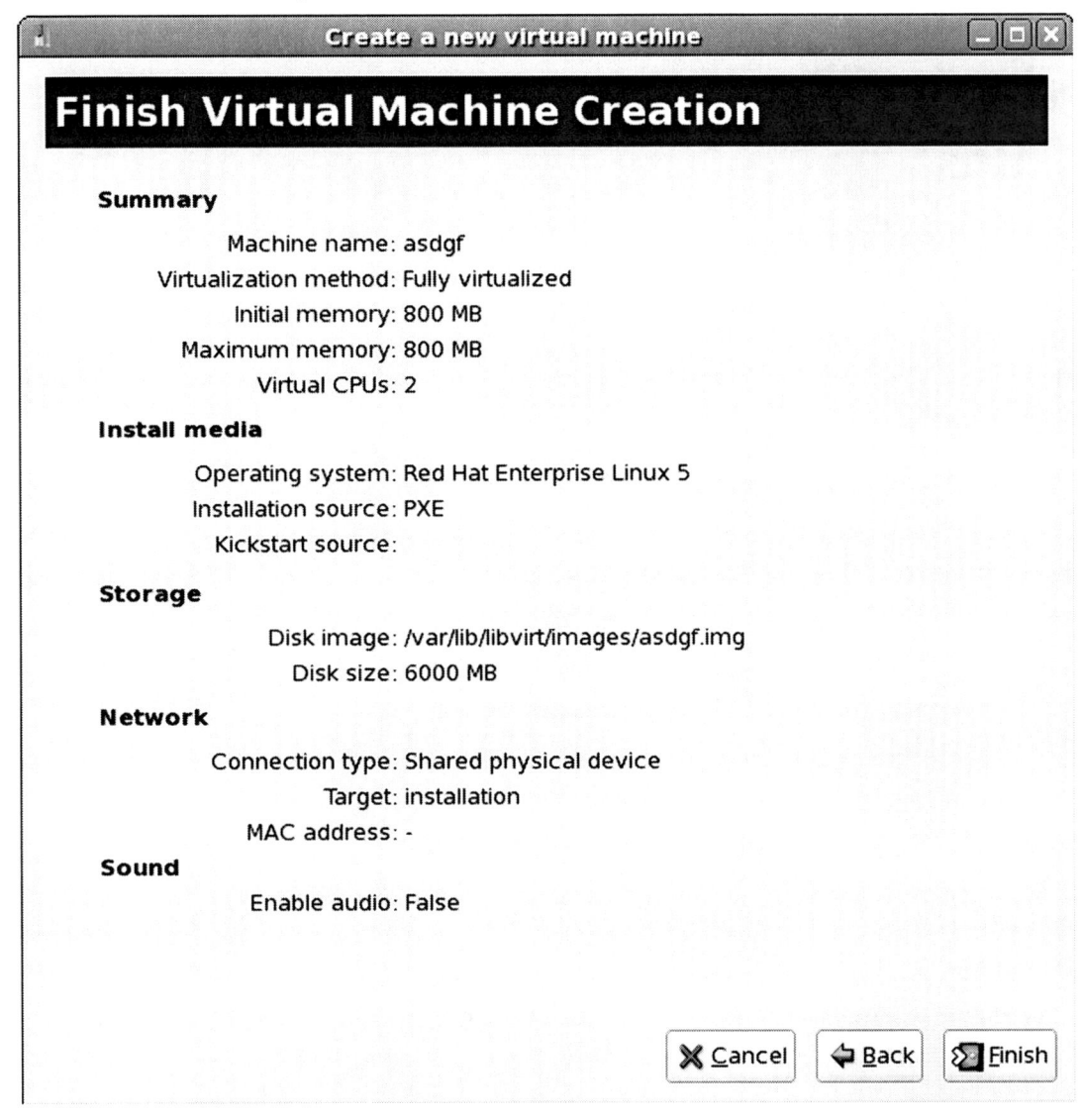

   ### Finish Virtual Machine Creation

   Summary
   - Machine name: asdgf
   - Virtualization method: Fully virtualized
   - Initial memory: 800 MB
   - Maximum memory: 800 MB
   - Virtual CPUs: 2

   Install media
   - Operating system: Red Hat Enterprise Linux 5
   - Installation source: PXE
   - Kickstart source:

   Storage
   - Disk image: /var/lib/libvirt/images/asdgf.img
   - Disk size: 6000 MB

   Network
   - Connection type: Shared physical device
   - Target: installation
   - MAC address: -

   Sound
   - Enable audio: False

   A DHCP request is sent and if a valid PXE server is found the guest installation processes will start.

Chapter 3.
Guest operating system installation procedures

This chapter covers how to install various guest operating systems in a virtualized environment on Fedora. To understand the basic processes, refer to *Chapter 2, Virtualized guest installation overview*.

3.1. Installing Red Hat Enterprise Linux 5 as a para-virtualized guest

This section describes how to install Red Hat Enterprise Linux 5 as a para-virtualized guest. Para-virtualization is a faster than full virtualization and supports all of the advantages of full virtualization. Para-virtualization requires a special, supported kernel, the `kernel-xen` kernel.

> **Important note on para-virtualization**
>
> Para-virtualization only works with the Xen hypervisor. Para-virtualization does not work with the KVM hypervisor.

Ensure you have root access before starting the installation.

This method installs Red Hat Enterprise Linux from a remote server. The installation instructions presented in this section are similar to installing from the minimal installation live CD-ROM.

Create para-virtualized Red Hat Enterprise Linux 5 guests using virt-manager or virt-install. For instructions on `virt-manager`, refer to the procedure in *Section 2.2, "Creating guests with virt-manager"*.

Create a para-virtualized guest with the command line based `virt-install` tool. The `--vnc` option shows the graphical installation. The name of the guest in the example is `rhel5PV`, the disk image file is `rhel5PV.dsk` and a local mirror of the Red Hat Enterprise Linux 5 installation tree is `ftp://10.1.1.1/trees/CentOS5-B2-Server-i386/`. Replace those values with values accurate for your system and network.

Virtualization Guide

```
# virt-install -n rhel5PV -r 500 \
-f /var/lib/libvirt/images/rhel5PV.dsk -s 3 --vnc -p \
-l ftp://10.1.1.1/trees/CentOS5-B2-Server-i386/
```

> **Automating installation**
>
> Red Hat Enterprise Linux can be installed without a graphical interface or manual input. Use Kickstart files to automate the installation process.

Using either method opens this window, displaying the initial boot phases of your guest:

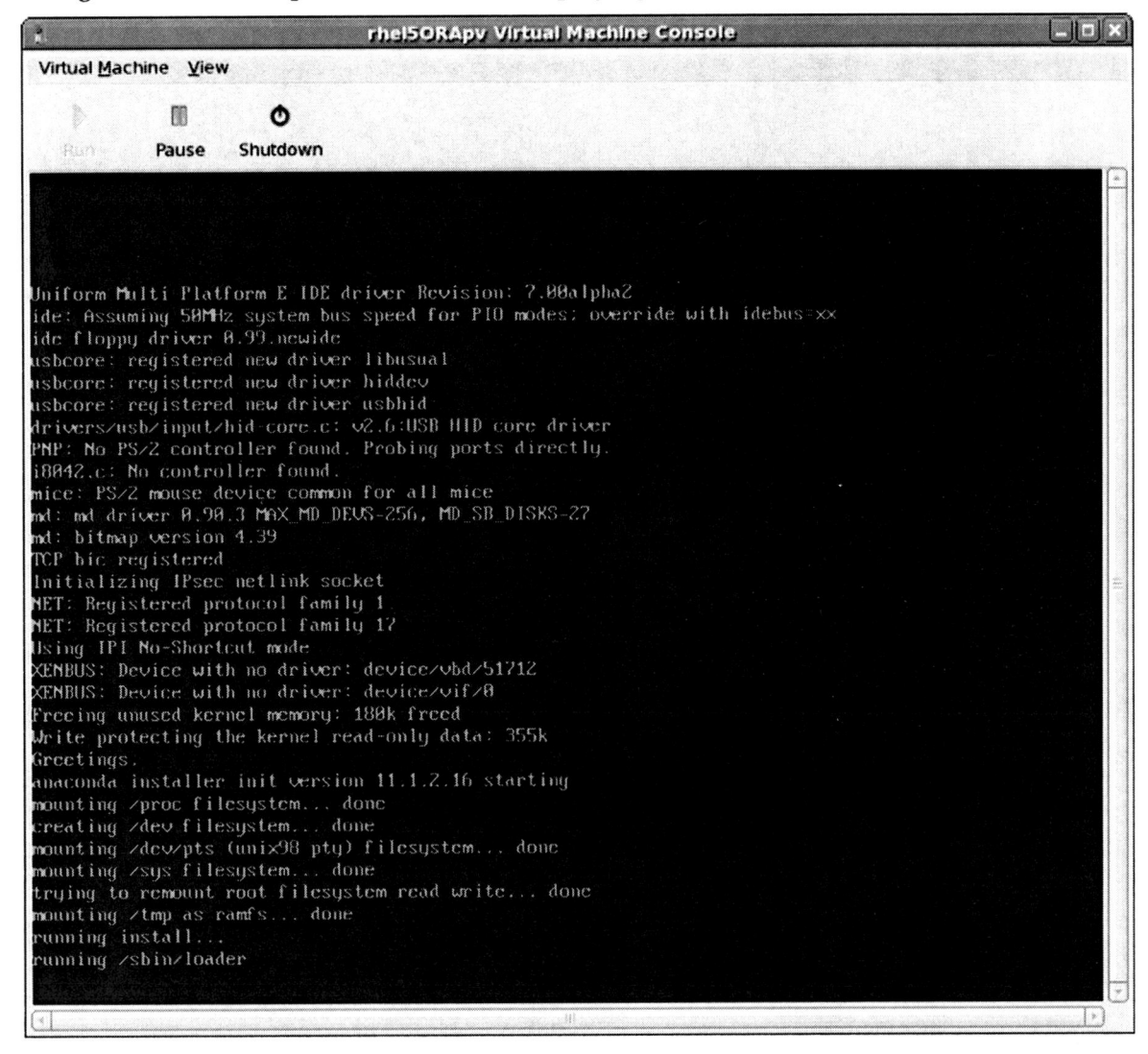

Fedora 12

After your guest has completed its initial boot, the standard installation process for Red Hat Enterprise Linux starts. For most systems the default answers are acceptable.

Procedure 3.1. Para-virtualized Red Hat Enterprise Linux guest installation procedure

1. Select the language and click **OK**.

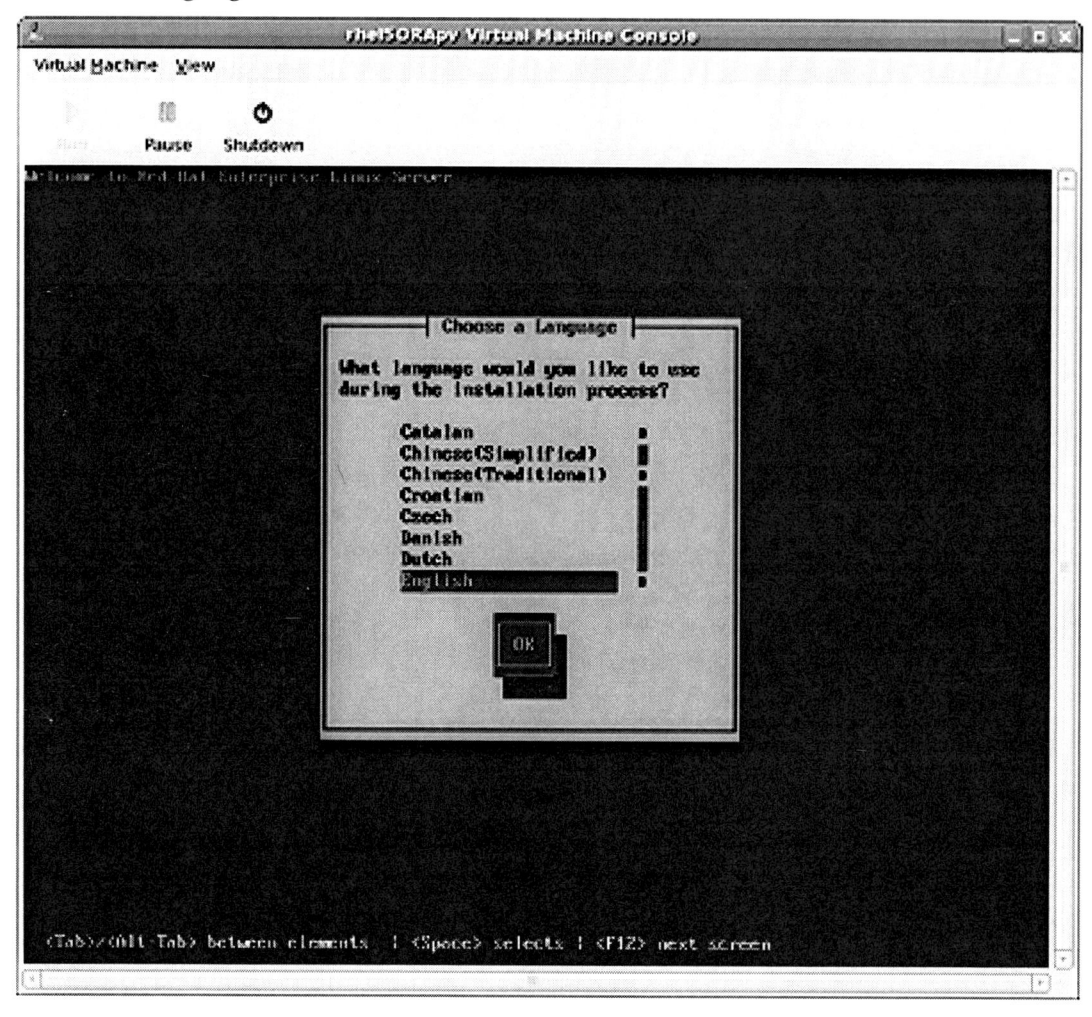

2. Select the keyboard layout and click **OK**.

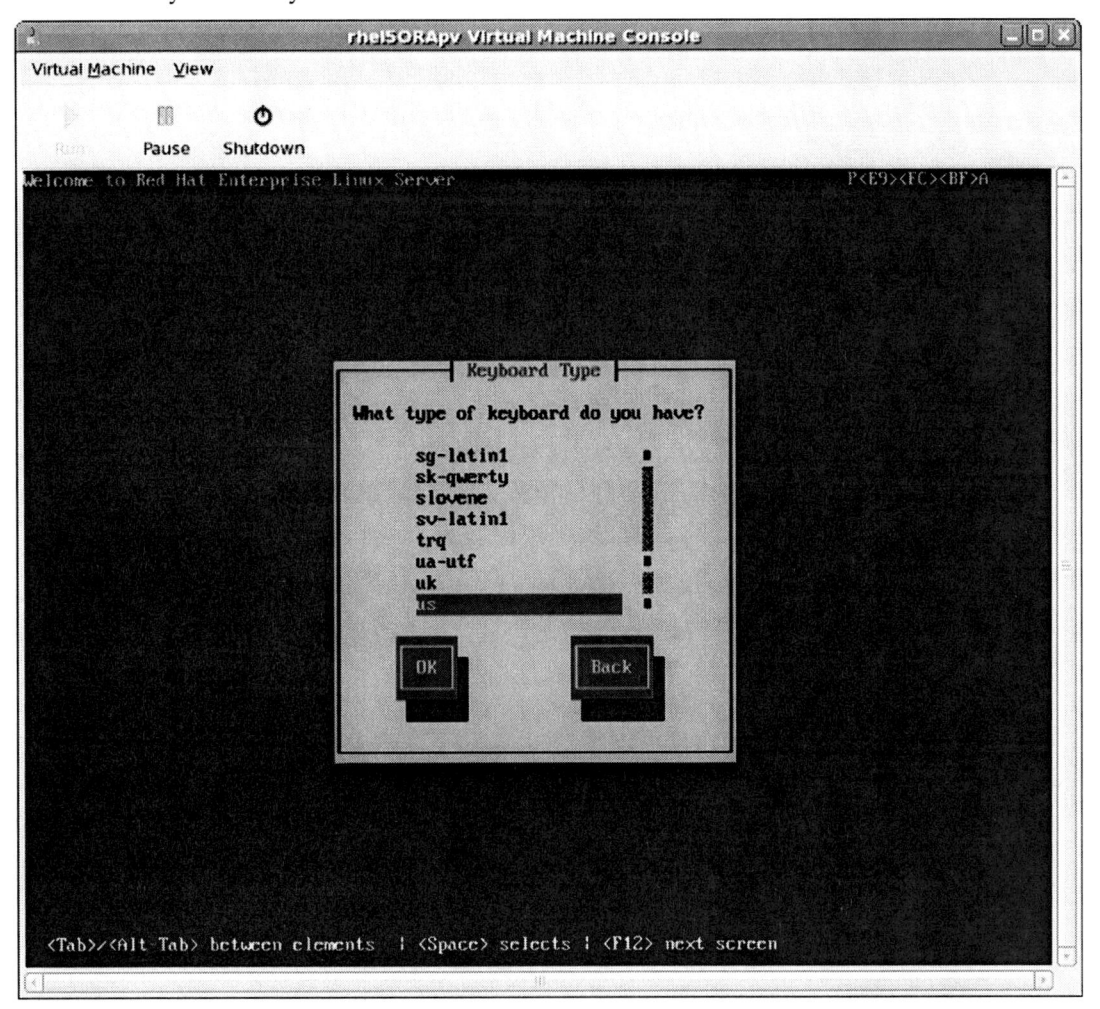

Fedora 12

3. Assign the guest's network address. Choose to use DHCP (as shown below) or a static IP address:

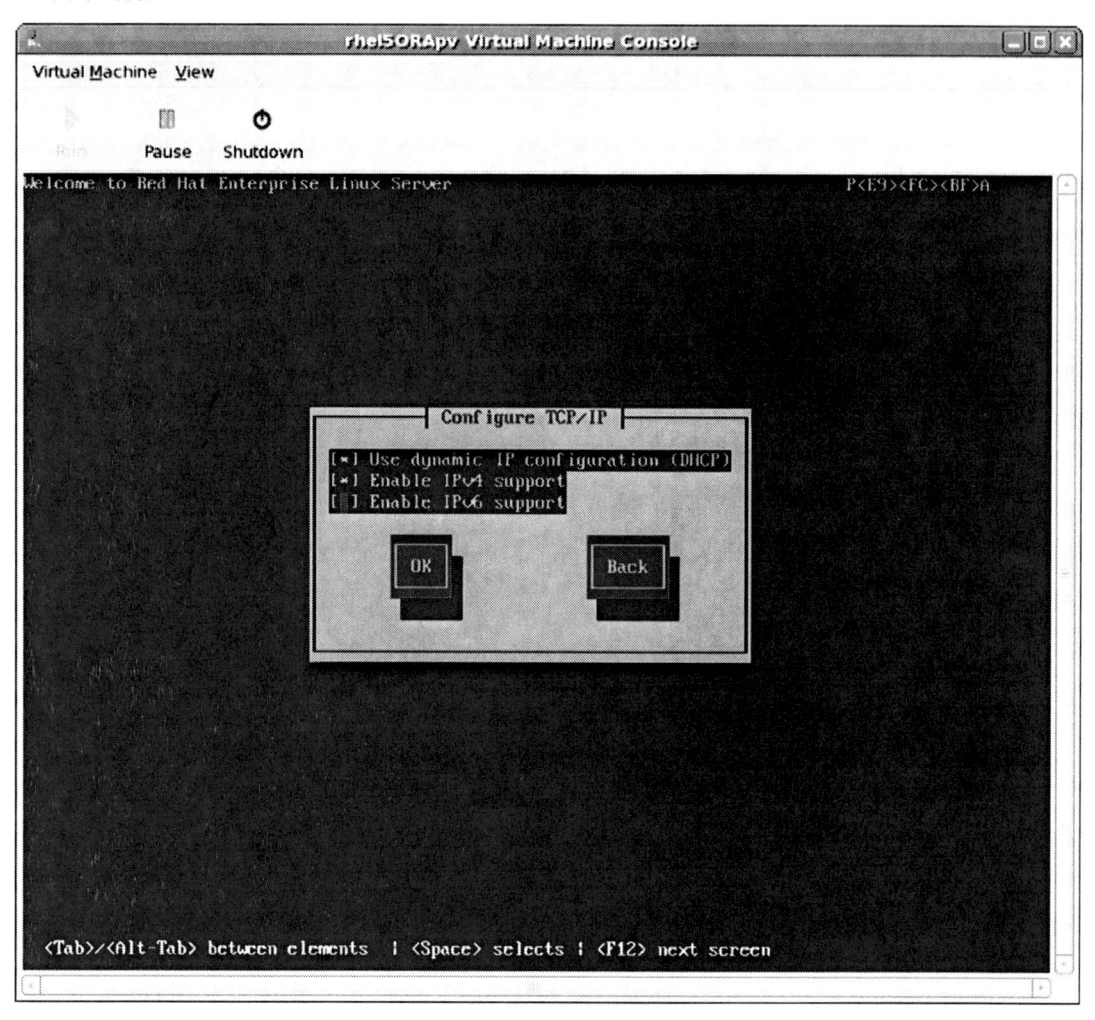

Virtualization Guide

4. If you select DHCP the installation process will now attempt to acquire an IP address:

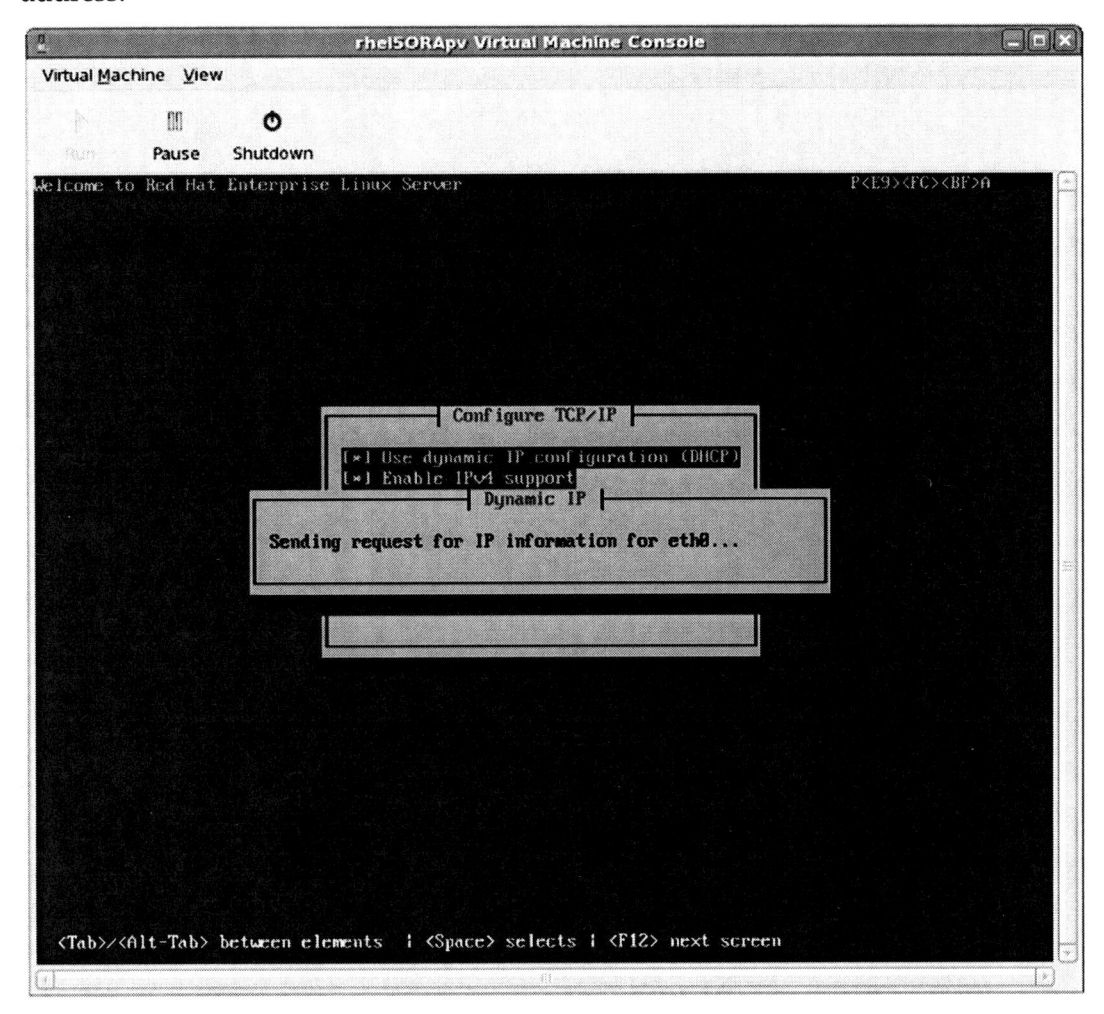

Fedora 12

5. If you chose a static IP address for your guest this prompt appears. Enter the details on the guest's networking configuration:

   1. Enter a valid IP address. Ensure the IP address you enter can reach the server with the installation tree.

   2. Enter a valid Subnet mask, default gateway and name server address.

   Select the language and click **OK**.

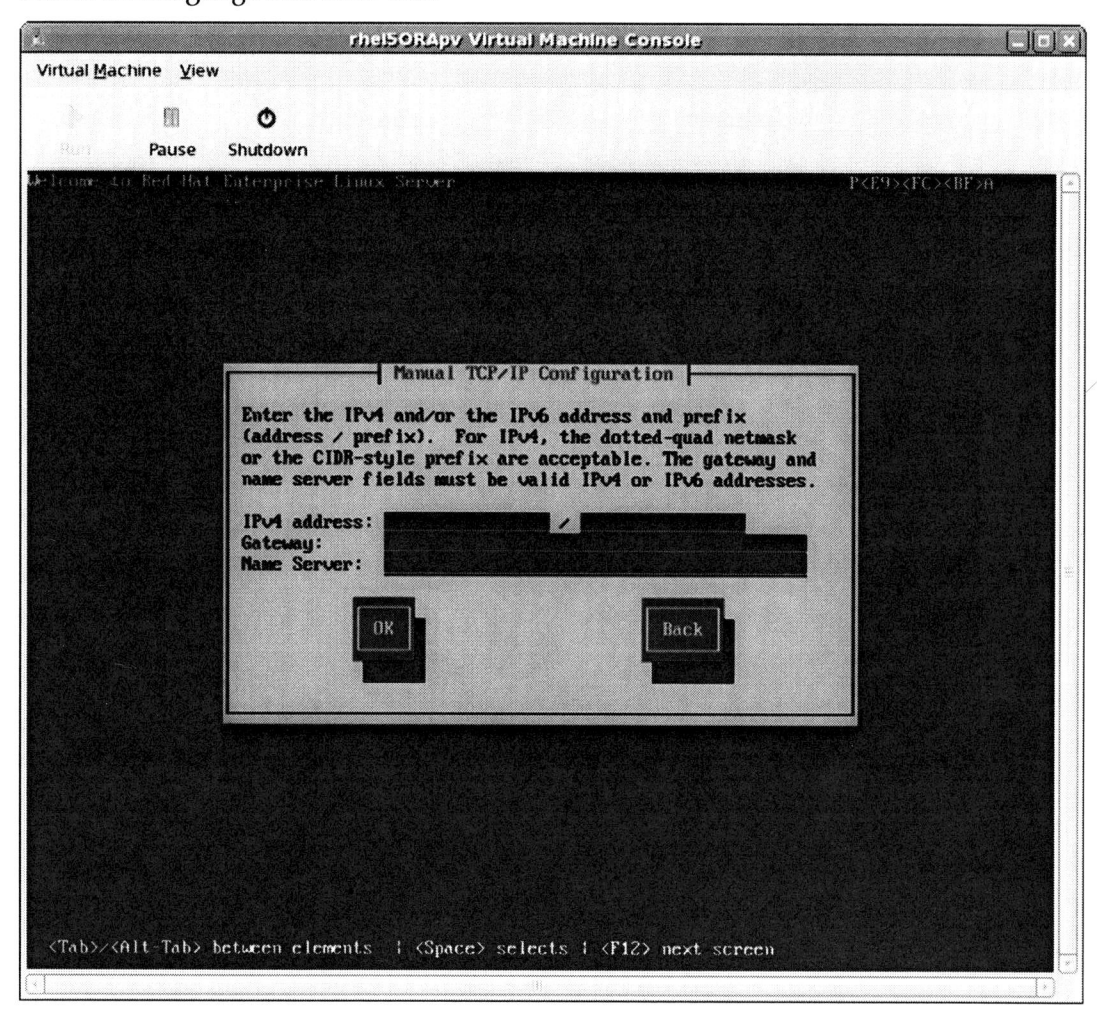

6. This is an example of a static IP address configuration:

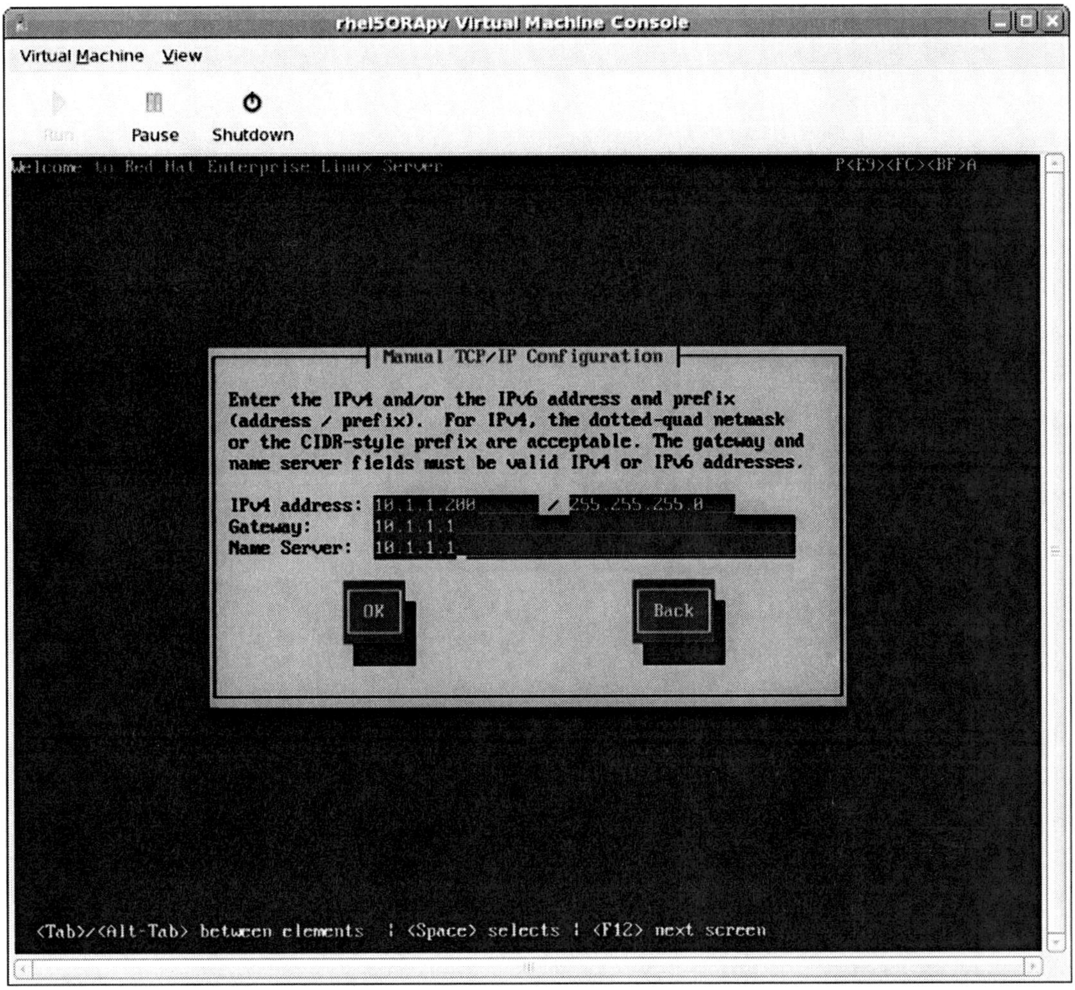
rhel5ORApv Virtual Machine Console
Virtual Machine View
Run
Pause
Shutdown
Welcome to Red Hat Enterprise Linux Server
Manual TCP/IP Configuration
Enter the IPv4 and/or the IPv6 address and prefix (address / prefix). For IPv4, the dotted-quad netmask or the CIDR-style prefix are acceptable. The gateway and name server fields must be valid IPv4 or IPv6 addresses.
IPv4 address: 10.1.1.200 / 255.255.255.0
Gateway: 10.1.1.1
Name Server: 10.1.1.1
OK
Back
<Tab>/<Alt-Tab> between elements | <Space> selects | <F12> next screen

Fedora 12

7. The installation process now retrieves the files it needs from the server:

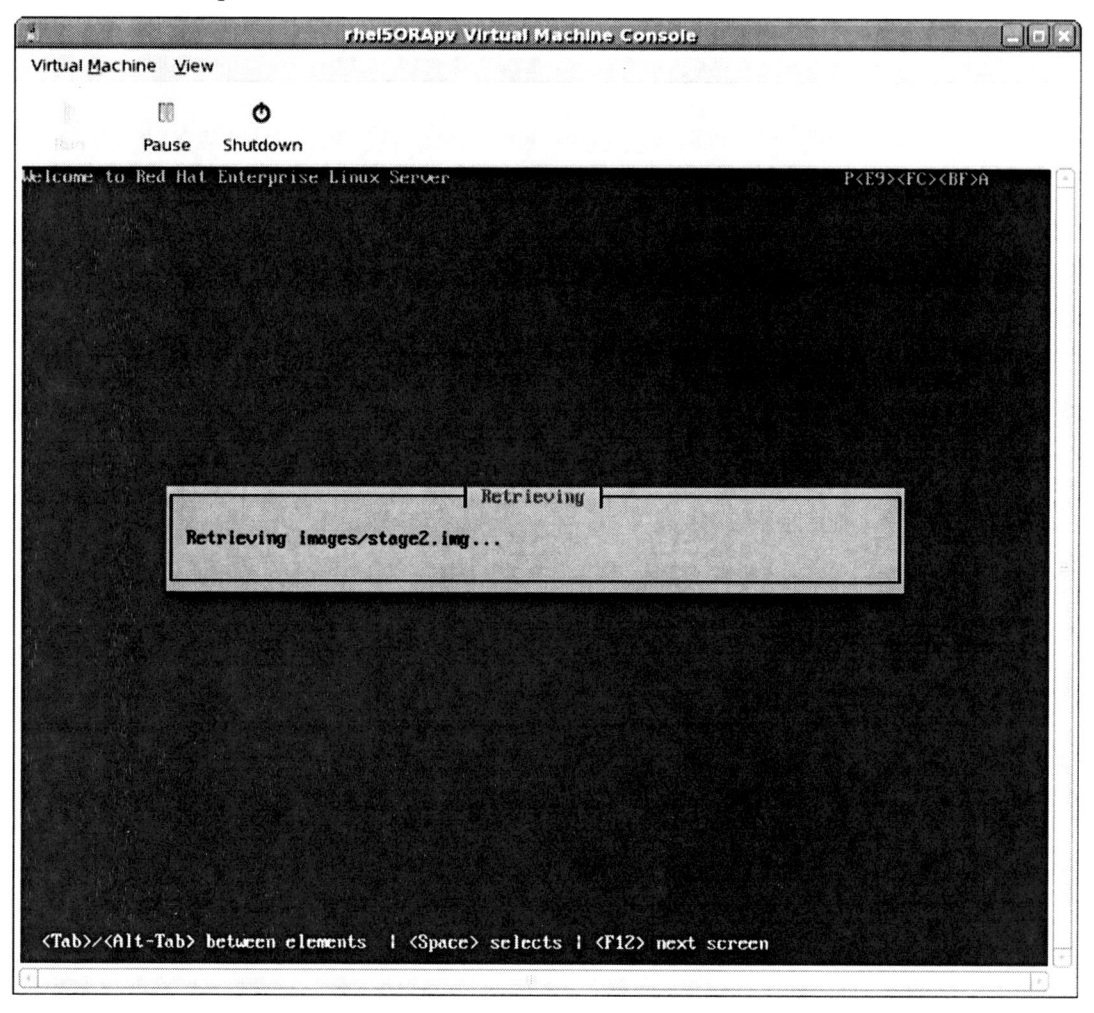

Virtualization Guide

Once the initial steps are complete the graphical installation process starts.

Fedora 12

If you are installing a Beta or early release distribution confirm that you want to install the operating system. Click **Install Anyway**, and then click **OK**:

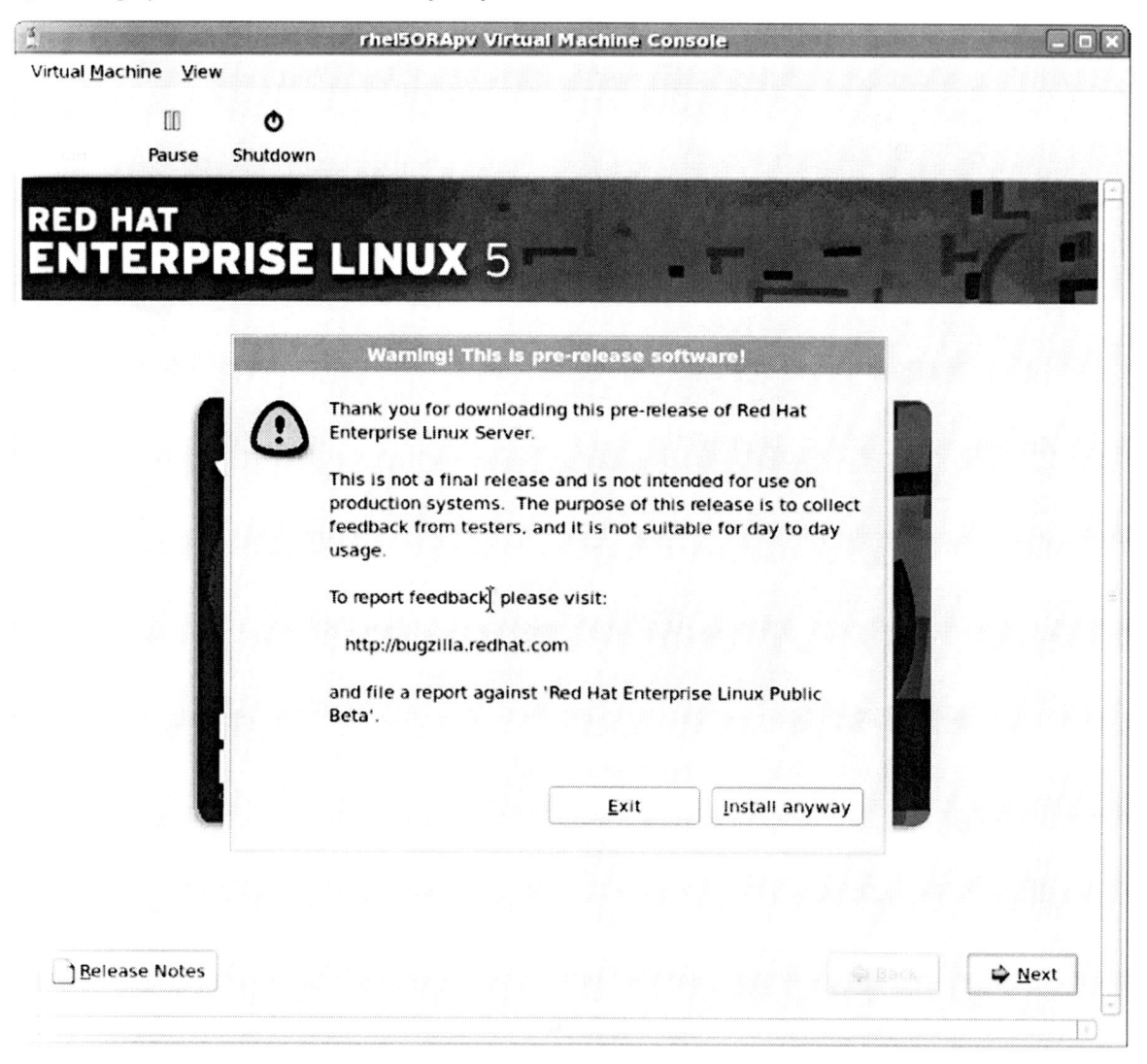

Procedure 3.2. The graphical installation process

1. Enter a valid registration code. If you have a valid RHN subscription key please enter in the `Installation Number` field:

rhel5ORApv Virtual Machine Console
Virtual Machine View
Run
Pause
Shutdown
RED HAT
ENTERPRISE LINUX 5
To install the full set of supported packages included in your subscription, please enter your Installation Number
Installation Number:
Skip entering Installation Number
Cancel
OK
Release Notes
Back
Next

Note

If you skip the registration step the you can confirm your fedora Network account details after the installation with the `rhn_register` command. The `rhn_register` command requires root access.

```
# rhn_register
```

Fedora 12

2. The installation prompts you to confirm erasure of all data on the storage you selected for the installation:

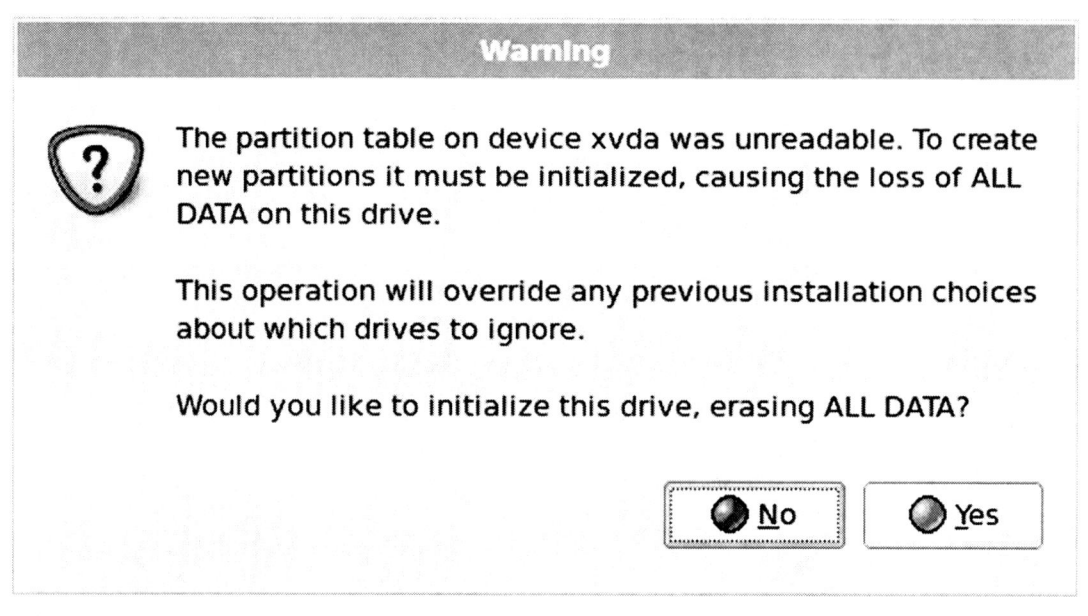

> **Warning**
>
> ❓ The partition table on device xvda was unreadable. To create new partitions it must be initialized, causing the loss of ALL DATA on this drive.
>
> This operation will override any previous installation choices about which drives to ignore.
>
> Would you like to initialize this drive, erasing ALL DATA?
>
> [No] [Yes]

Click **Yes** to continue.

Virtualization Guide

3. Review the storage configuration and partition layout. You can chose to select the advanced storage configuration if you want to use iSCSI for the guest's storage.

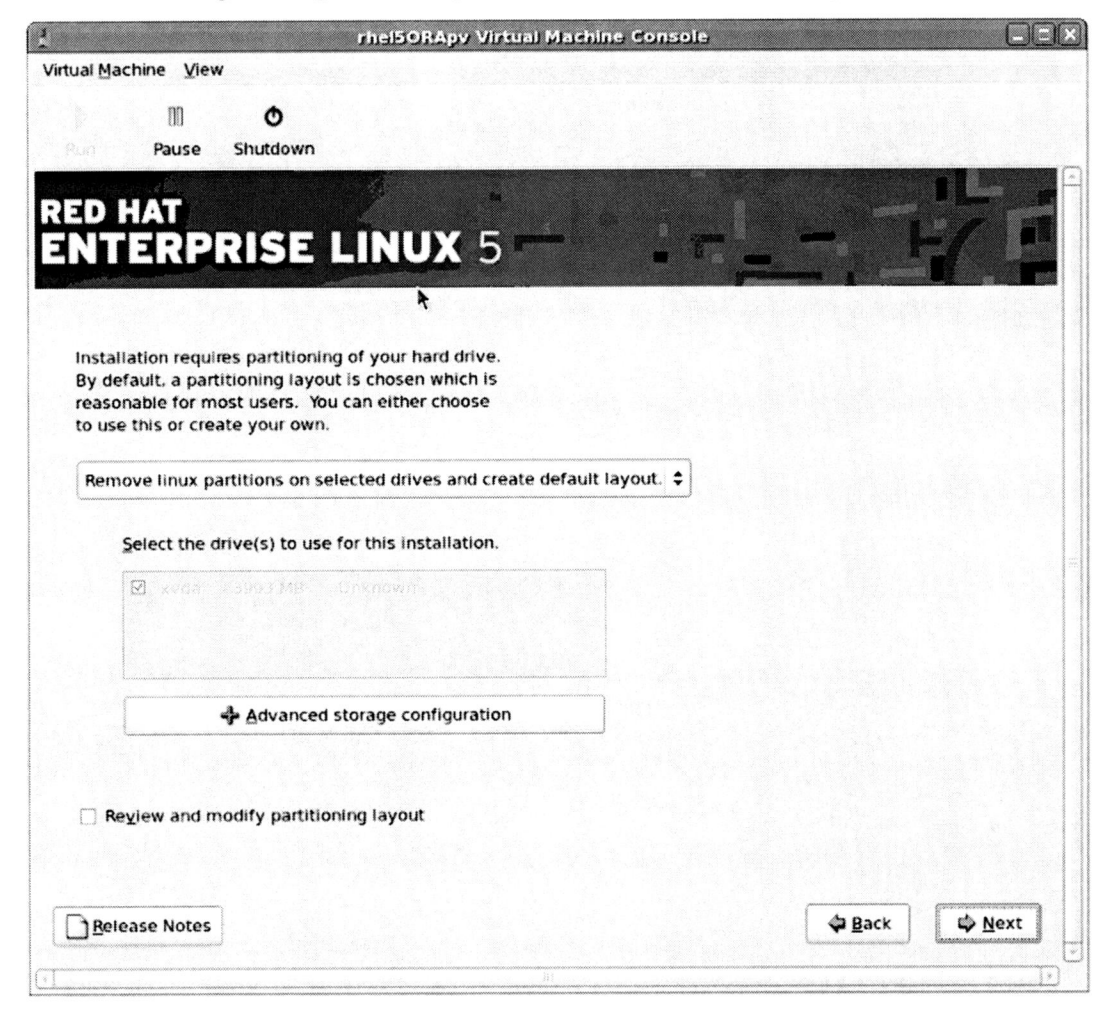

Make your selections then click **Next**.

Fedora 12

4. Confirm the selected storage for the installation.

   Warning

   You have chosen to remove all Linux partitions (and ALL DATA on them) on the following drives:

   /dev/xvda

   Are you sure you want to do this?

   [No]   [Yes]

Click **Yes** to continue.

5. Configure networking and hostname settings. These settings are populated with the data entered earlier in the installation process. Change these settings if necessary.

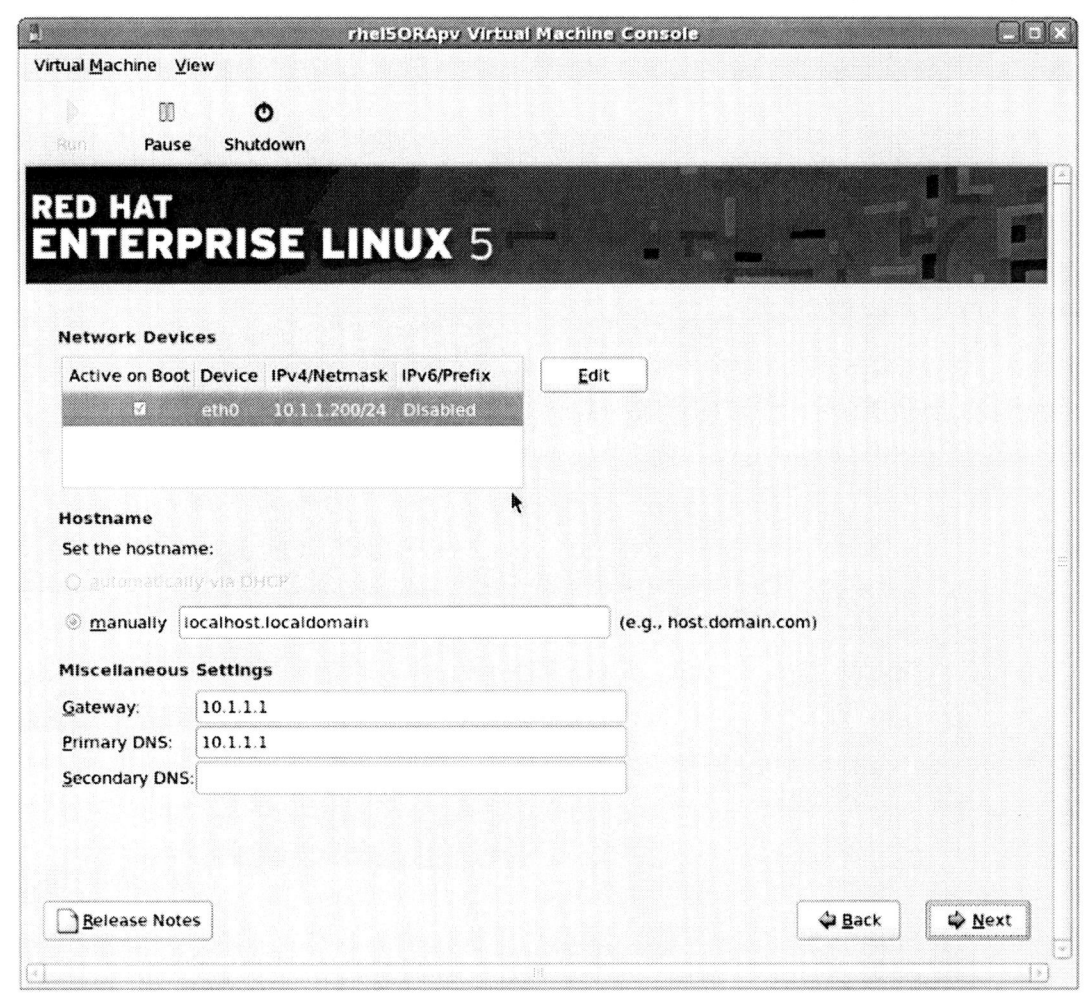

Click **OK** to continue.

Fedora 12

6. Select the appropriate time zone for your environment.

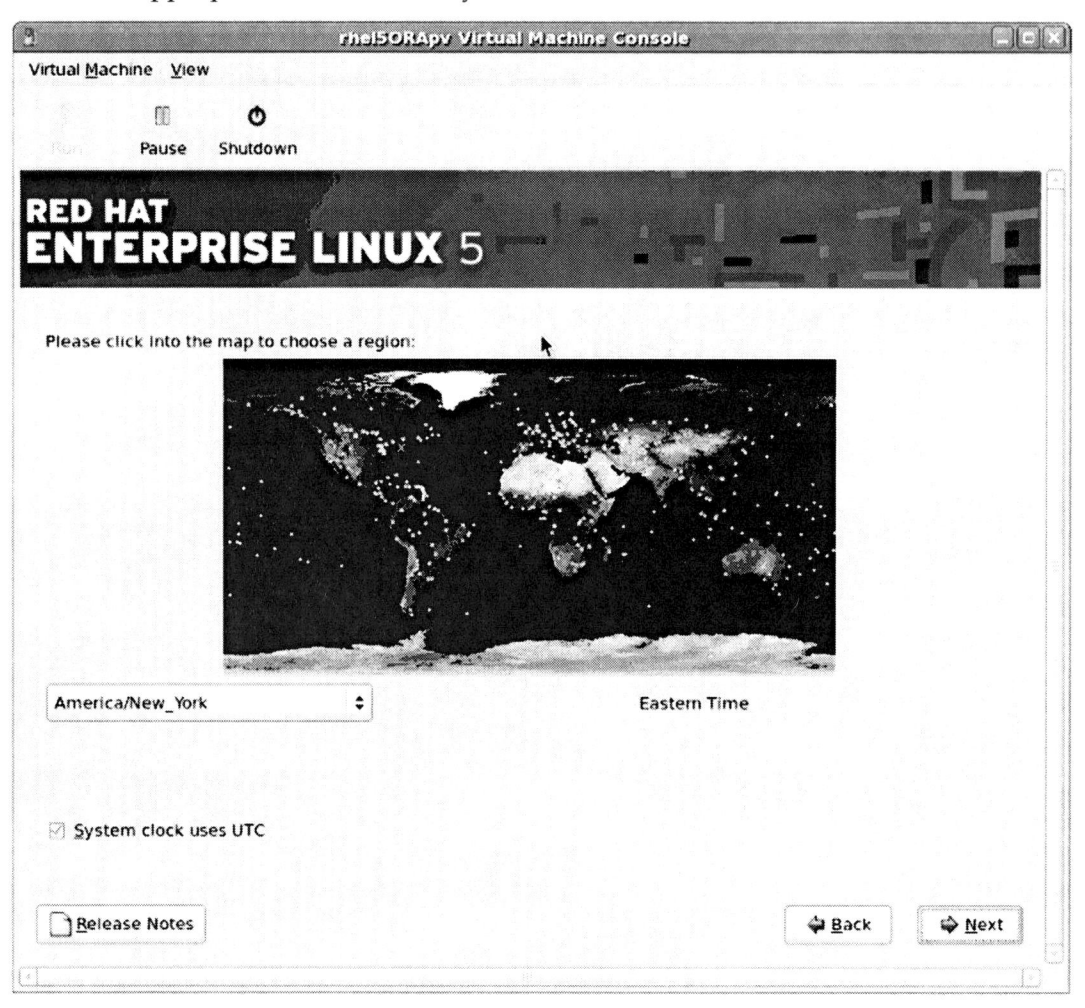

7. Enter the root password for the guest.

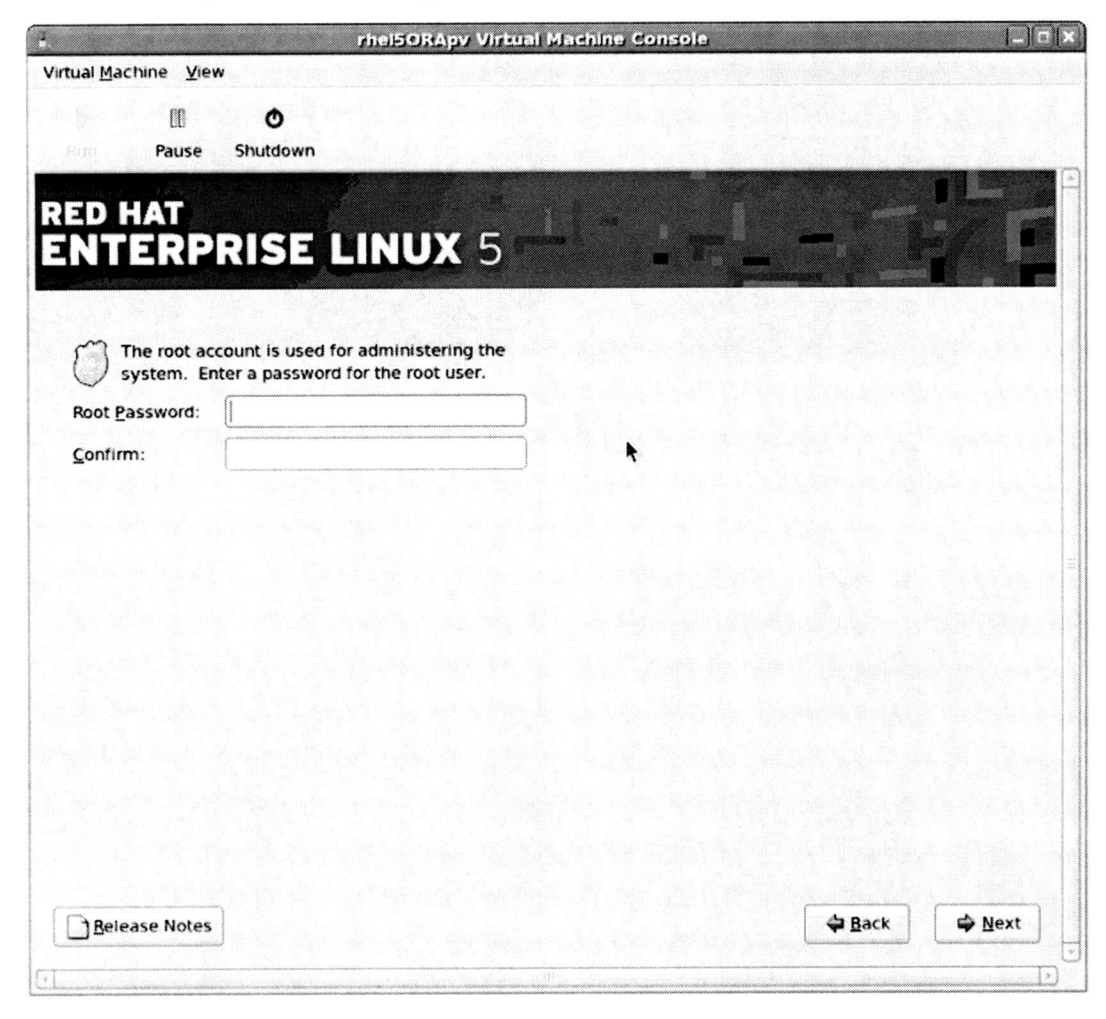

Click **Next** to continue.

Fedora 12

8. Select the software packages to install. Select the **Customize Now** button. You must install the **kernel-xen** package in the **System** directory. The **kernel-xen** package is required for para-virtualization.

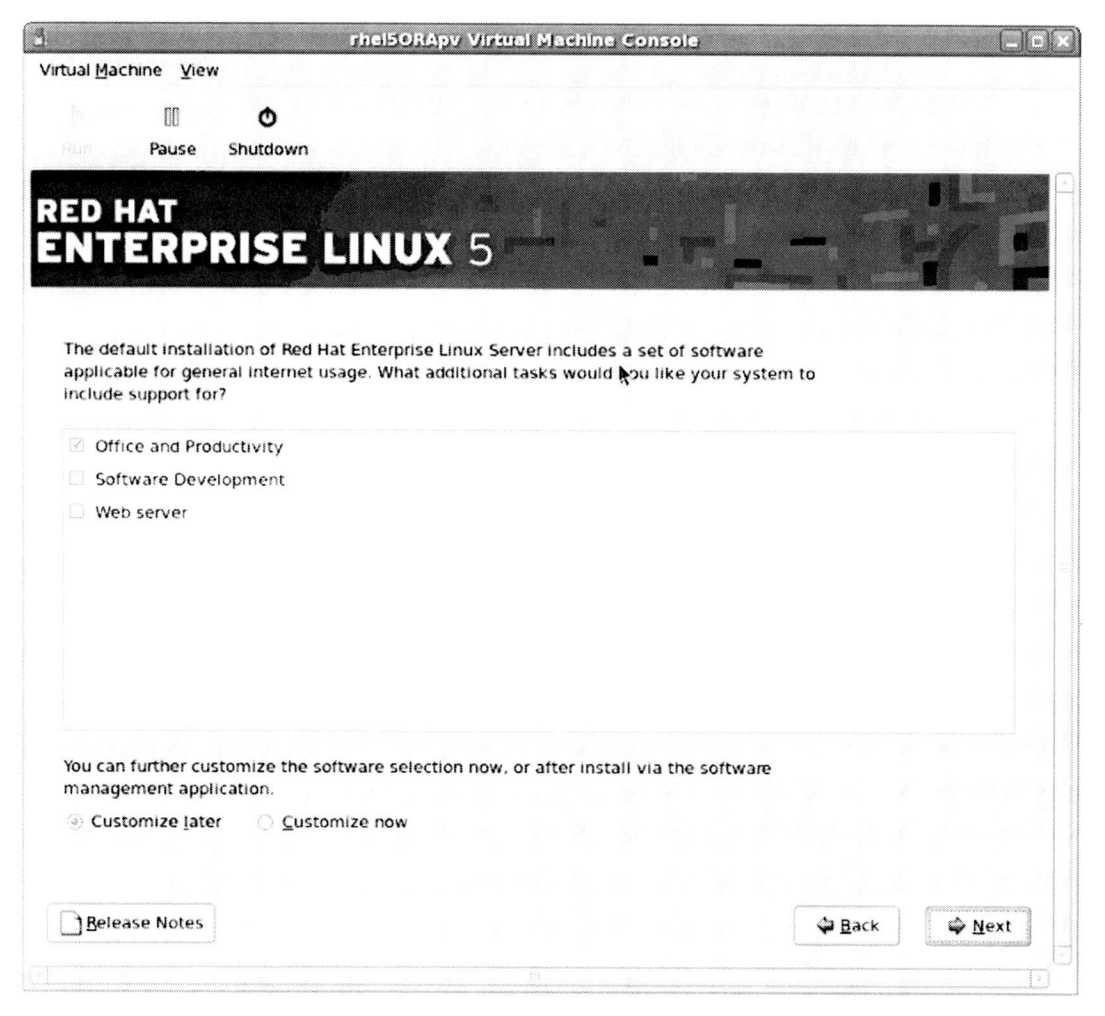

Click **Next**.

Virtualization Guide

9. Dependencies and space requirements are calculated.

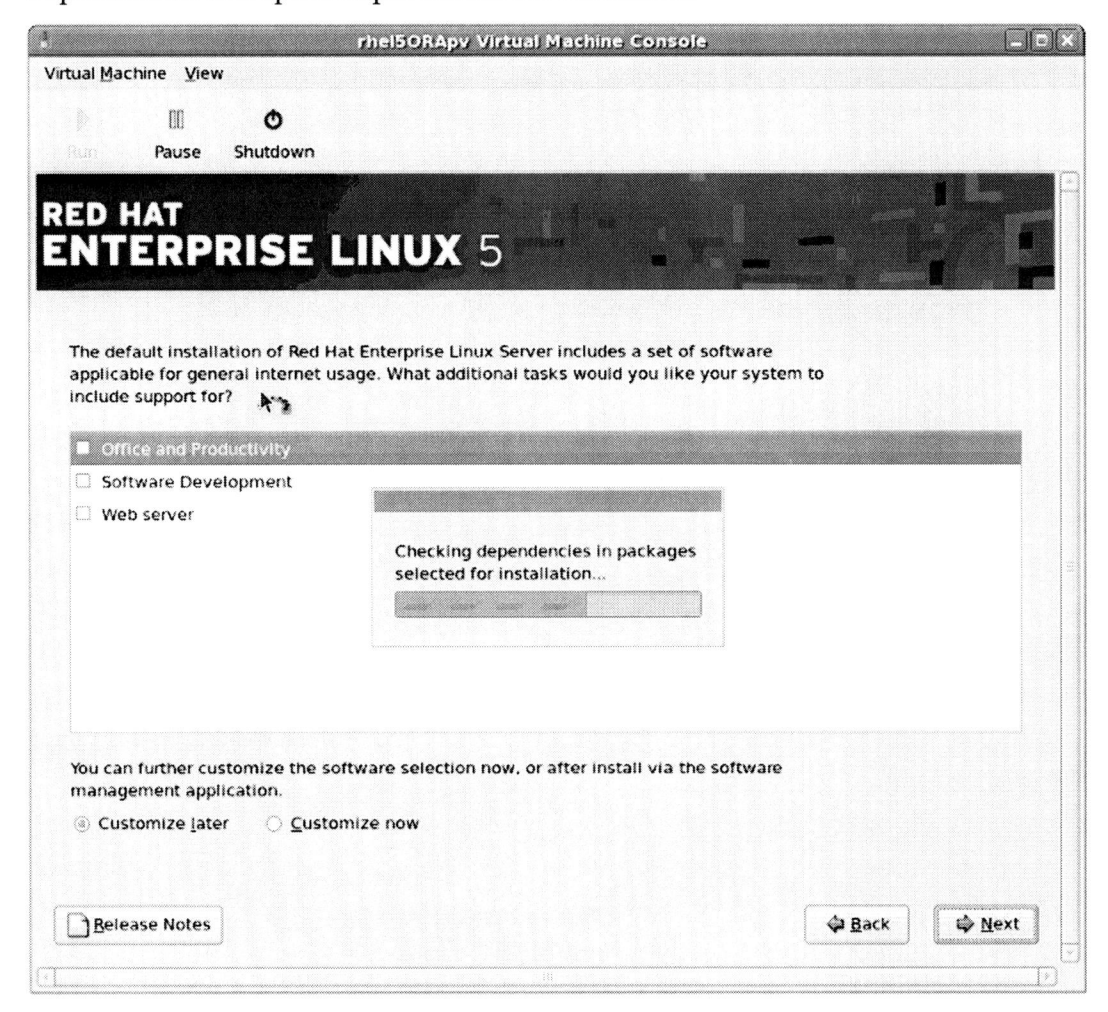

Fedora 12

10. After the installation dependencies and space requirements have been verified click **Next** to start the actual installation.

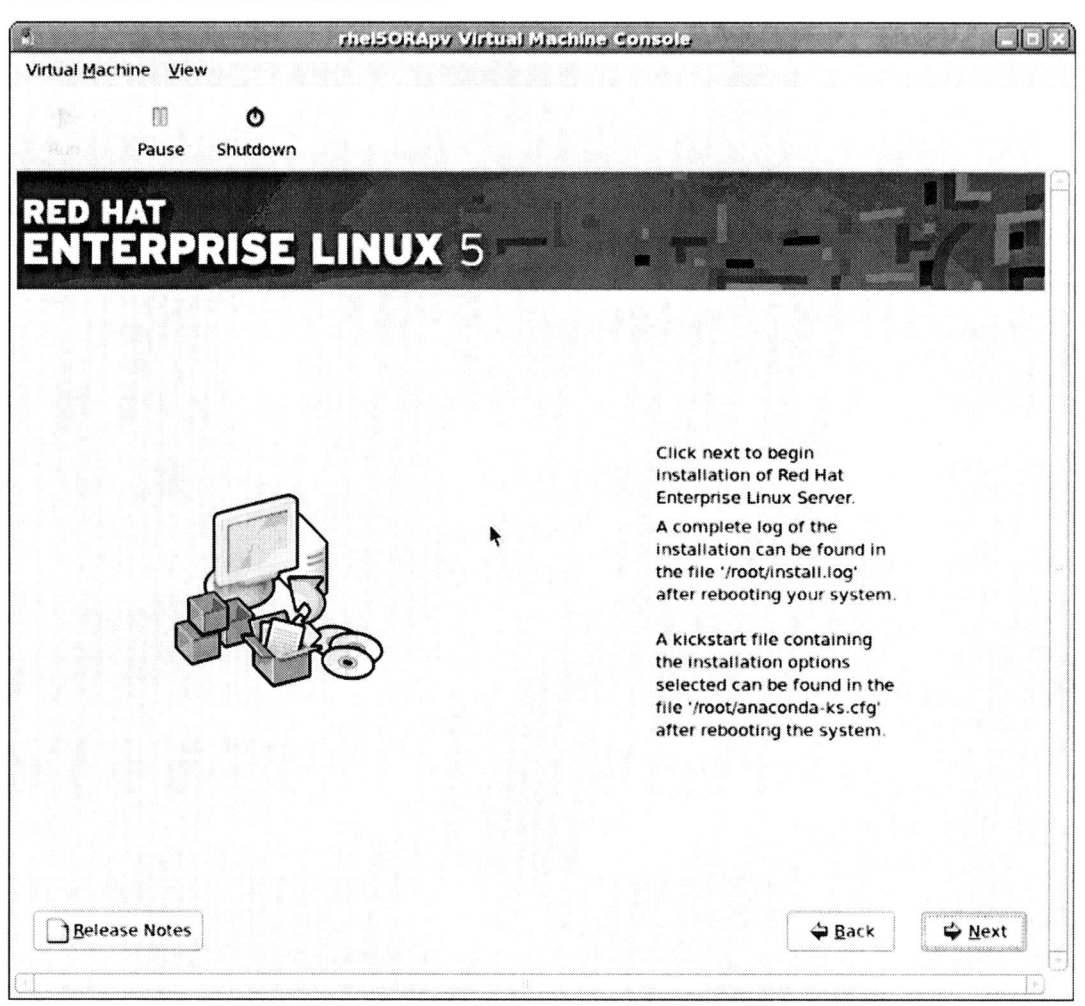

Virtualization Guide

11. All of the selected software packages are installed automatically.

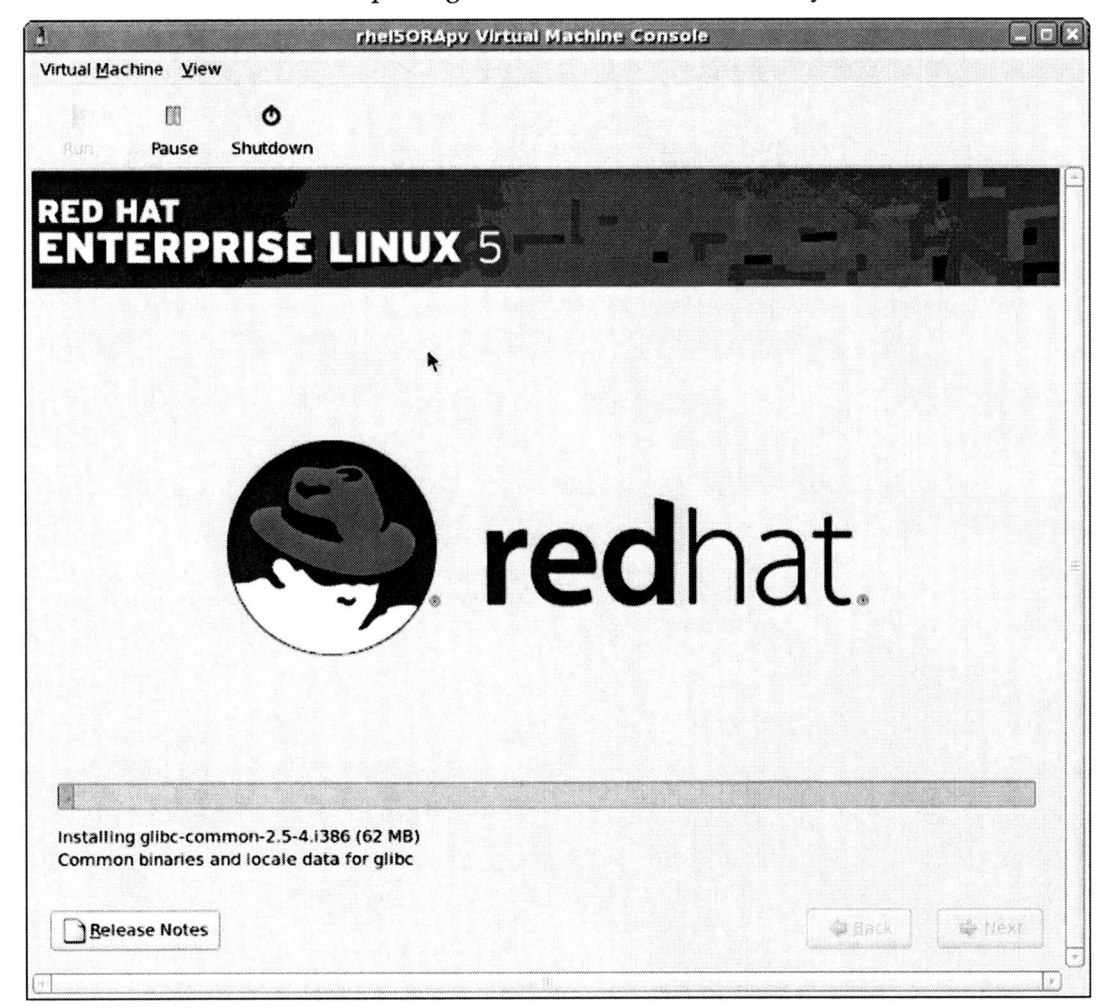

Fedora 12

12. After the installation has finished reboot your guest:

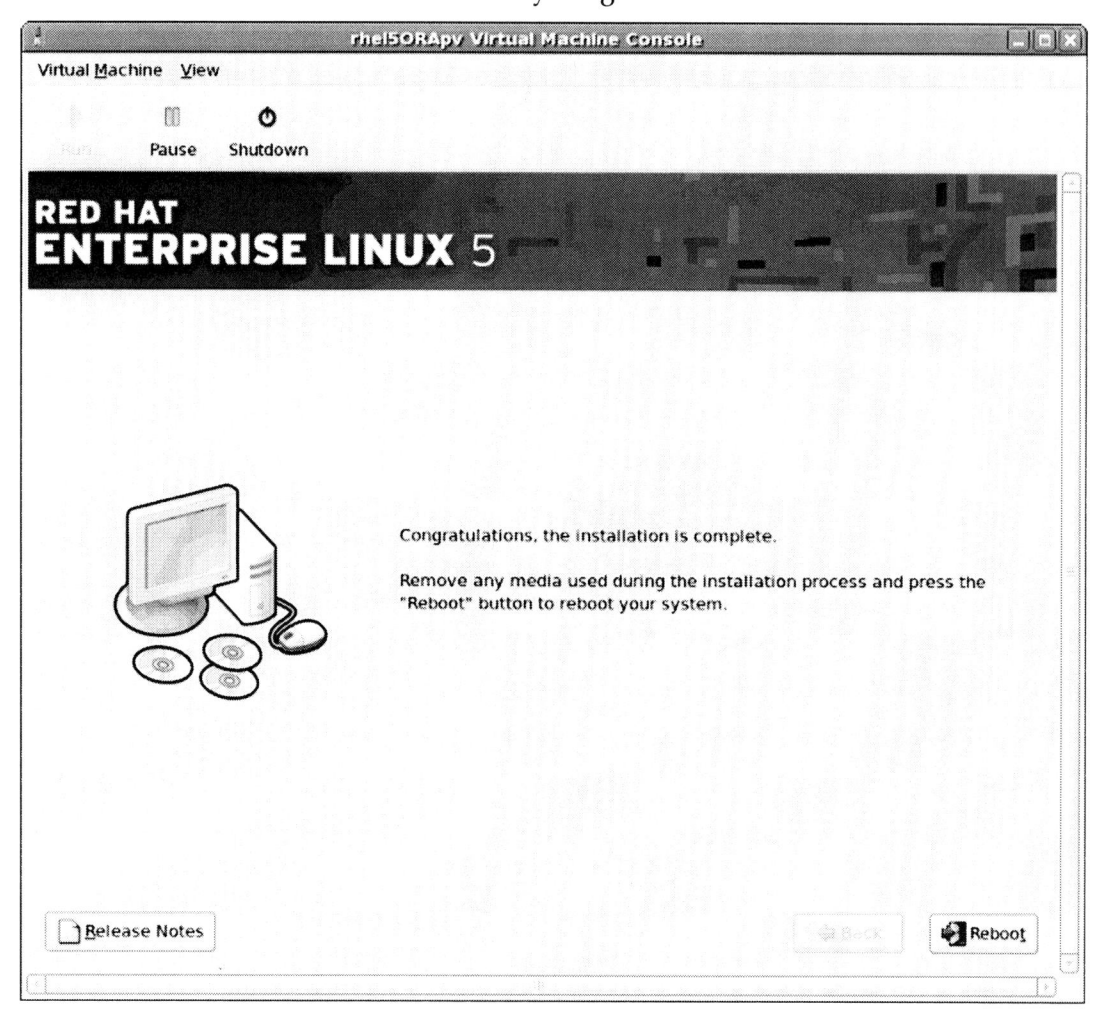

Virtualization Guide

13. The guest will not reboot, instead it will shutdown..

Fedora 12

14. Boot the guest. The guest's name was chosen when you used the `virt-install` in *Section 3.1, "Installing Red Hat Enterprise Linux 5 as a para-virtualized guest"*. If you used the default example the name is *rhel5PV*.

    Run:

    `virsh reboot rhel5PV`

    Alternatively, open `virt-manager`, select the name of your guest, click **Open**, then click **Run**.

    A **VNC** window displaying the guest's boot processes now opens.

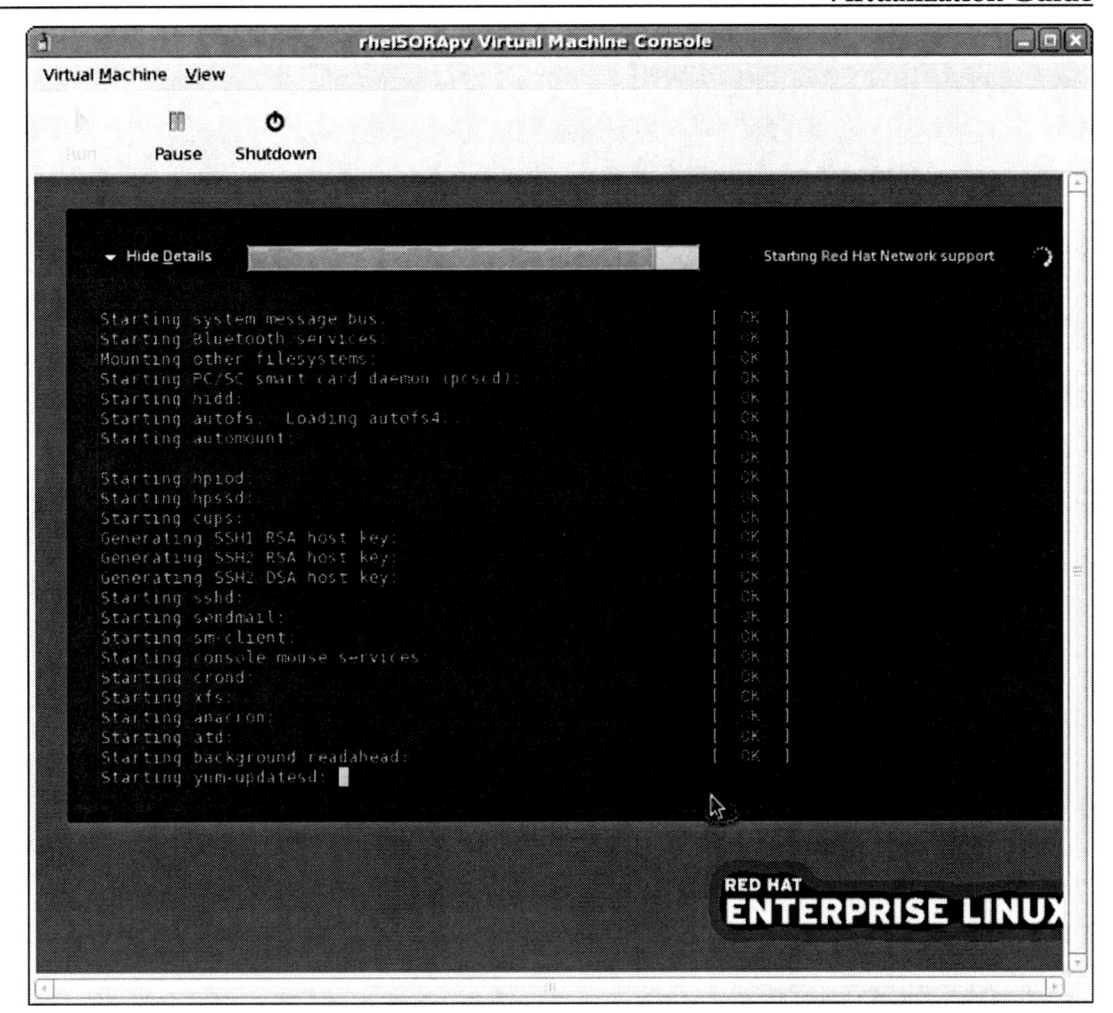

Virtualization Guide

Fedora 12

15. Booting the guest starts the *First Boot* configuration screen. This wizard prompts you for some basic configuration choices for your guest.

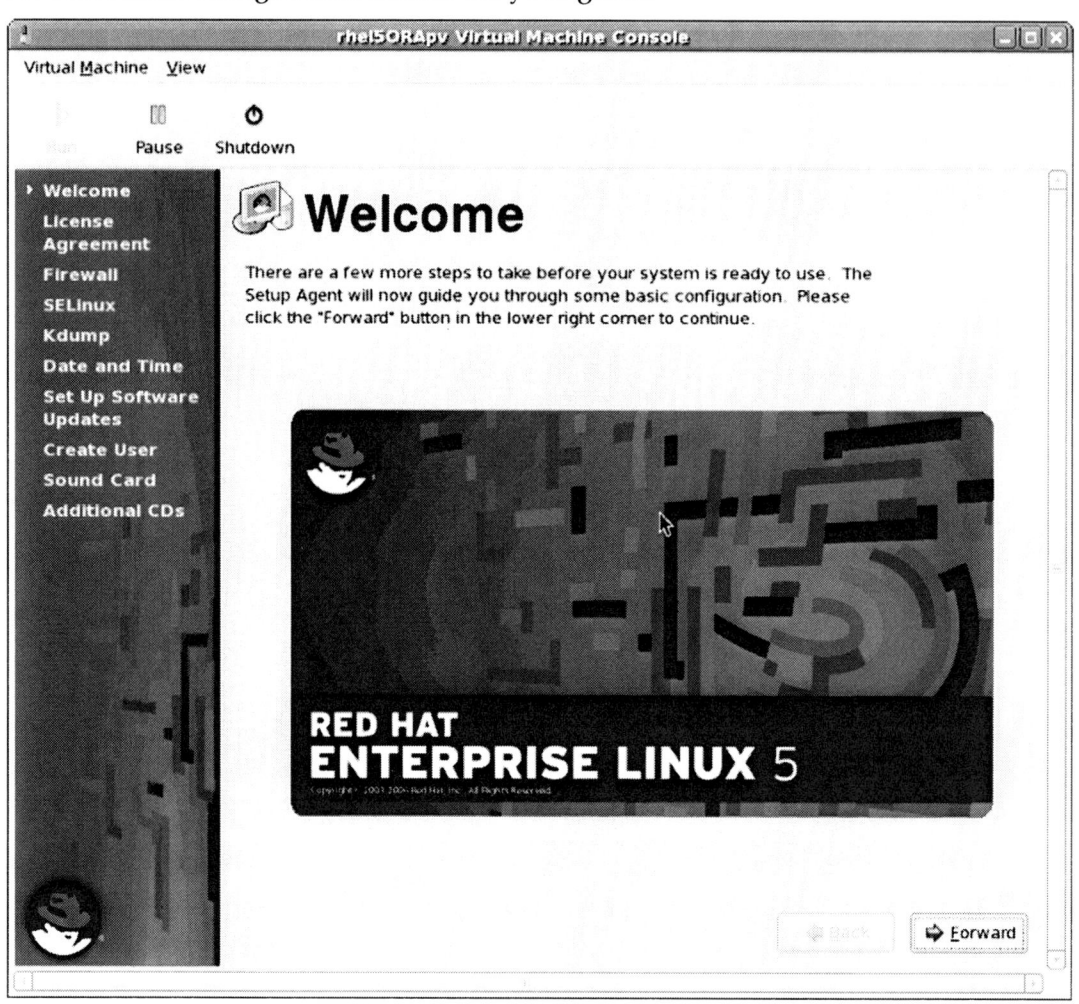

Virtualization Guide

16. Read and agree to the license agreement.

    Click **Forward** on the license agreement windows.

Fedora 12

17. Configure the firewall.

Click **Forward** to continue.

Virtualization Guide

1. If you disable the firewall prompted to confirm your choice. Click **Yes** to confirm and continue.

Fedora 12

18. Configure SELinux. It is strongly recommended you run SELinux in **enforcing mode**. You can choose to either run SELinux in permissive mode or completely disable it.

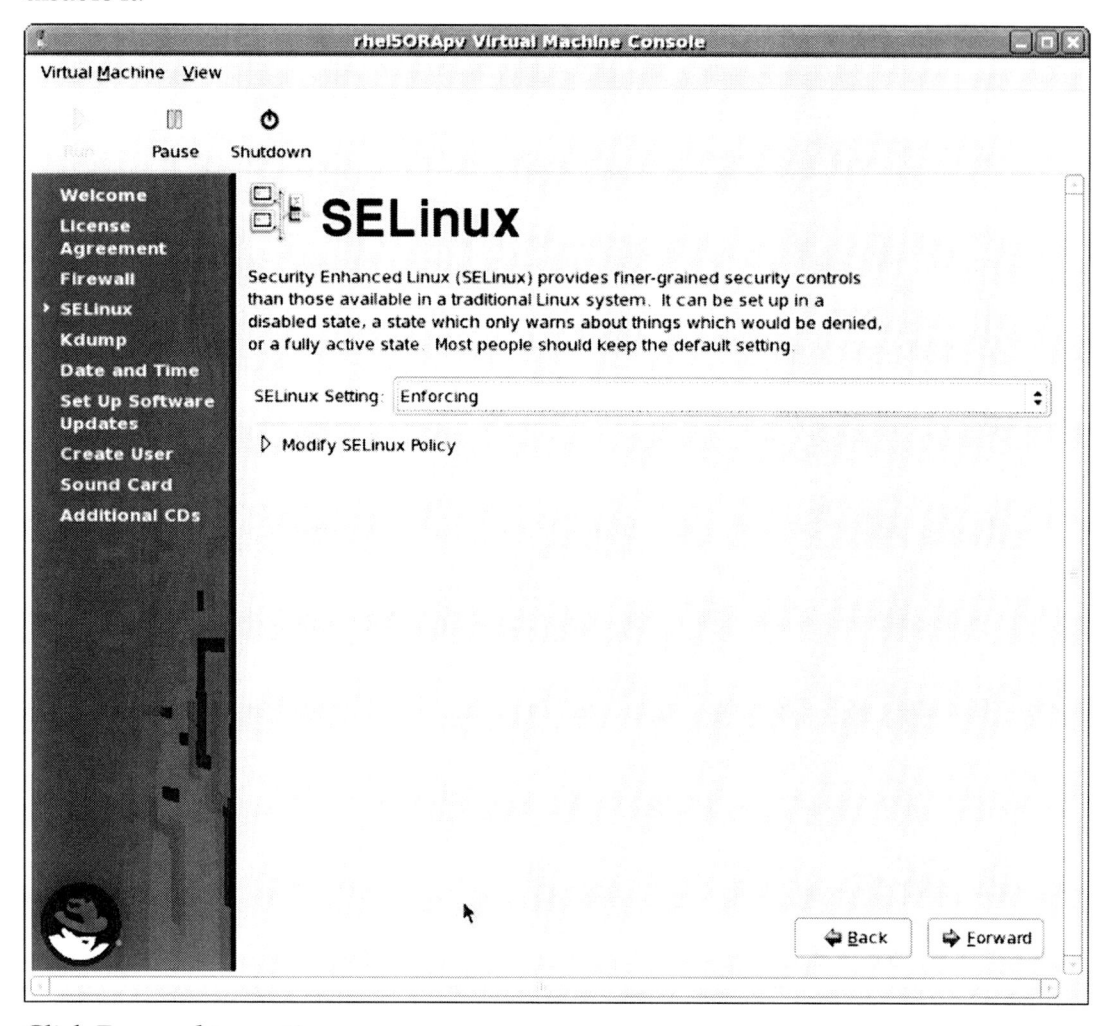

Click **Forward** to continue.

Virtualization Guide

1. If you choose to disable SELinux this warning displays. Click **Yes** to disable SELinux.

Fedora 12

19. Enable `kdump` if necessary.

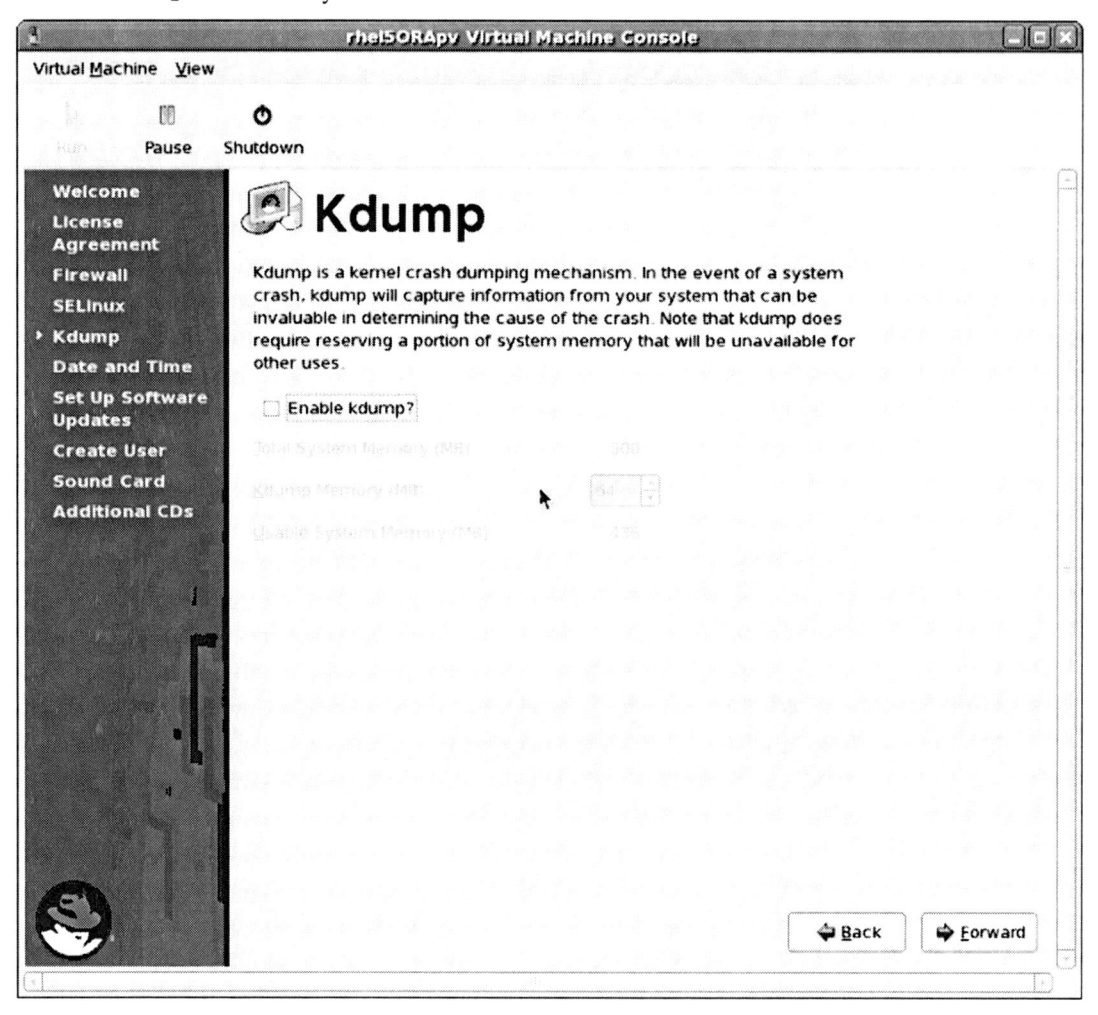

Click **Forward** to continue.

20. Confirm time and date are set correctly for your guest. If you install a paravirtualized guest time and date should sync with the hypervisor.

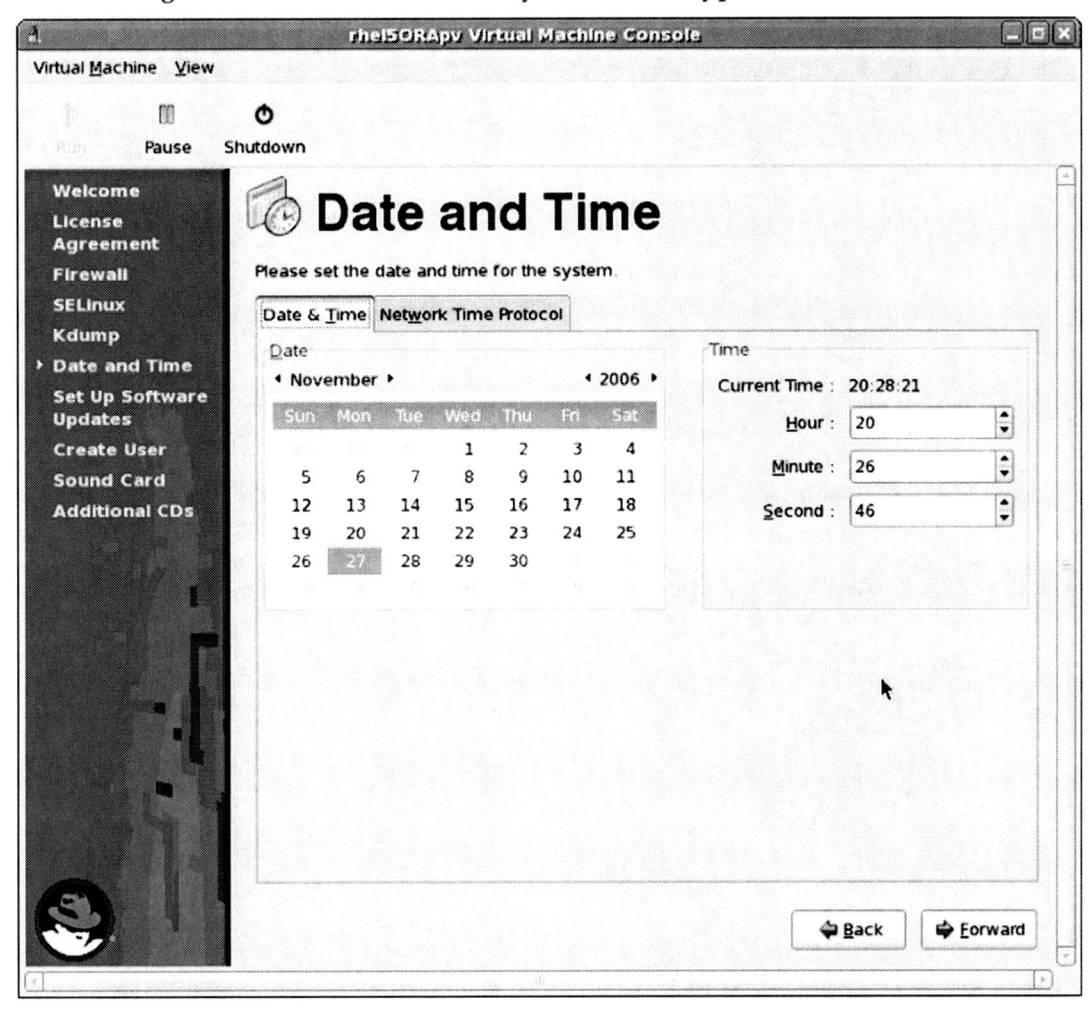

Click **Forward** to continue.

Fedora 12

21. Set up software updates. If you have a fedora Network subscription or want to trial one use the screen below to register your newly installed guest in RHN.

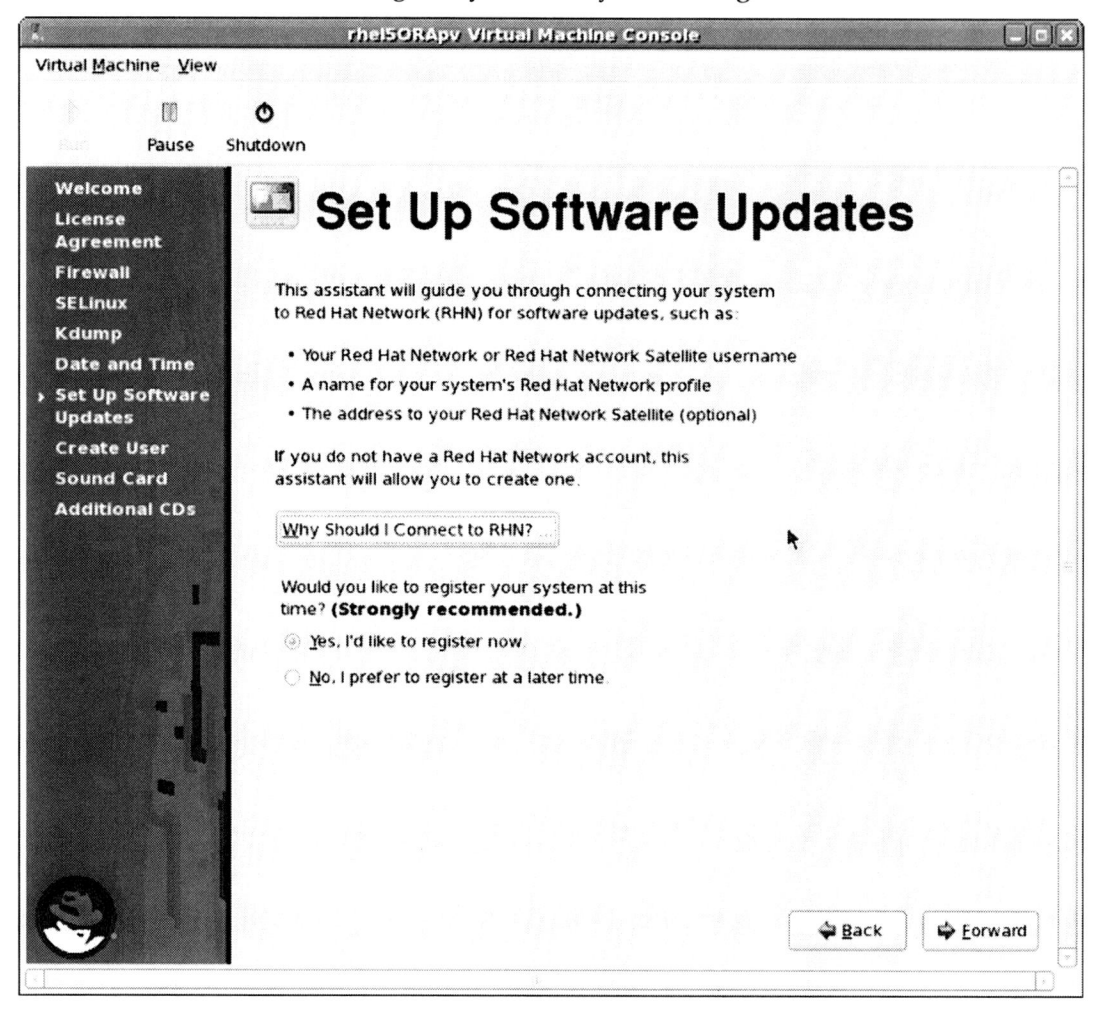

Click **Forward** to continue.

Virtualization Guide

1. Confirm your choices for RHN.

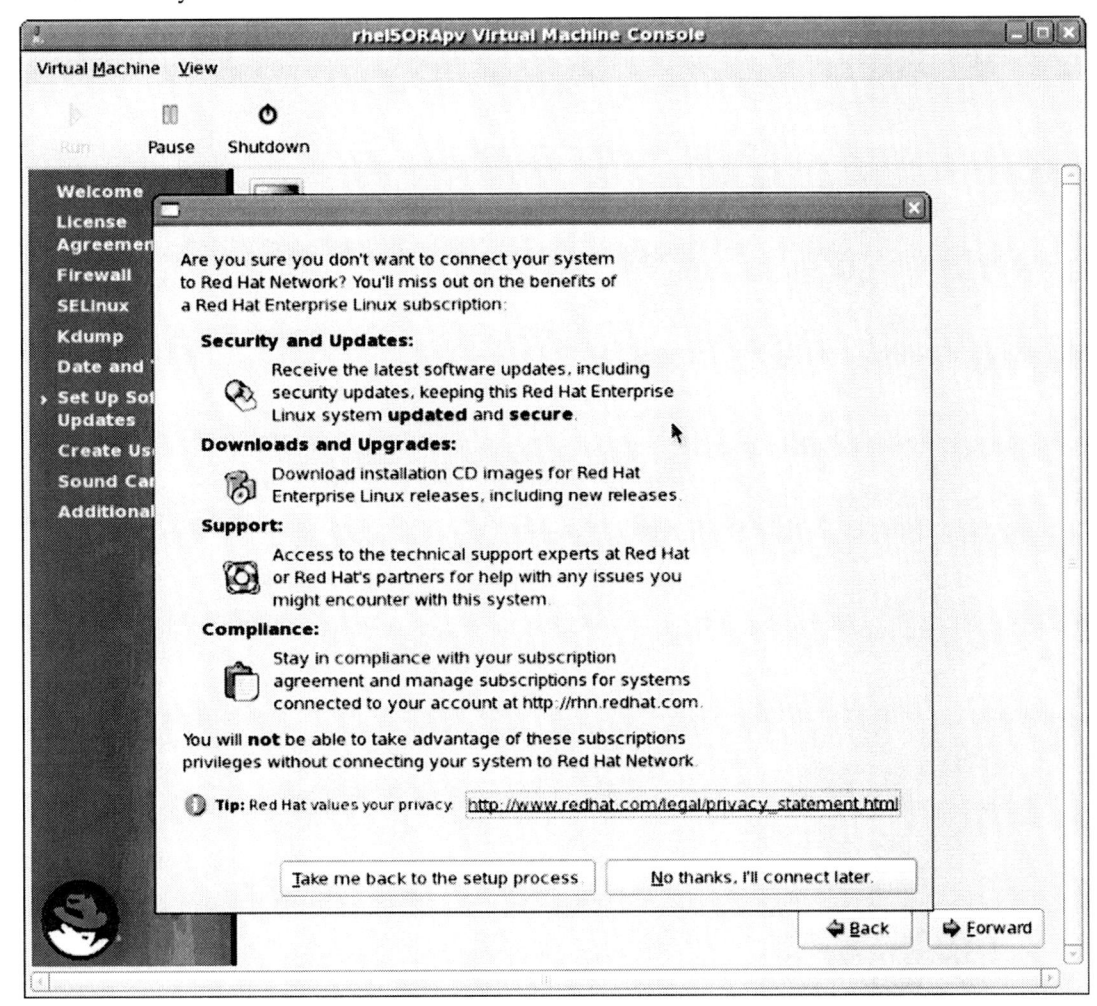

Fedora 12

2. Once setup has finished you may see one more screen if you opted out of RHN at this time. You will not receive software updates.

Click the **Forward** button.

Virtualization Guide

22. Create a non root user account. It is advised to create a non root user for normal usage and enhanced security. Enter the Username, Name and password.

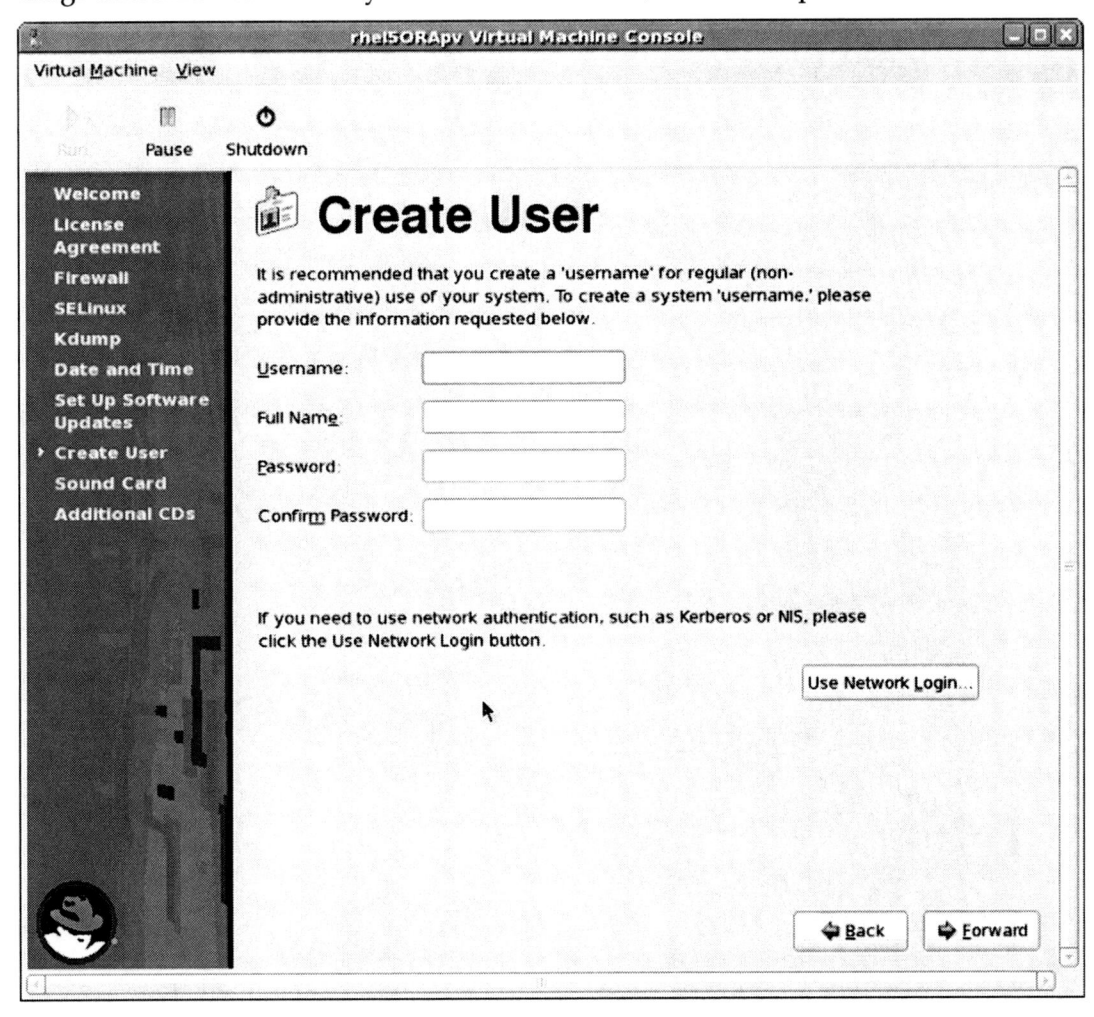

Click the **Forward** button.

73

Fedora 12

23. If a sound device is detected and you require sound, calibrate it. Complete the process and click **Forward**.

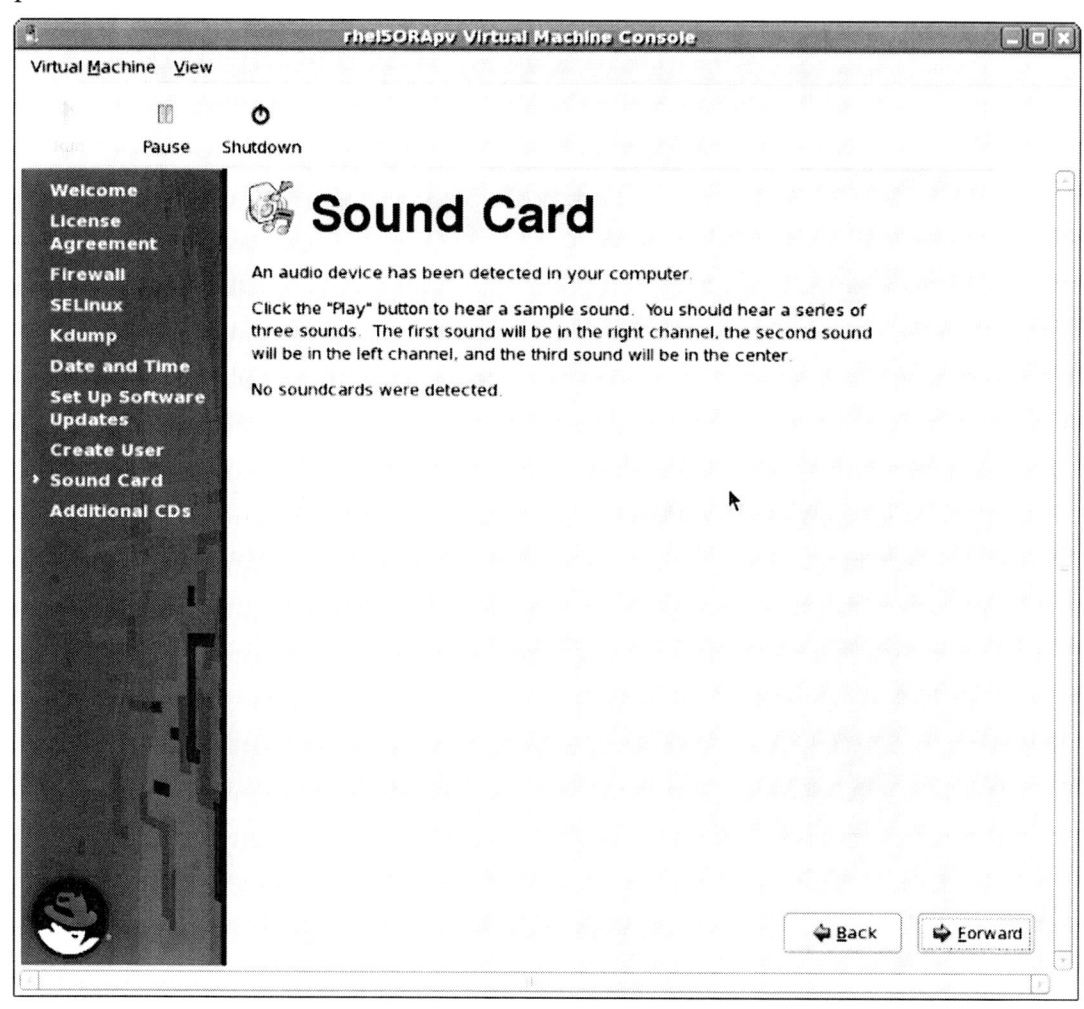

24. You can to install any additional software packages from CD you could do so on this screen. It it often more efficient to not install any additional software at this point but add it later using yum. Click **Finish**.

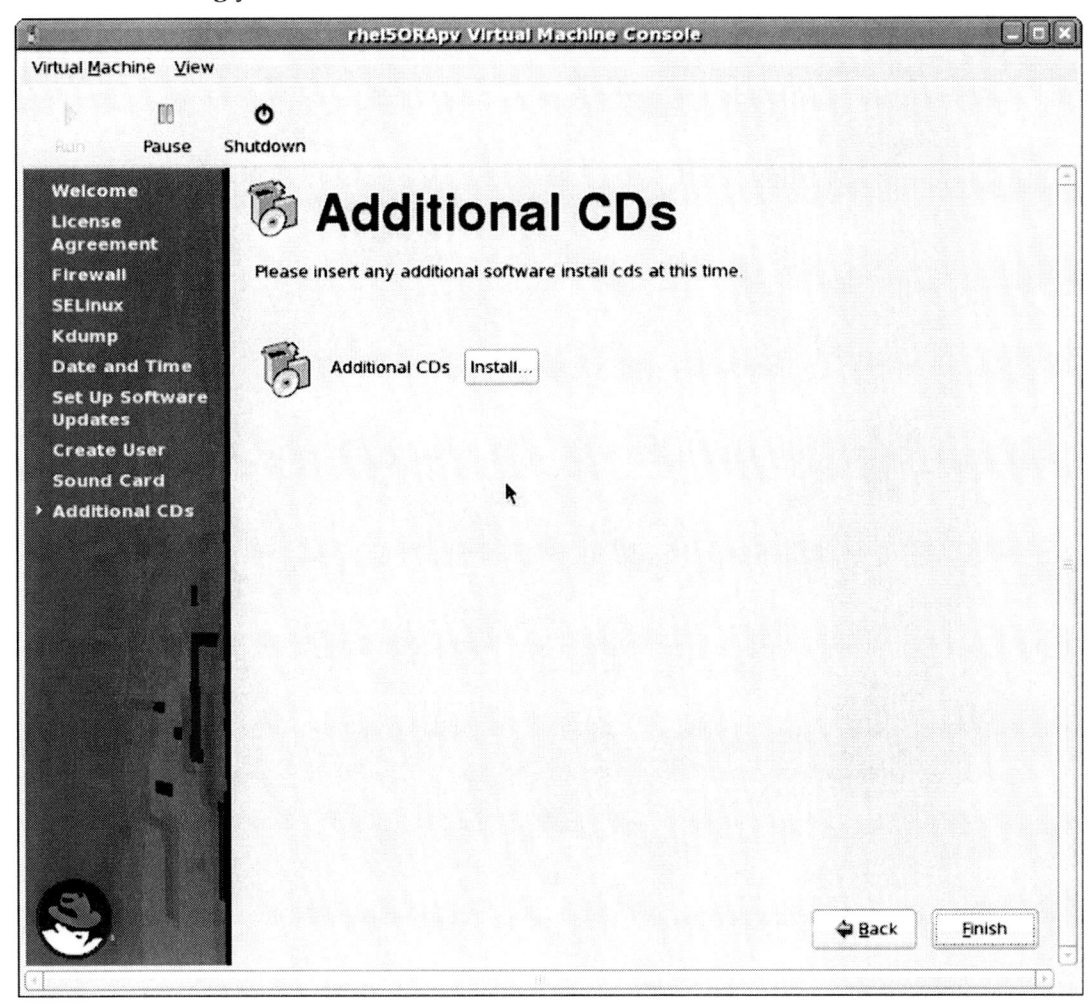

Fedora 12

25. The guest now configure any settings you changed and continues the boot process.

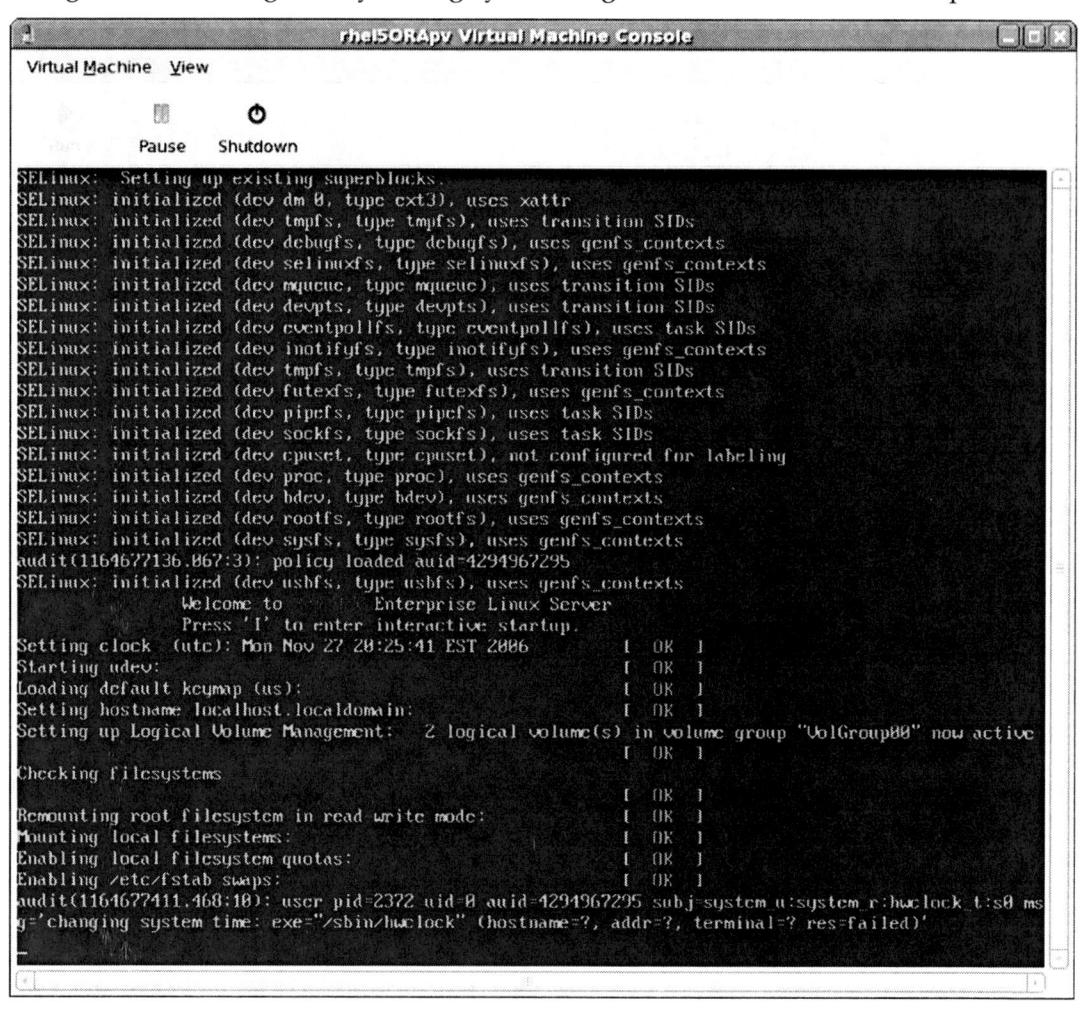

26. The Red Hat Enterprise Linux 5 login screen displays. Log in using the username created in the previous steps.

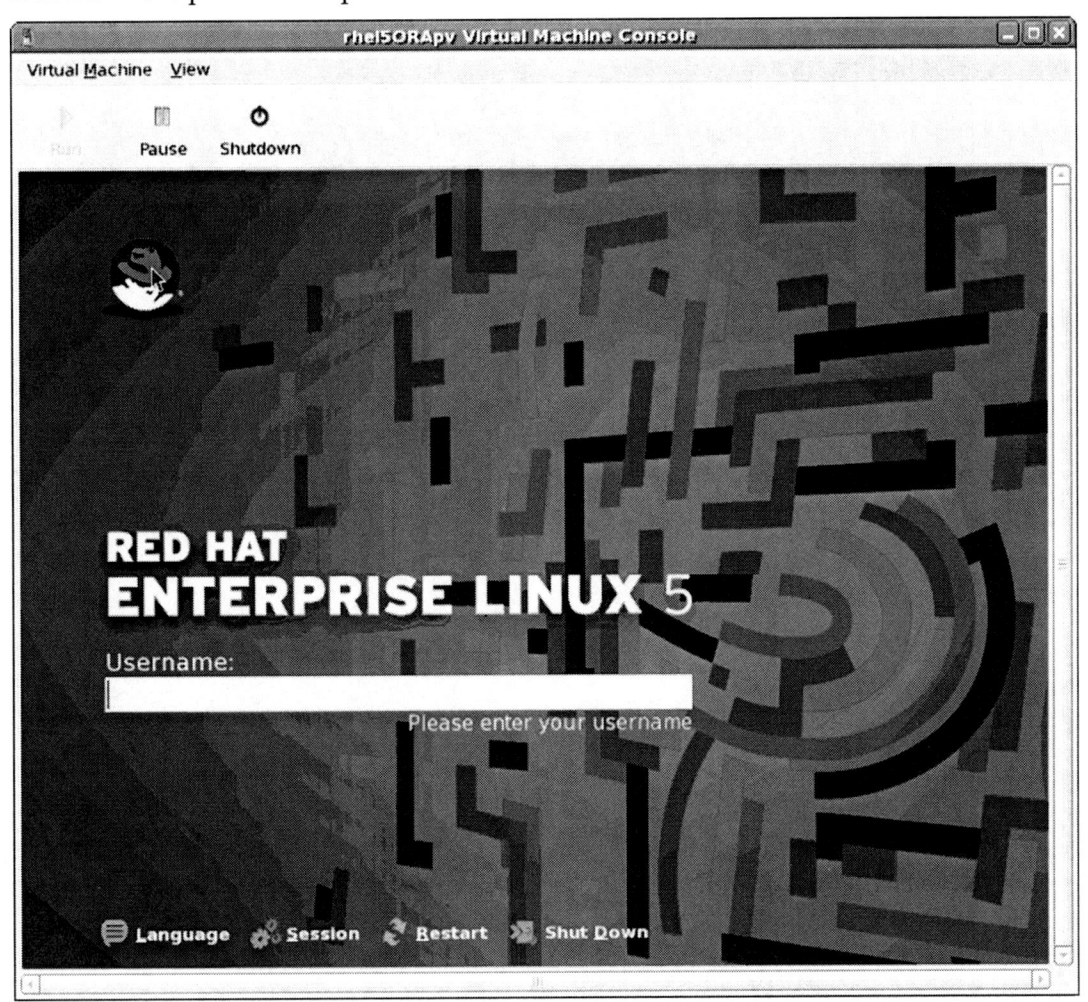

Fedora 12

27. You have now successfully installed a para-virtualized Red Hat Enterprise Linux 5 guest.

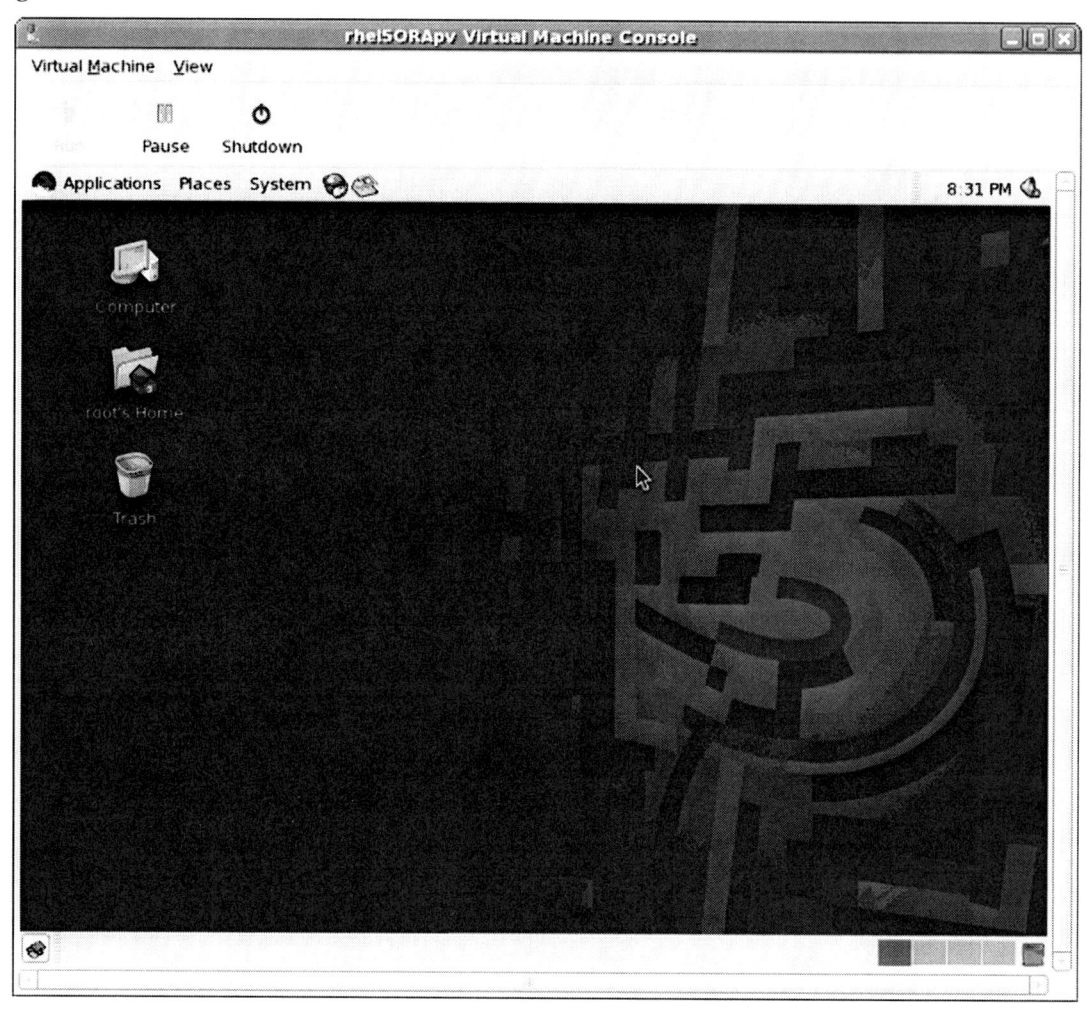

3.2. Installing Red Hat Enterprise Linux as a fully virtualized guest

This section covers installing a fully virtualized Red Hat Enterprise Linux 5 guest.

Procedure 3.3.
Creating a fully virtualized Red Hat Enterprise Linux 5 guest with virt-manager

1. Open virt-manager

    Start `virt-manager`. Launch the **Virtual Machine Manager** application from the **Applications** menu and **System Tools** submenu. Alternatively, run the `virt-manager` command as root.

2. Select the hypervisor

    Select the hypervisor. If installed, select Xen or KVM. For this example, select KVM. Note that presently KVM is named qemu.

    Connect to a hypervisor if you have not already done so. Open the **File** menu and select the **Add Connection...** option. Refer to *Section 16.1, "The open connection window"*.

    Once a hypervisor connection is selected the **New** button becomes available. Press the **New** button.

3. Start the new virtual machine wizard

    Pressing the **New** button starts the virtual machine creation wizard.

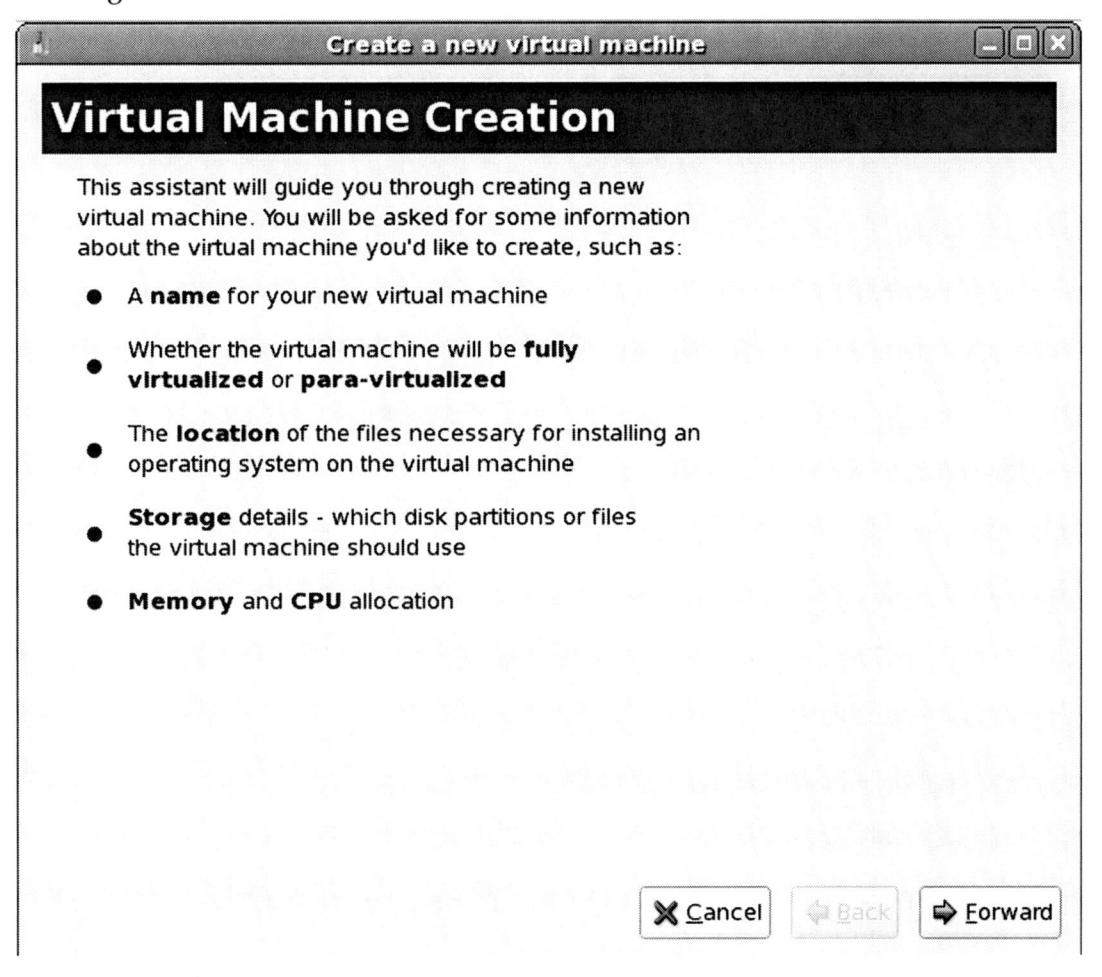

    Virtual Machine Creation

    This assistant will guide you through creating a new virtual machine. You will be asked for some information about the virtual machine you'd like to create, such as:

    - A **name** for your new virtual machine
    - Whether the virtual machine will be **fully virtualized** or **para-virtualized**
    - The **location** of the files necessary for installing an operating system on the virtual machine
    - **Storage** details - which disk partitions or files the virtual machine should use
    - **Memory** and **CPU** allocation

    Press **Forward** to continue.

Fedora 12

4. Name the virtual machine

   Provide a name for your virtualized guest. Punctuation and whitespace characters are not permitted.

   Press **Forward** to continue.

Virtualization Guide

5. Choose a virtualization method

    Choose the virtualization method for the virtualized guest. Note you can only select an installed virtualization method. If you selected KVM or Xen earlier (*Step 4*) you must use the hypervisor you selected. This example uses the KVM hypervisor.

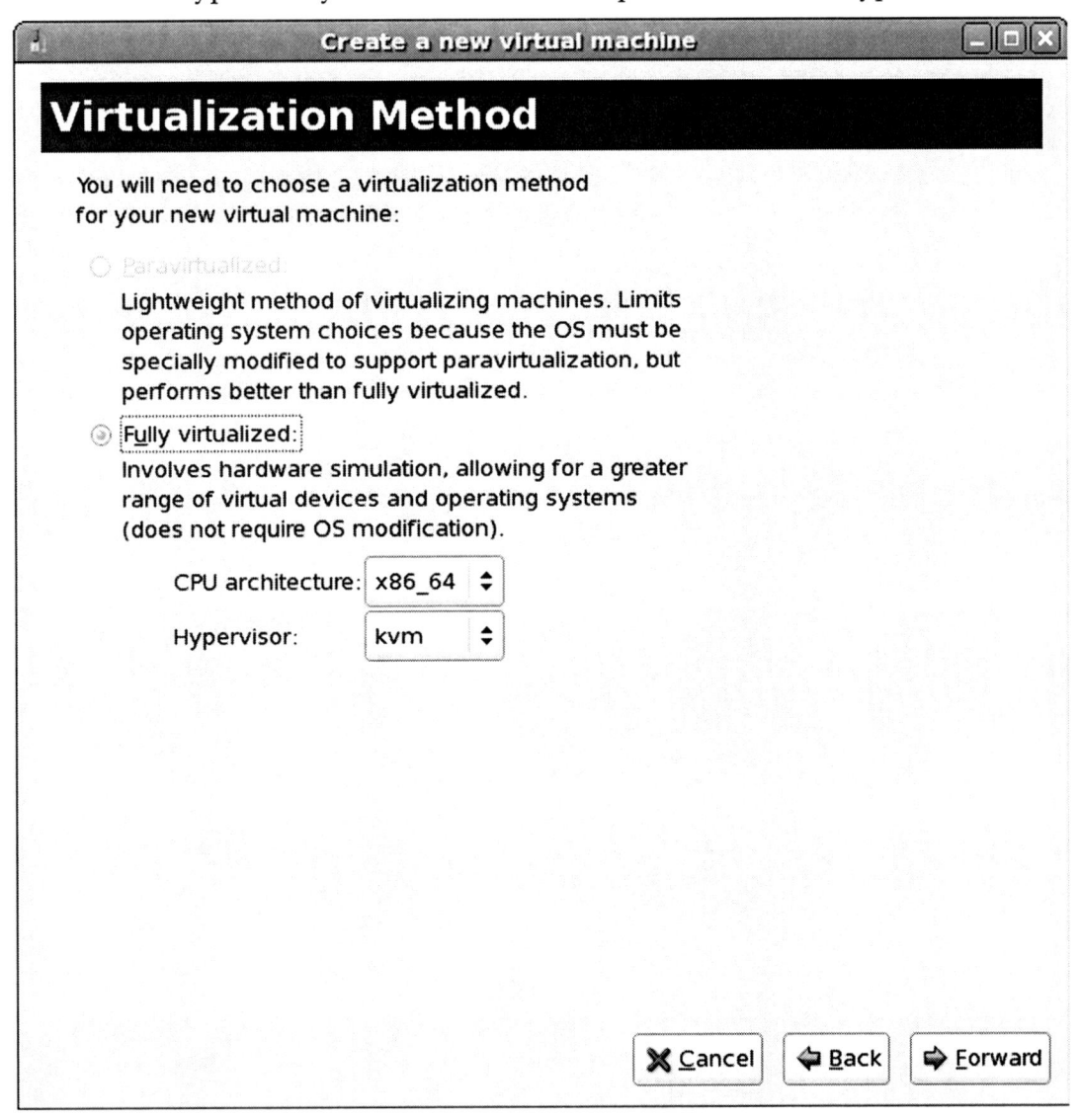

    ### Create a new virtual machine

    ## Virtualization Method

    You will need to choose a virtualization method for your new virtual machine:

    ○ Paravirtualized:
    Lightweight method of virtualizing machines. Limits operating system choices because the OS must be specially modified to support paravirtualization, but performs better than fully virtualized.

    ⦿ Fully virtualized:
    Involves hardware simulation, allowing for a greater range of virtual devices and operating systems (does not require OS modification).

    CPU architecture: x86_64
    Hypervisor: kvm

    [✖ Cancel]   [⬅ Back]   [➡ Forward]

    Press **Forward** to continue.

81

6. Select the installation method

   Select **Local install media** for installing from an optical disc or ISO image; **Network install tree** to install from a HTTP, FTP, or NFS server; or **Network boot** to install from a PXE server.

   Set **OS Type** to **Linux** and **OS Variant** to **Red Hat Enterprise Linux 5** as shown in the screenshot.

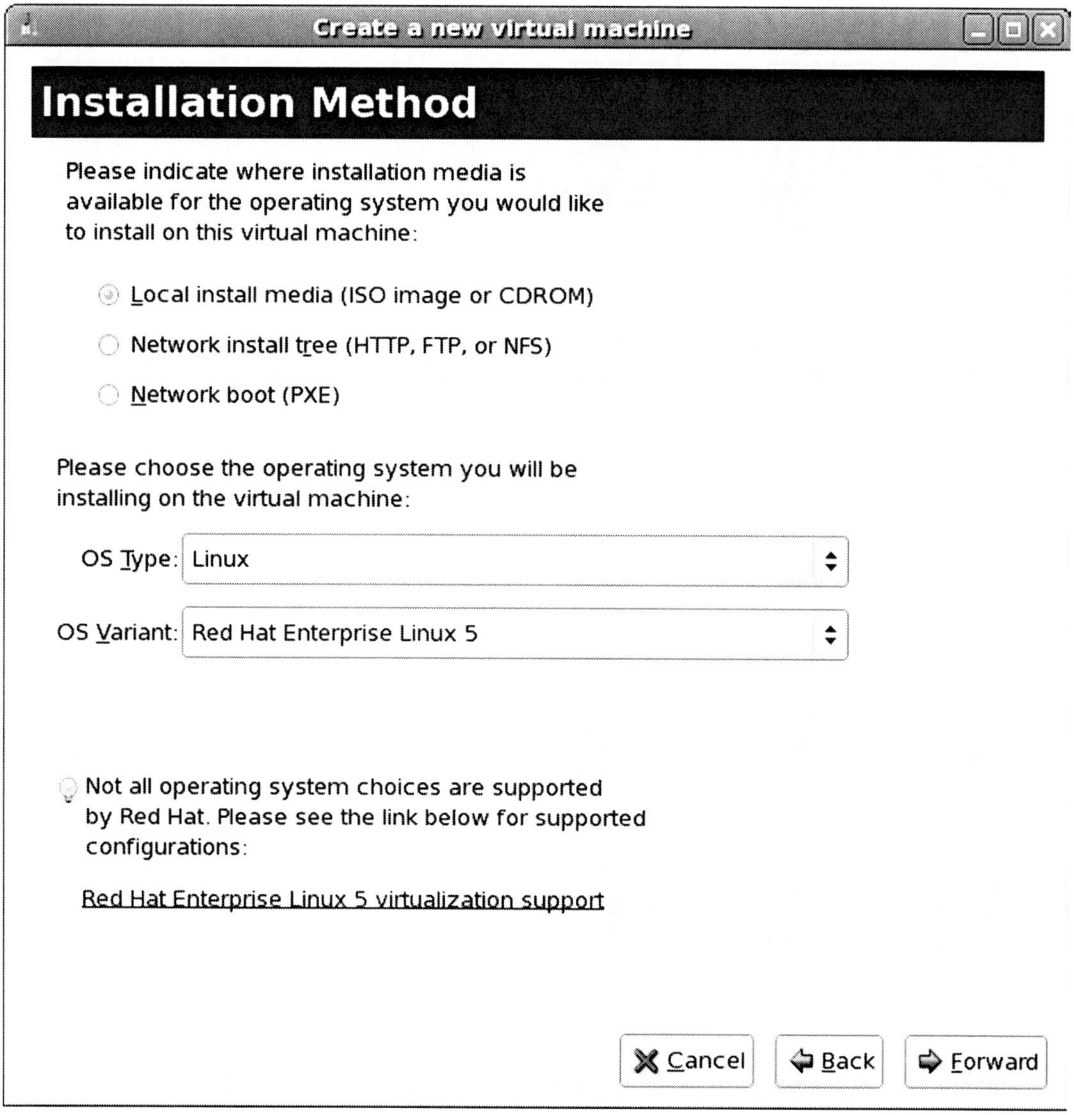

   Press **Forward** to continue.

Virtualization Guide

7. Locate installation media

   Select ISO image location or CD-ROM or DVD device. This example uses an ISO file image of the Red Hat Enterprise Linux 5 installation DVD.

   1. Press the **Browse** button.
   2. Search to the location of the ISO file and select the ISO image. Press **Open** to confirm your selection.
   3. The file is selected and ready to install from.

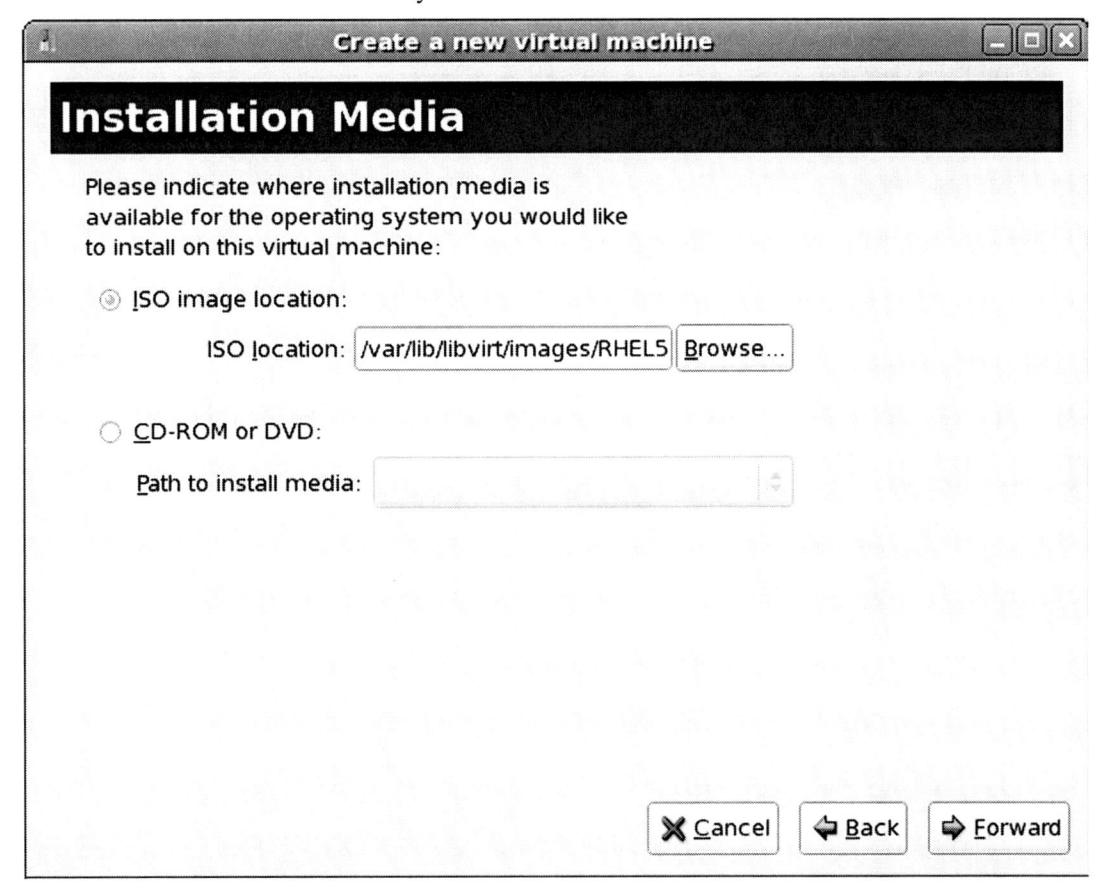

   ![Installation Media dialog showing ISO image location set to /var/lib/libvirt/images/RHEL5]

   Press **Forward** to continue.

   > **Image files and SELinux**
   >
   > For ISO image files and guest storage images, use the `/var/lib/libvirt/images/` directory. Any other location may require additional configuration for SELinux, refer to *Section 7.1, "SELinux and virtualization"* for details.

Fedora 12

8. Storage setup

    Assign a physical storage device (**Block device**) or a file-based image (**File**). File-based images must be stored in the /var/lib/libvirt/images/ directory. Assign sufficient storage for your virtualized guest. Assign sufficient space for your virtualized guest and any application it requires.

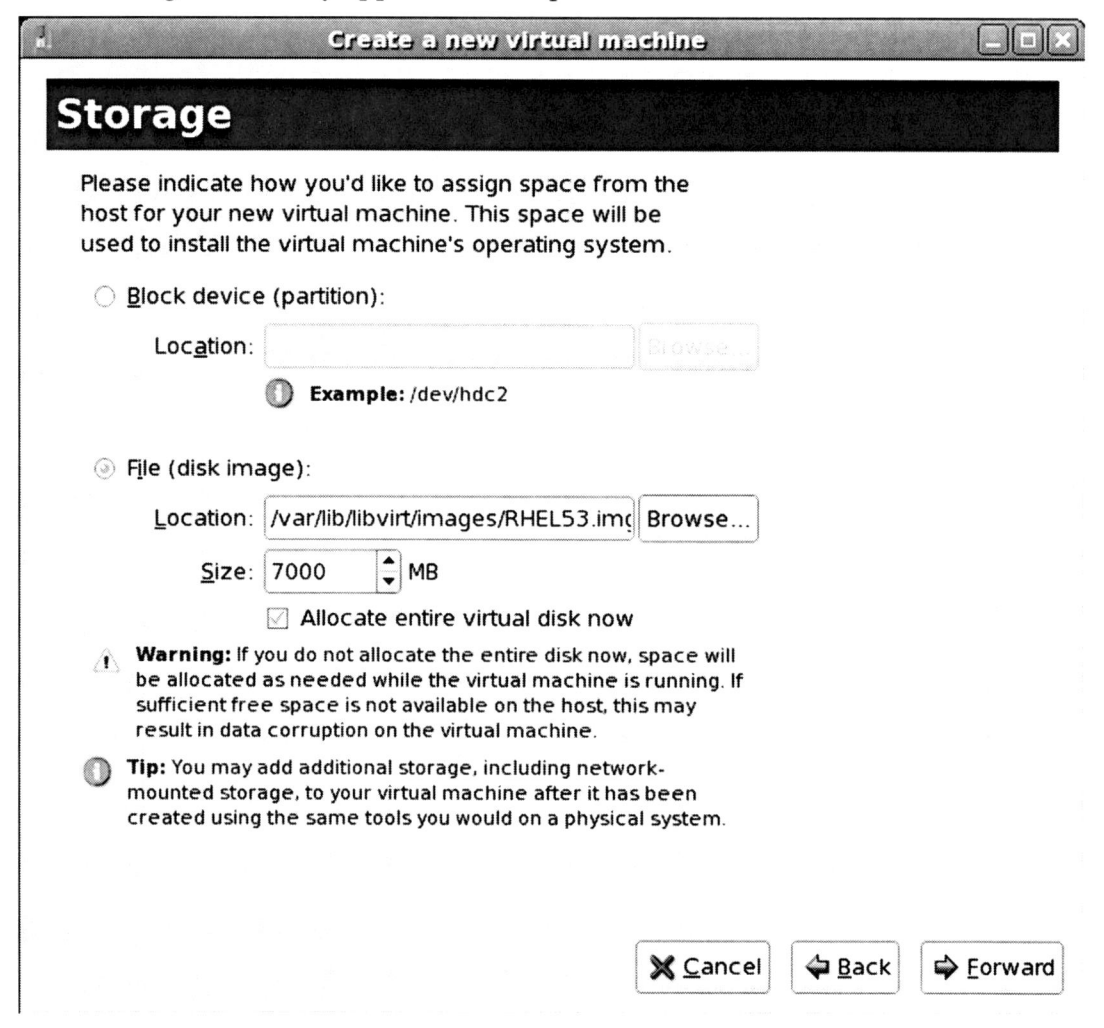

    Press **Forward** to continue.

    To migrating this guest

    Live and offline migrations require guests to be installed on shared network storage. For information on setting up shared storage for guests refer to *Chapter 5, Shared storage and virtualization*.

9. Network setup

    Select either **Virtual network** or **Shared physical device**.

    The virtual network option uses Network Address Translation (NAT) to share the default network device with the virtualized guest. Use the virtual network option for wireless networks.

    The shared physical device option uses a network bond to give the virtualized guest full access to a network device.

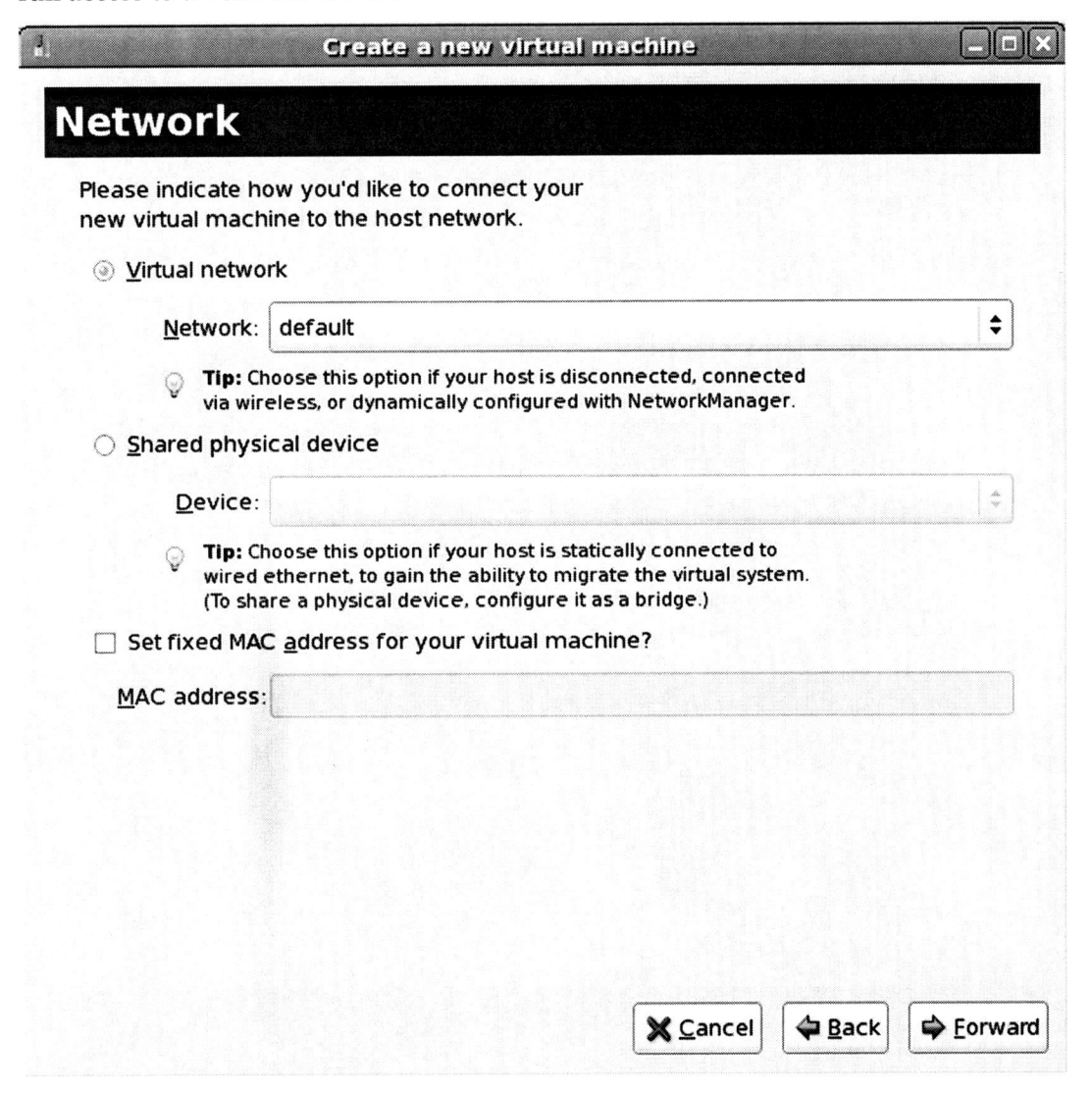

    Press **Forward** to continue.

10. Memory and CPU allocation

    The Allocate memory and CPU window displays. Choose appropriate values for the virtualized CPUs and RAM allocation. These values affect the host's and guest's performance.

    Virtualized guests require sufficient physical memory (RAM) to run efficiently and effectively. Choose a memory value which suits your guest operating system and application requirements. Windows Server 2008. Remember, guests use physical RAM. Running too many guests or leaving insufficient memory for the host system results in significant usage of virtual memory and swapping. Virtual memory is significantly slower causing degraded system performance and responsiveness. Ensure to allocate sufficient memory for all guests and the host to operate effectively.

    Assign sufficient virtual CPUs for the virtualized guest. If the guest runs a multithreaded application assign the number of virtualized CPUs it requires to run most efficiently. Do not assign more virtual CPUs than there are physical processors (or hyper-threads) available on the host system. It is possible to over allocate virtual processors, however, over allocating has a significant, negative affect on guest and host performance due to processor context switching overheads.

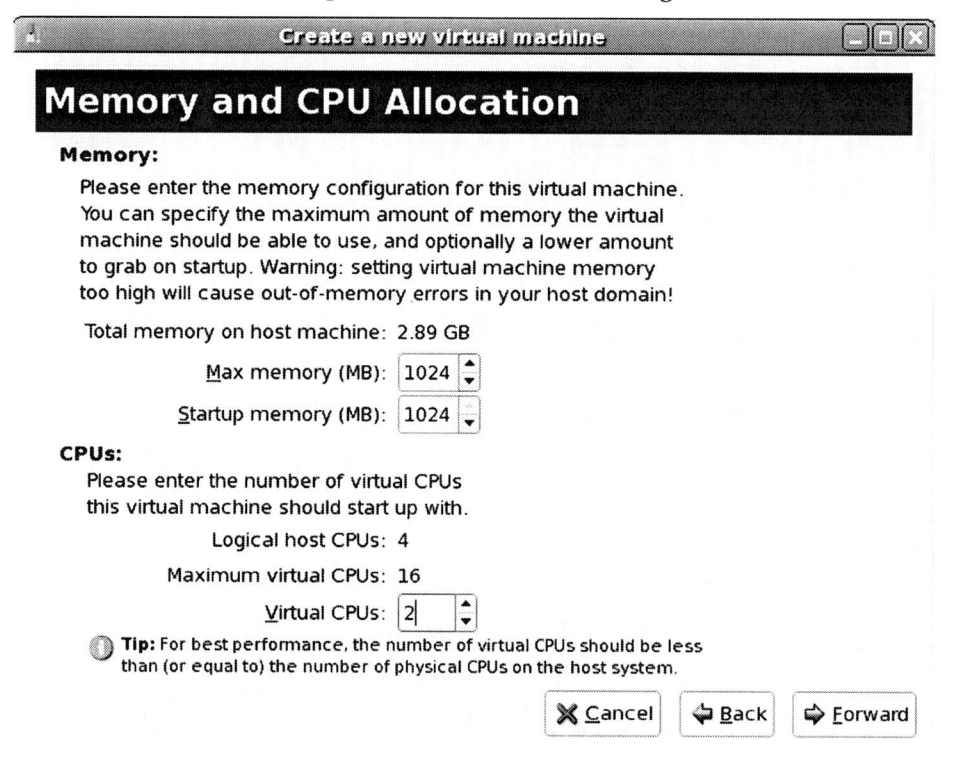

    Press **Forward** to continue.

11. Verify and start guest installation

    Verify the configuration.

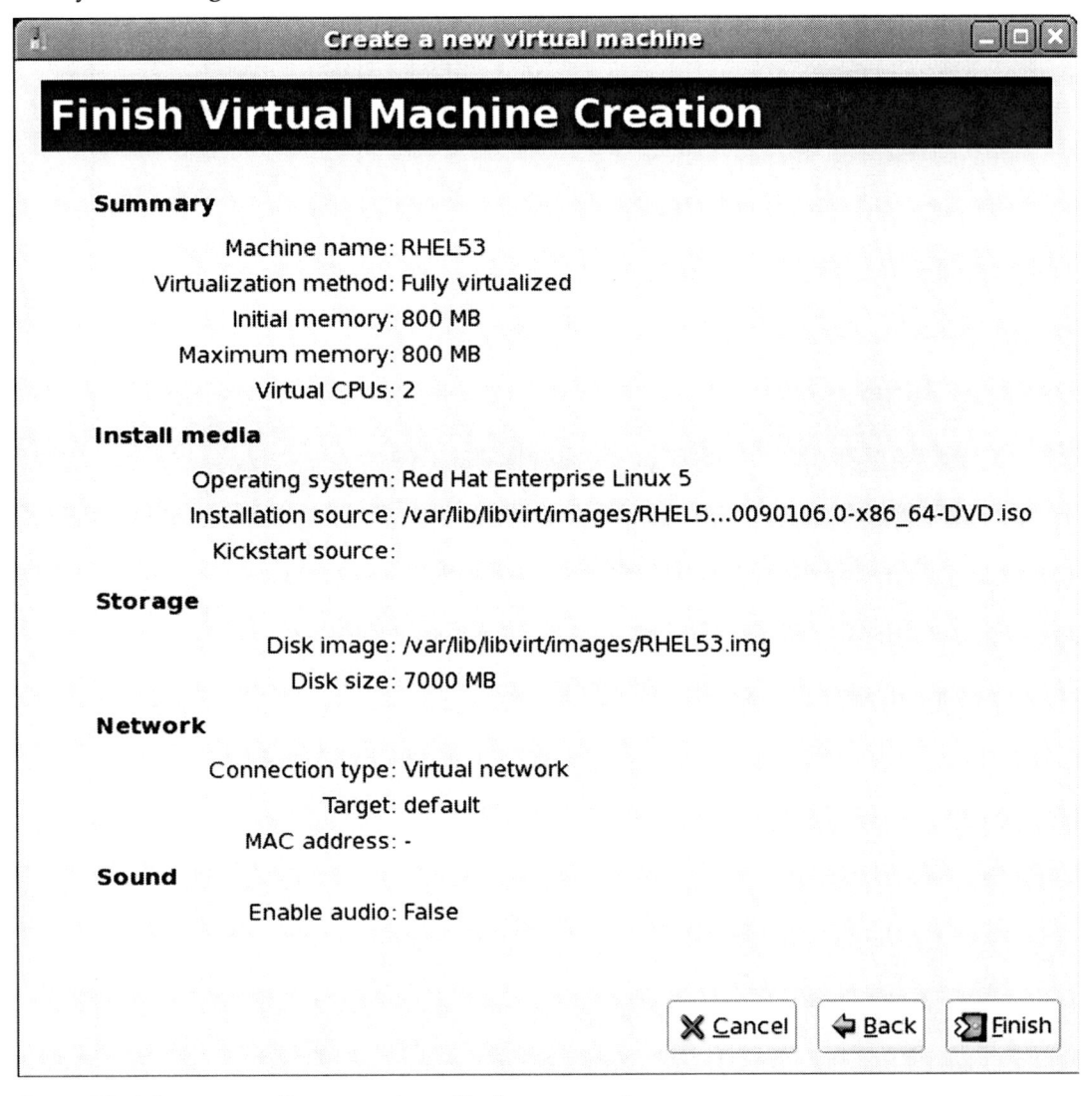

    ![Finish Virtual Machine Creation dialog]

    Summary
    - Machine name: RHEL53
    - Virtualization method: Fully virtualized
    - Initial memory: 800 MB
    - Maximum memory: 800 MB
    - Virtual CPUs: 2

    Install media
    - Operating system: Red Hat Enterprise Linux 5
    - Installation source: /var/lib/libvirt/images/RHEL5...0090106.0-x86_64-DVD.iso
    - Kickstart source:

    Storage
    - Disk image: /var/lib/libvirt/images/RHEL53.img
    - Disk size: 7000 MB

    Network
    - Connection type: Virtual network
    - Target: default
    - MAC address: -

    Sound
    - Enable audio: False

    Press **Finish** to start the guest installation procedure.

12. Installing Linux

    Complete the Red Hat Enterprise Linux 5 installation sequence. The installation sequence is covered by the *Red Hat Enterprise Linux Installation Guide*, available from *http://redhat.com/docs*.

A fully virtualized Red Hat Enterprise Linux 5 Guest is now installed.

Fedora 12

3.3. Installing Windows XP as a fully virtualized guest

Windows XP can be installed as a fully virtualized guest. This section describes how to install Windows XP as a fully virtualized guest on Linux.

Before commencing this procedure ensure you must have root access.

1. Starting virt-manager

    Open **Applications > System Tools > Virtual Machine Manager**. Open a connection to the host (click **File > Open Connection**). Click the **New** button to create a new virtual machine.

2. Naming your virtual system

    Enter the **System Name** and click the **Forward** button.

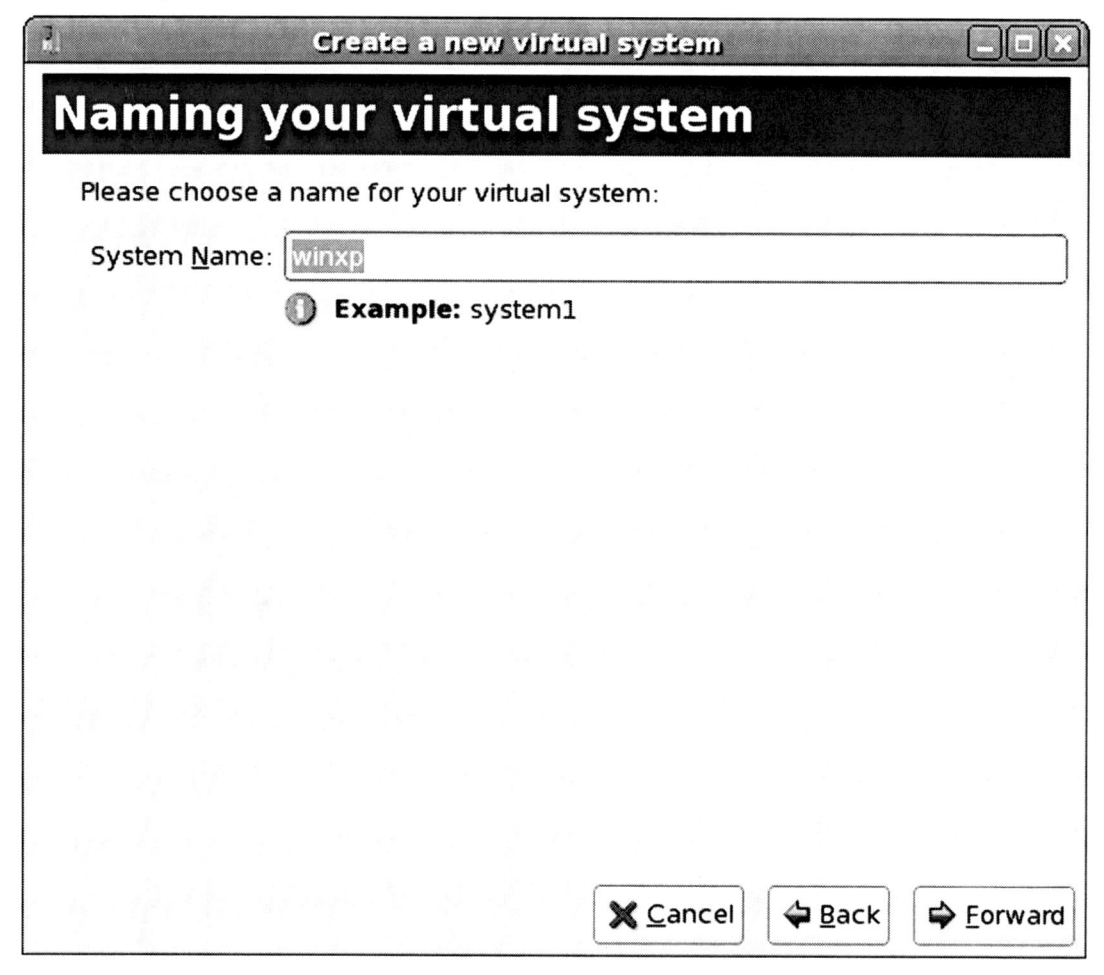

Virtualization Guide

3. Choosing a virtualization method

    If you selected KVM or Xen earlier (step *Step 1*) you must use the hypervisor you selected. This example uses the KVM hypervisor.

    Windows can only be installed using full virtualization.

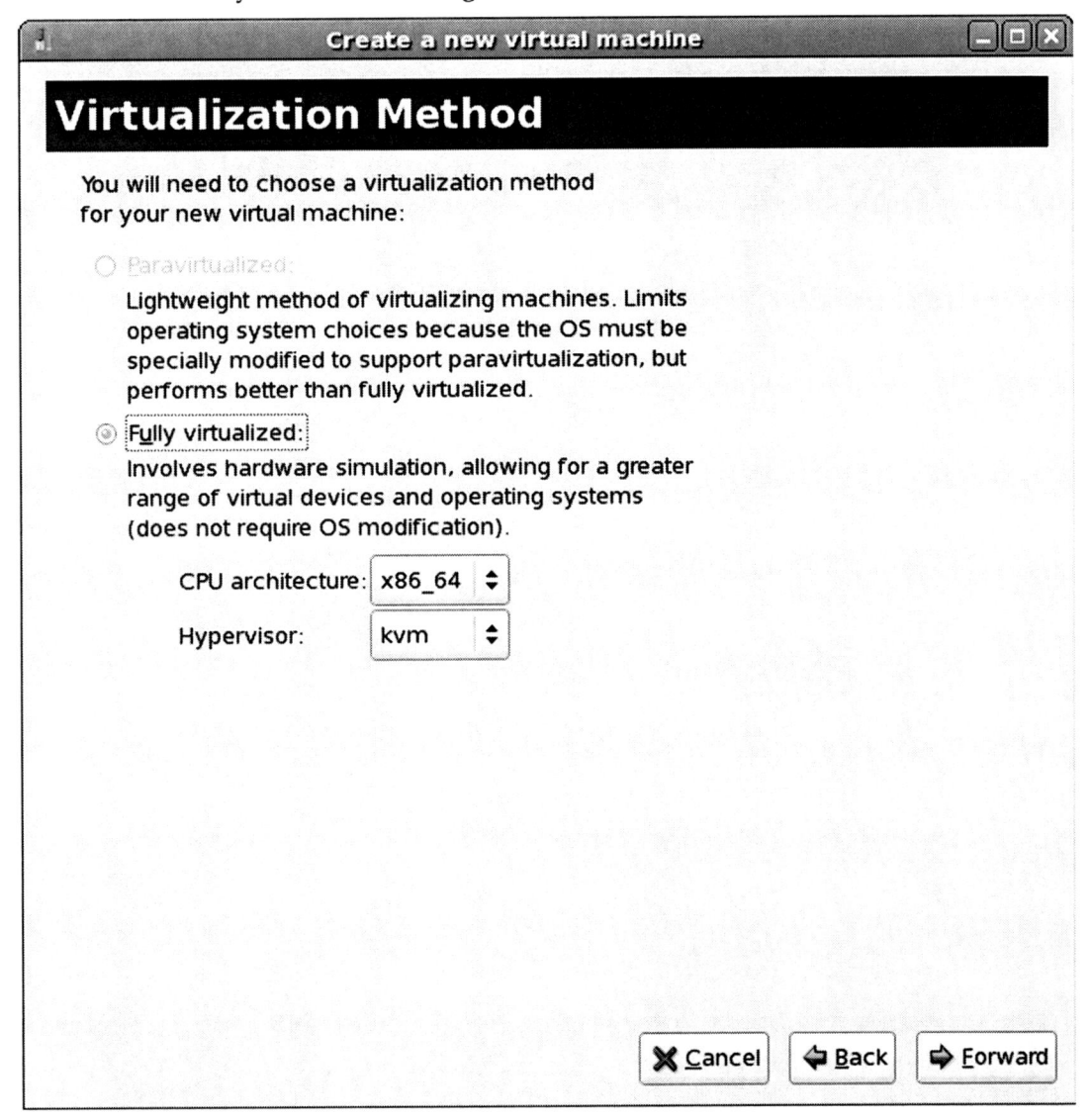

    ## Virtualization Method

    You will need to choose a virtualization method for your new virtual machine:

    ○ Paravirtualized:
    Lightweight method of virtualizing machines. Limits operating system choices because the OS must be specially modified to support paravirtualization, but performs better than fully virtualized.

    ◉ Fully virtualized:
    Involves hardware simulation, allowing for a greater range of virtual devices and operating systems (does not require OS modification).

    CPU architecture: x86_64
    Hypervisor: kvm

    [Cancel] [Back] [Forward]

4. Choosing an installation method

    This screen enables you to specify the installation method and the type of operating system.

Fedora 12

For CD-ROM or DVD installation select the device with the Windows installation disc in it. If you chose **ISO Image Location** enter the path to a Windows installation .iso image.

Select **Windows** from the **OS Type** list and **Microsoft Windows XP** from the **OS Variant** list.

PXE installation is not covered by this chapter.

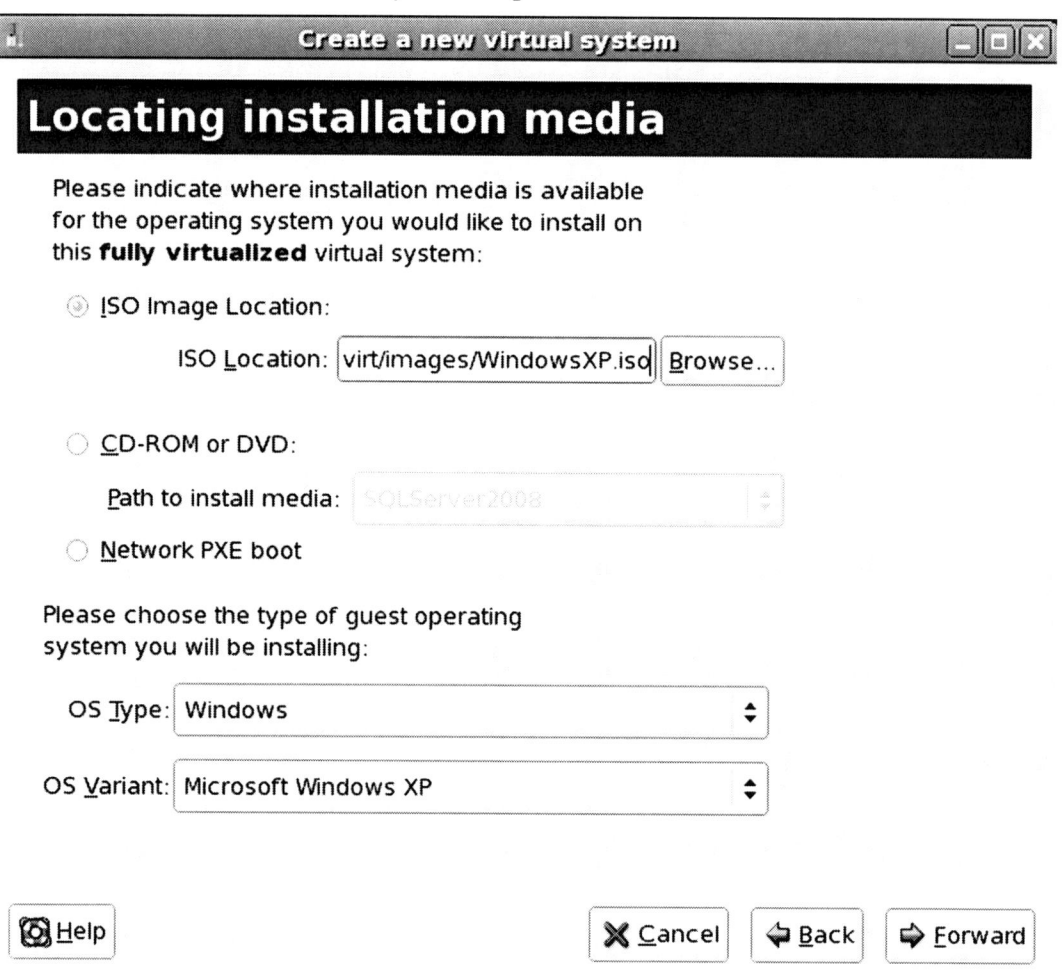

Locating installation media

Please indicate where installation media is available for the operating system you would like to install on this **fully virtualized** virtual system:

- ⦿ ISO Image Location:
    - ISO Location: `virt/images/WindowsXP.iso` [Browse...]
- ○ CD-ROM or DVD:
    - Path to install media: SQLServer2008
- ○ Network PXE boot

Please choose the type of guest operating system you will be installing:

- OS Type: Windows
- OS Variant: Microsoft Windows XP

[Help] [Cancel] [Back] [Forward]

Press **Forward** to continue.

> **Image files and SELinux**
>
> For ISO image files and guest storage images the the recommended to use the `/var/lib/libvirt/images/` directory. Any other location may require additional configuration for SELinux, refer to *Section 7.1, "SELinux and virtualization"* for details.

90

5. The **Assigning storage space** window displays. Choose a disk partition, LUN or create a file based image for the guest storage.

    The convention for file based images in Fedora is that all file based guest images are in the /var/lib/libvirt/images/ directory. Other directory locations for file based images are prohibited by SELinux. If you run SELinux in enforcing mode, refer to *Section 7.1, "SELinux and virtualization"* for more information on installing guests.

    Your guest storage image should be larger than the size of the installation, any additional packages and applications, and the size of the guests swap file. The installation process will choose the size of the guest's swap file based on size of the RAM allocated to the guest.

    Allocate extra space if the guest needs additional space for applications or other data. For example, web servers require additional space for log files.

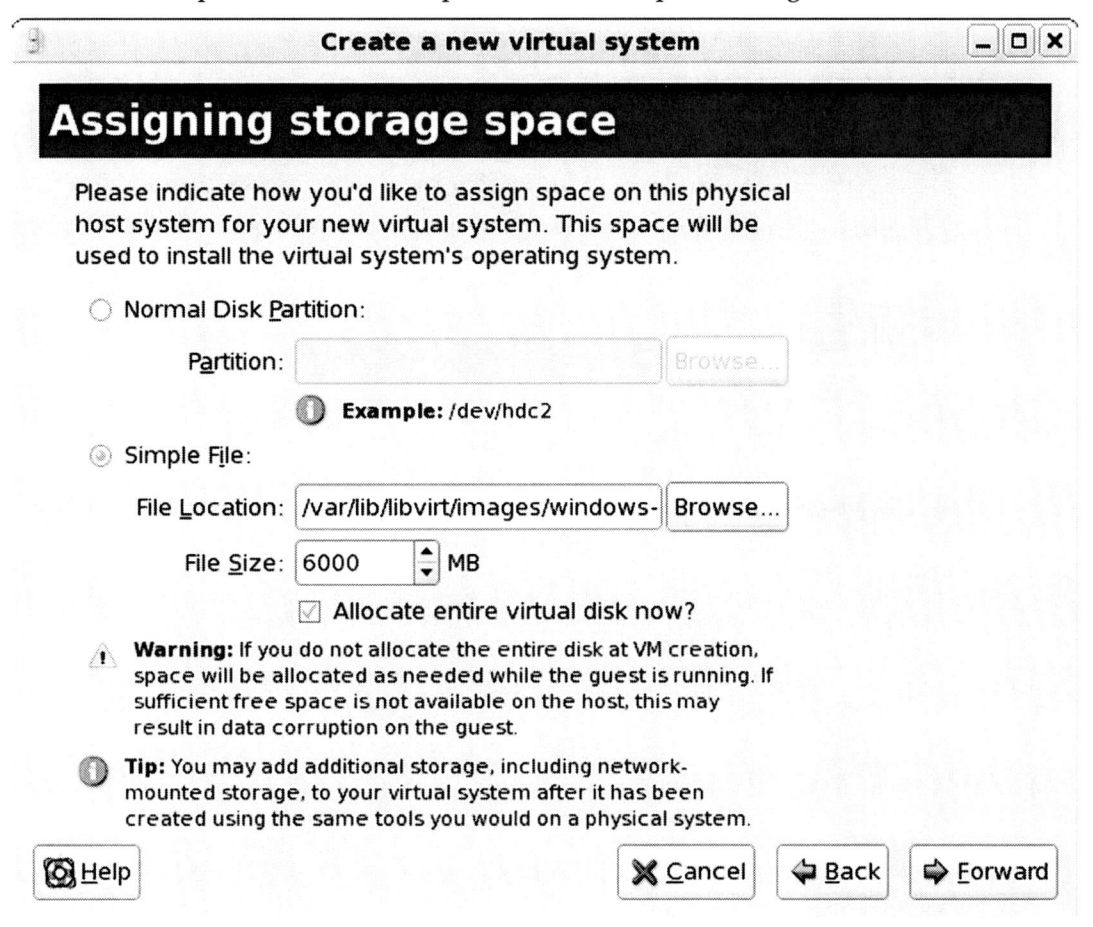

Virtualization Guide

91

Fedora 12

Choose the appropriate size for the guest on your selected storage type and click the **Forward** button.

> **Note**
>
> It is recommend that you use the default directory for virtual machine images, `/var/lib/libvirt/images/`. If you are using a different location (such as `/images/` in this example) make sure it is added to your SELinux policy and relabeled before you continue with the installation (later in the document you will find information on how to modify your SELinux policy)

6. Network setup

    Select either **Virtual network** or **Shared physical device**.

    The virtual network option uses Network Address Translation (NAT) to share the default network device with the virtualized guest. Use the virtual network option for wireless networks.

    The shared physical device option uses a network bond to give the virtualized guest full access to a network device.

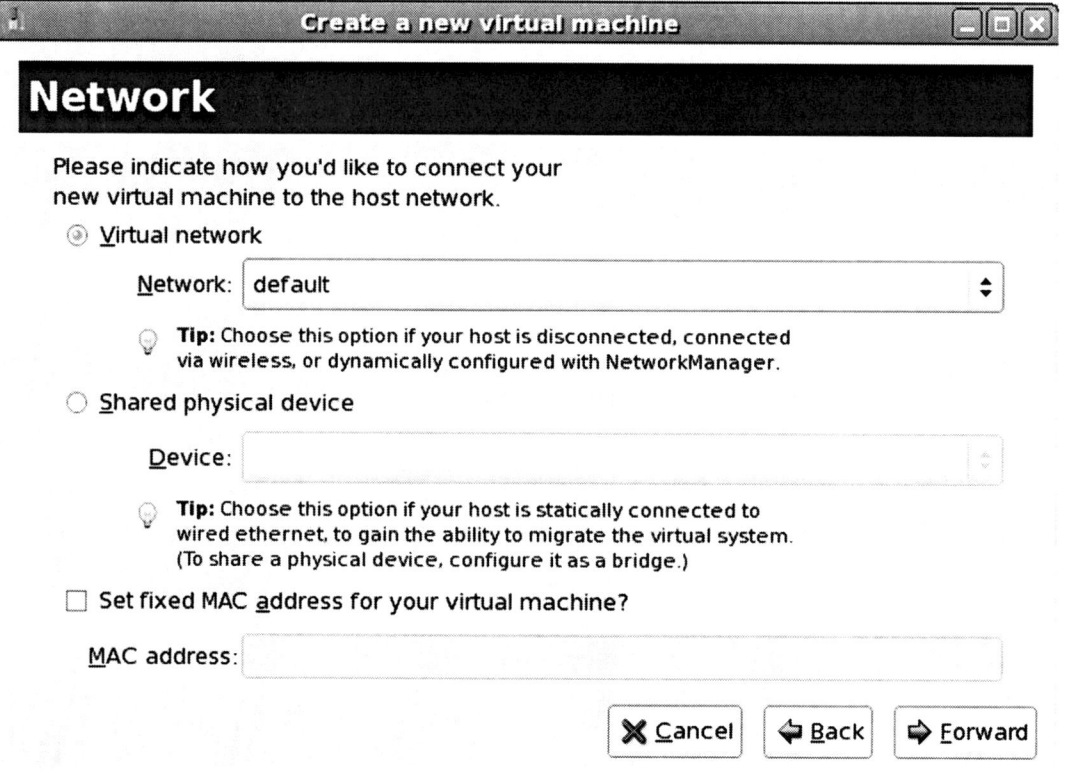

    Press **Forward** to continue.

Virtualization Guide

7. The Allocate memory and CPU window displays. Choose appropriate values for the virtualized CPUs and RAM allocation. These values affect the host's and guest's performance.

   Virtualized guests require sufficient physical memory (RAM) to run efficiently and effectively. Choose a memory value which suits your guest operating system and application requirements. Most operating system require at least 512MB of RAM to work responsively. Remember, guests use physical RAM. Running too many guests or leaving insufficient memory for the host system results in significant usage of virtual memory and swapping. Virtual memory is significantly slower causing degraded system performance and responsiveness. Ensure to allocate sufficient memory for all guests and the host to operate effectively.

   Assign sufficient virtual CPUs for the virtualized guest. If the guest runs a multithreaded application assign the number of virtualized CPUs it requires to run most efficiently. Do not assign more virtual CPUs than there are physical processors (or hyper-threads) available on the host system. It is possible to over allocate virtual processors, however, over allocating has a significant, negative affect on guest and host performance due to processor context switching overheads.

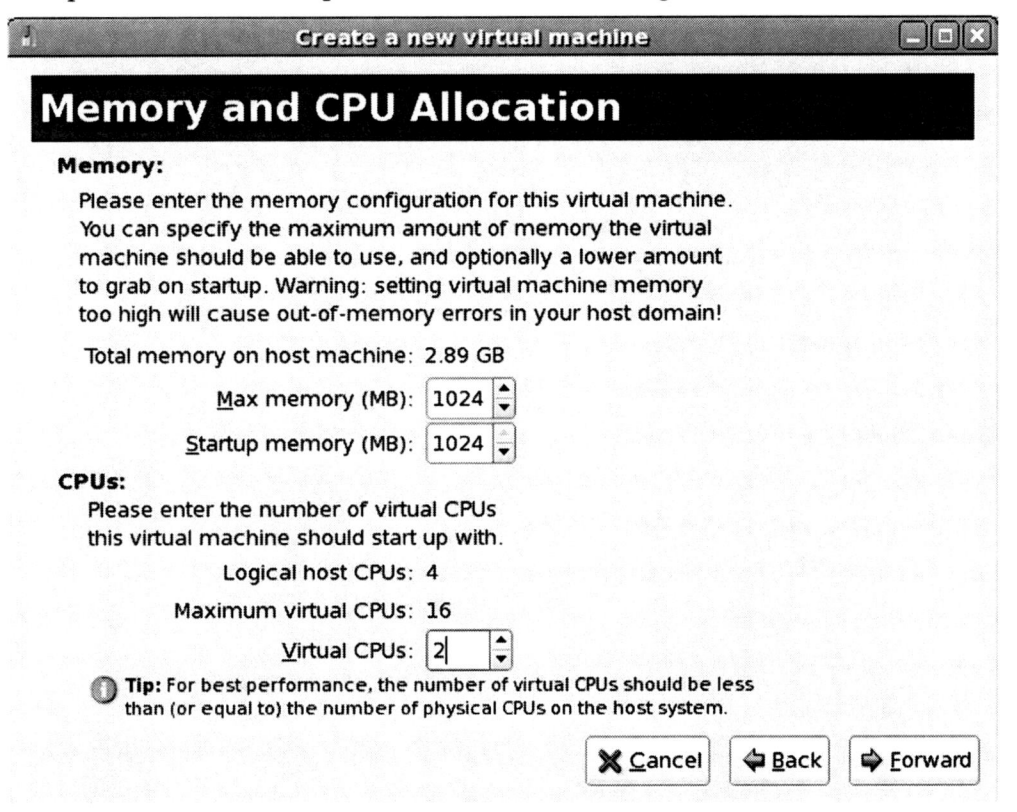

Create a new virtual machine

Memory and CPU Allocation

Memory:
Please enter the memory configuration for this virtual machine. You can specify the maximum amount of memory the virtual machine should be able to use, and optionally a lower amount to grab on startup. Warning: setting virtual machine memory too high will cause out-of-memory errors in your host domain!

Total memory on host machine: 2.89 GB

Max memory (MB): 1024

Startup memory (MB): 1024

CPUs:
Please enter the number of virtual CPUs this virtual machine should start up with.

Logical host CPUs: 4

Maximum virtual CPUs: 16

Virtual CPUs: 2

Tip: For best performance, the number of virtual CPUs should be less than (or equal to) the number of physical CPUs on the host system.

[Cancel] [Back] [Forward]

93

Fedora 12

8. Before the installation continues you will see the summary screen. Press **Finish** to proceed to the guest installation:

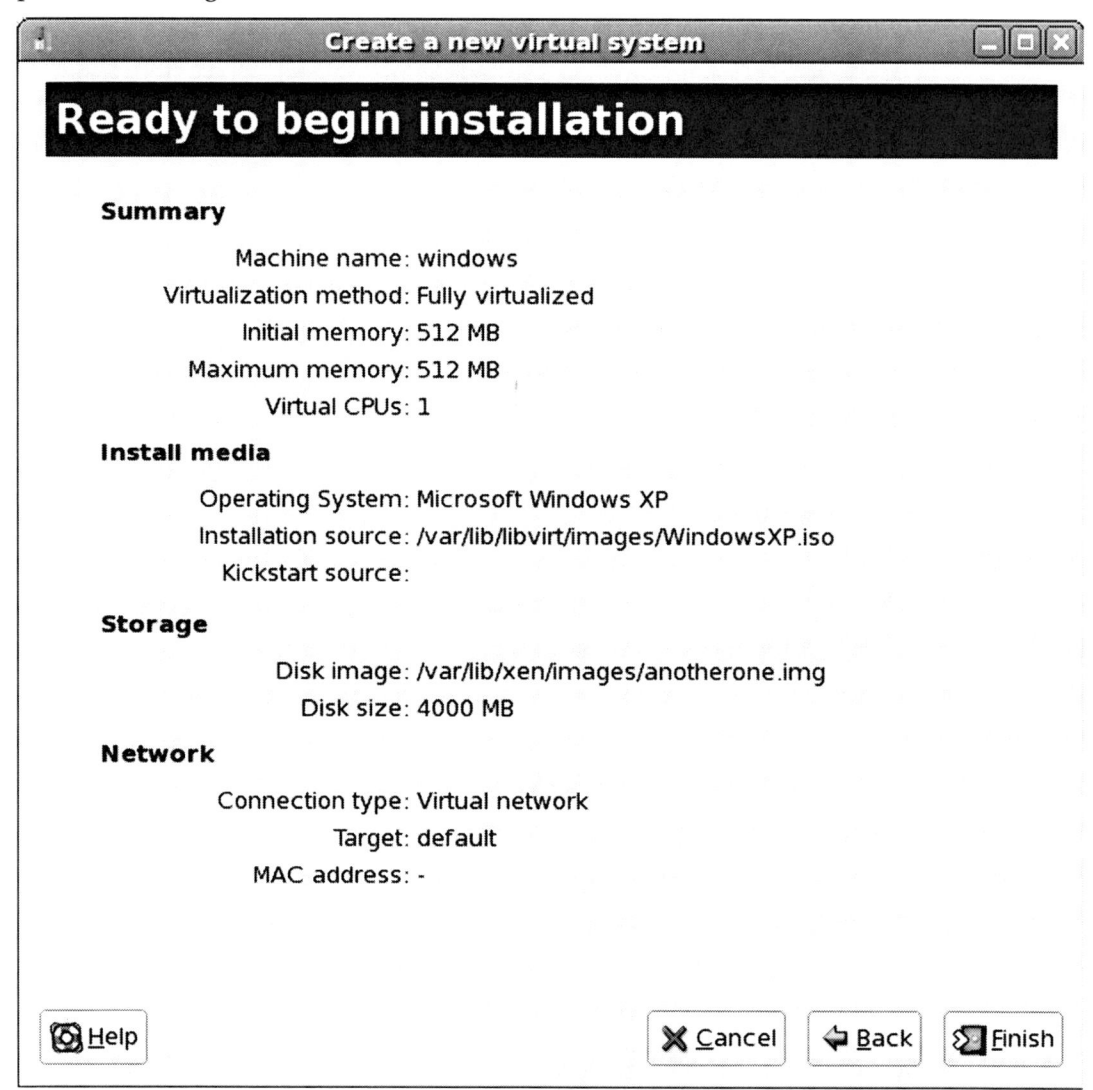

Create a new virtual system

Ready to begin installation

Summary

    Machine name: windows
    Virtualization method: Fully virtualized
    Initial memory: 512 MB
    Maximum memory: 512 MB
    Virtual CPUs: 1

Install media

    Operating System: Microsoft Windows XP
    Installation source: /var/lib/libvirt/images/WindowsXP.iso
    Kickstart source:

Storage

    Disk image: /var/lib/xen/images/anotherone.img
    Disk size: 4000 MB

Network

    Connection type: Virtual network
    Target: default
    MAC address: -

[Help]   [Cancel] [Back] [Finish]

Virtualization Guide

9. You must make a hardware selection so open a console window quickly after the installation starts. Click **Finish** then switch to the **virt-manager** summary window and select your newly started Windows guest. Double click on the system name and the console window opens. Quickly and repeatedly press **F5** to select a new `HAL`, once you get the dialog box in the Windows install select the `'Generic i486 Platform'` tab (scroll through selections with the **Up** and **Down** arrows.

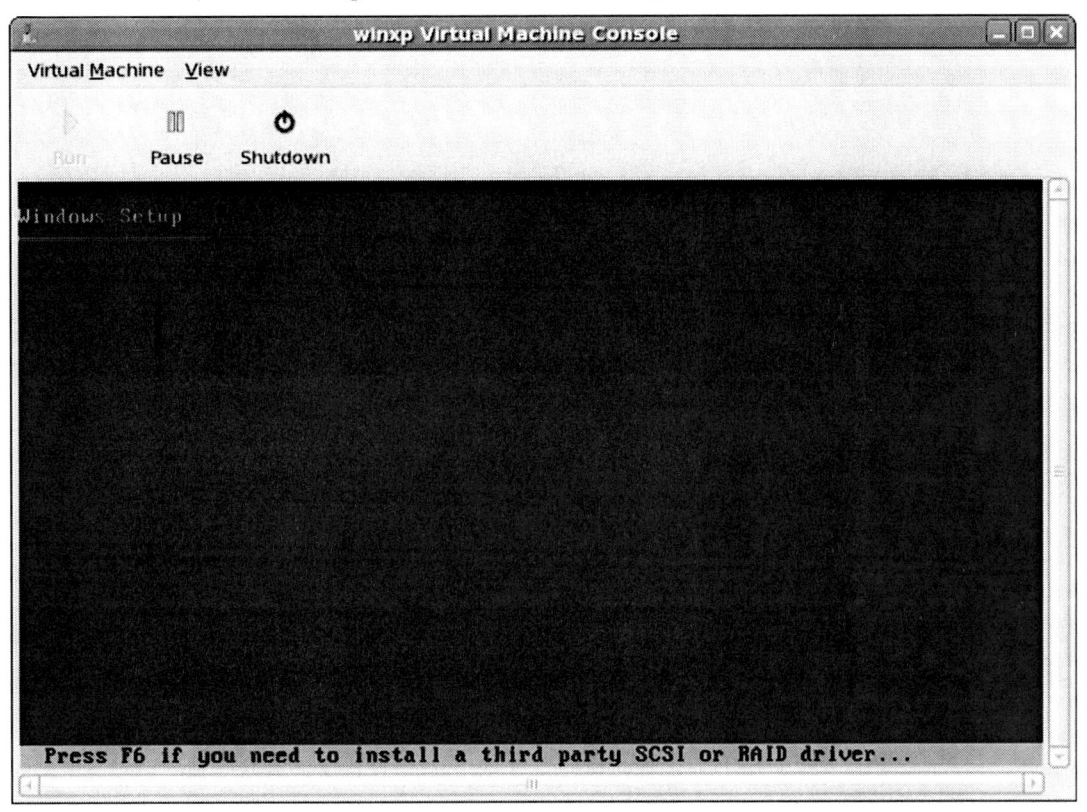

95

Fedora 12

10. The installation continues with the standard Windows installation.

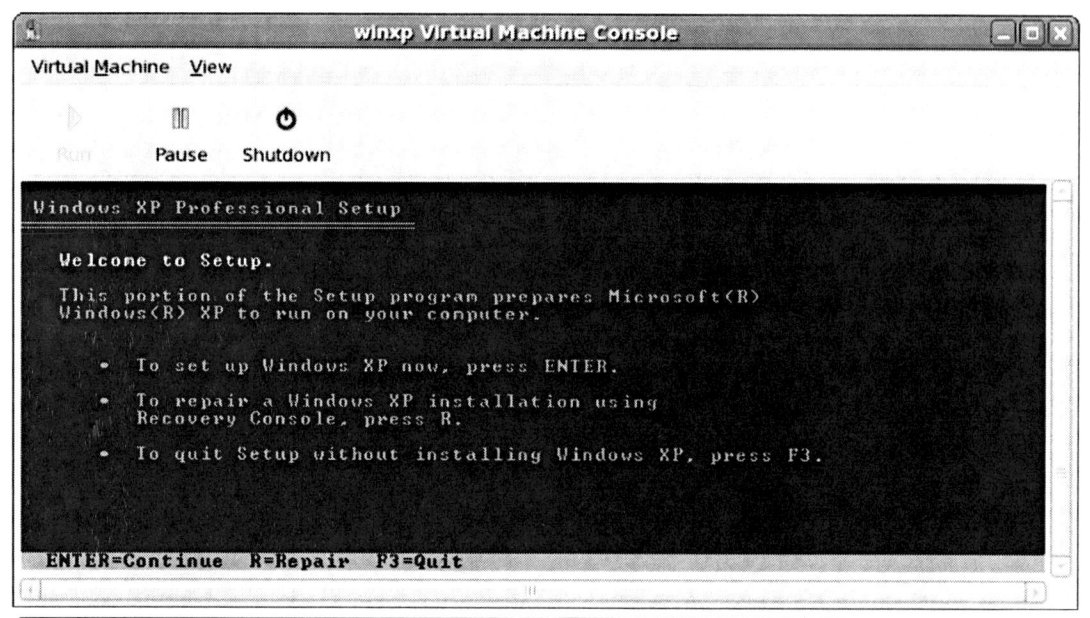

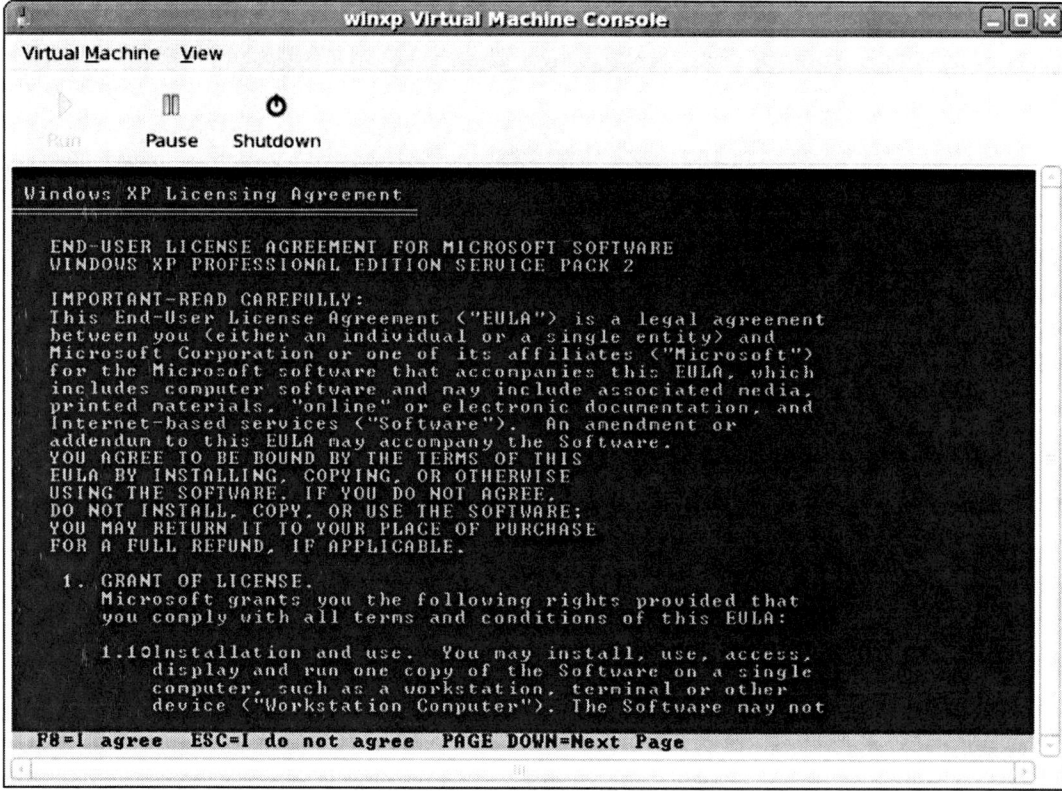

Virtualization Guide

11. Partition the hard drive when prompted.

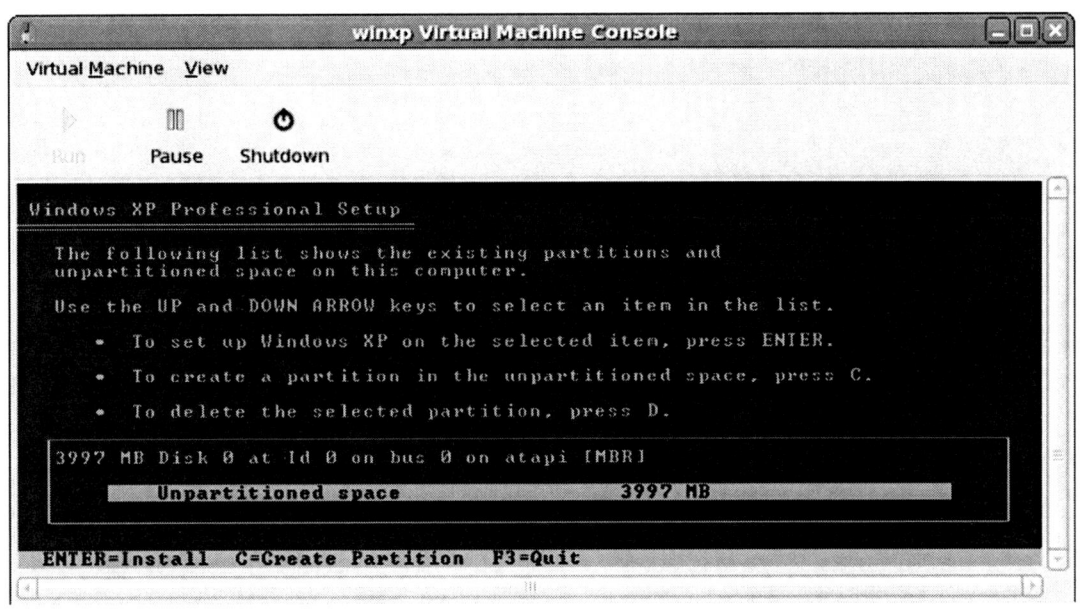

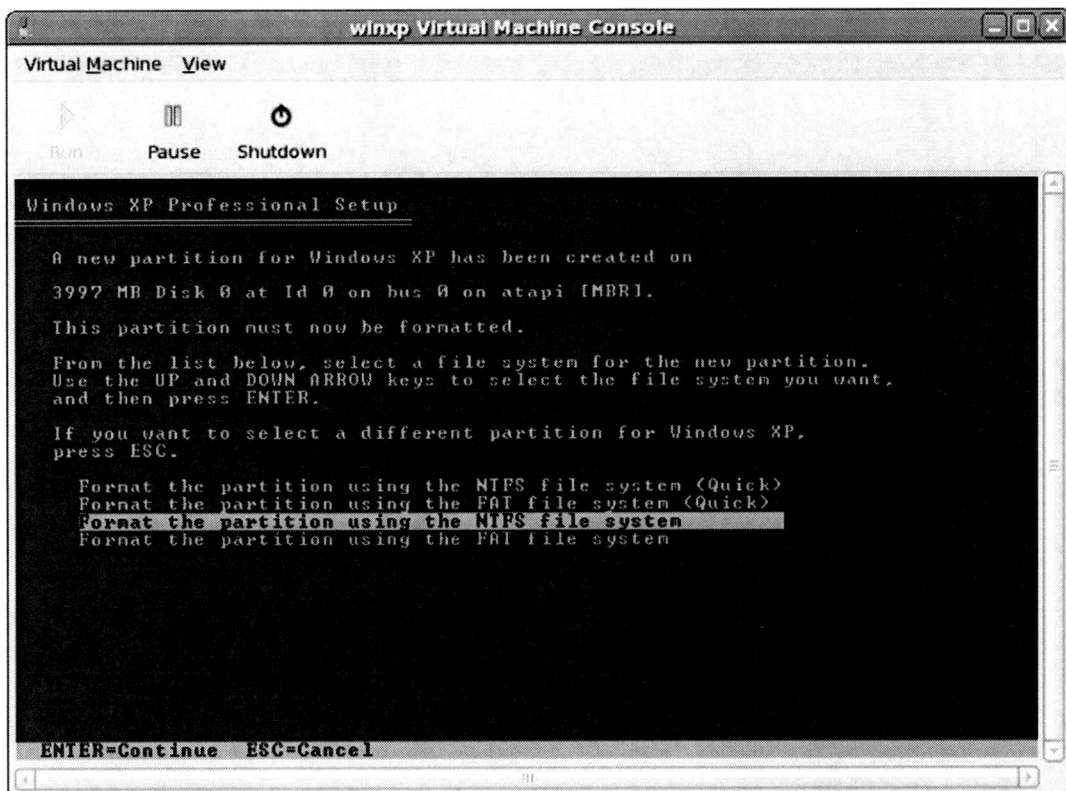

Fedora 12

12. After the drive is formatted Windows starts copying the files to the hard drive.

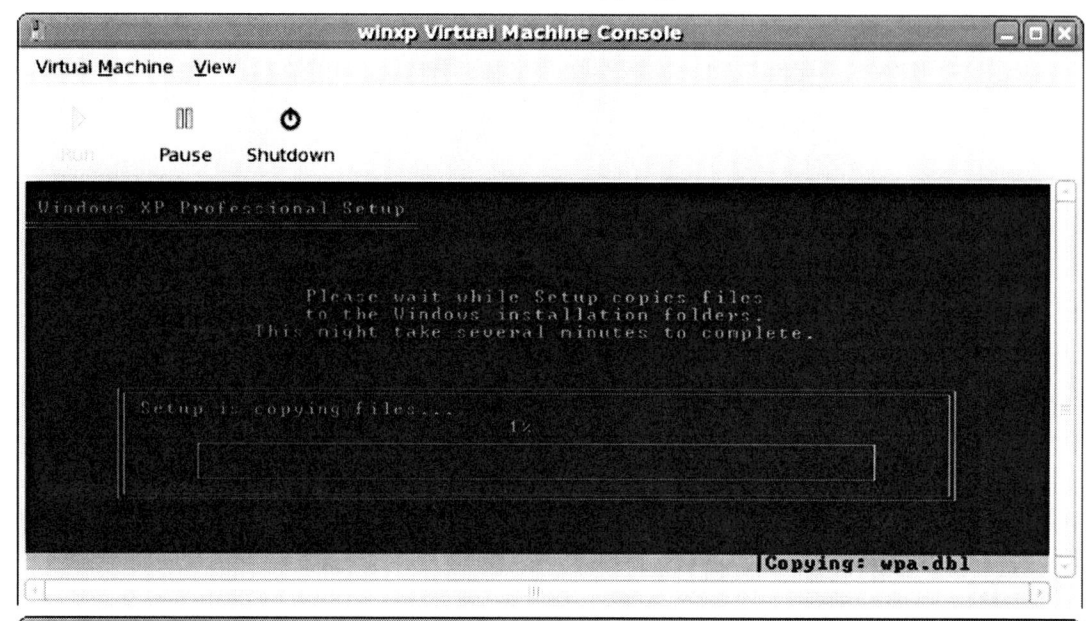

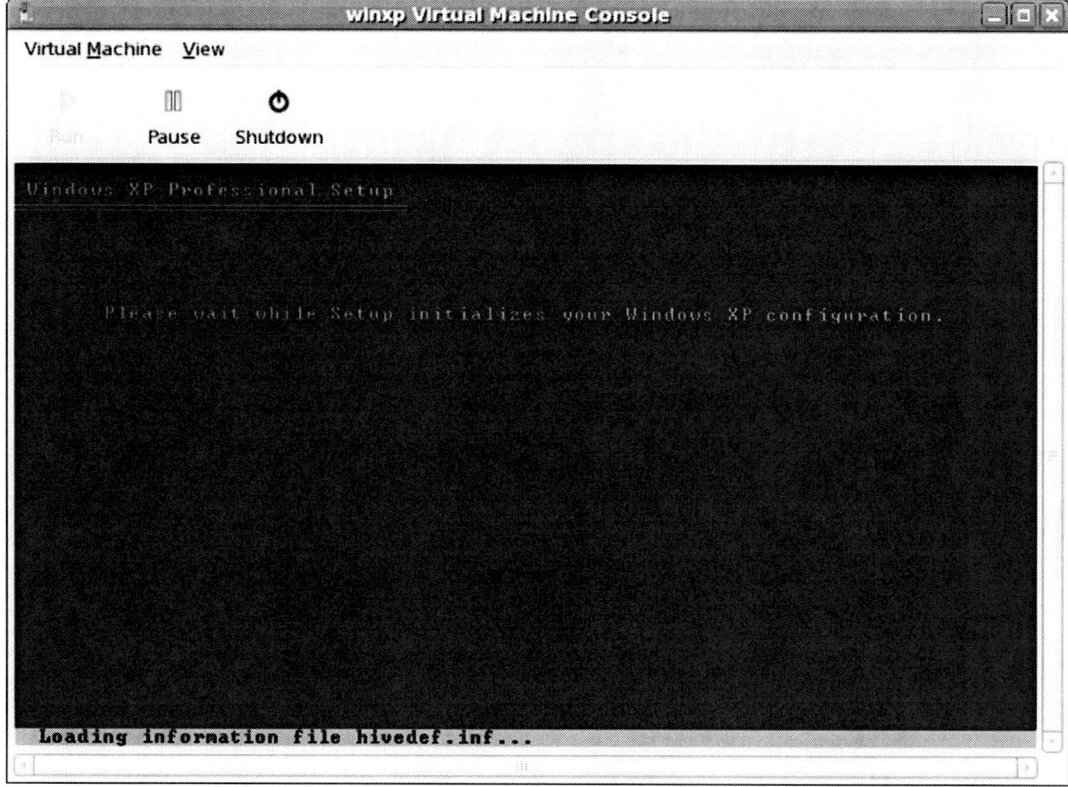

Virtualization Guide

13. The files are copied to the storage device, Windows now reboots.

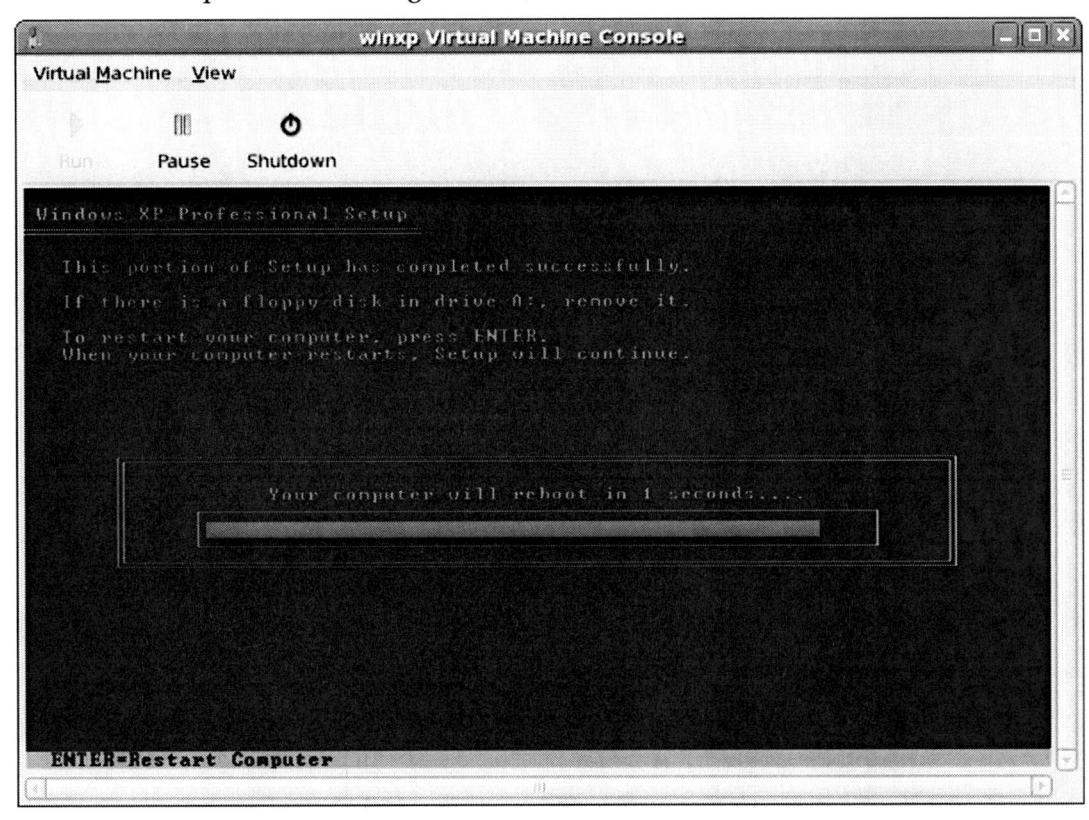

14. Restart your Windows guest:

    ```
    # virsh start WindowsGuest
    ```

    Where `WindowsGuest` is the name of your virtual machine.

Fedora 12

15. When the console window opens, you will see the setup phase of the Windows installation.

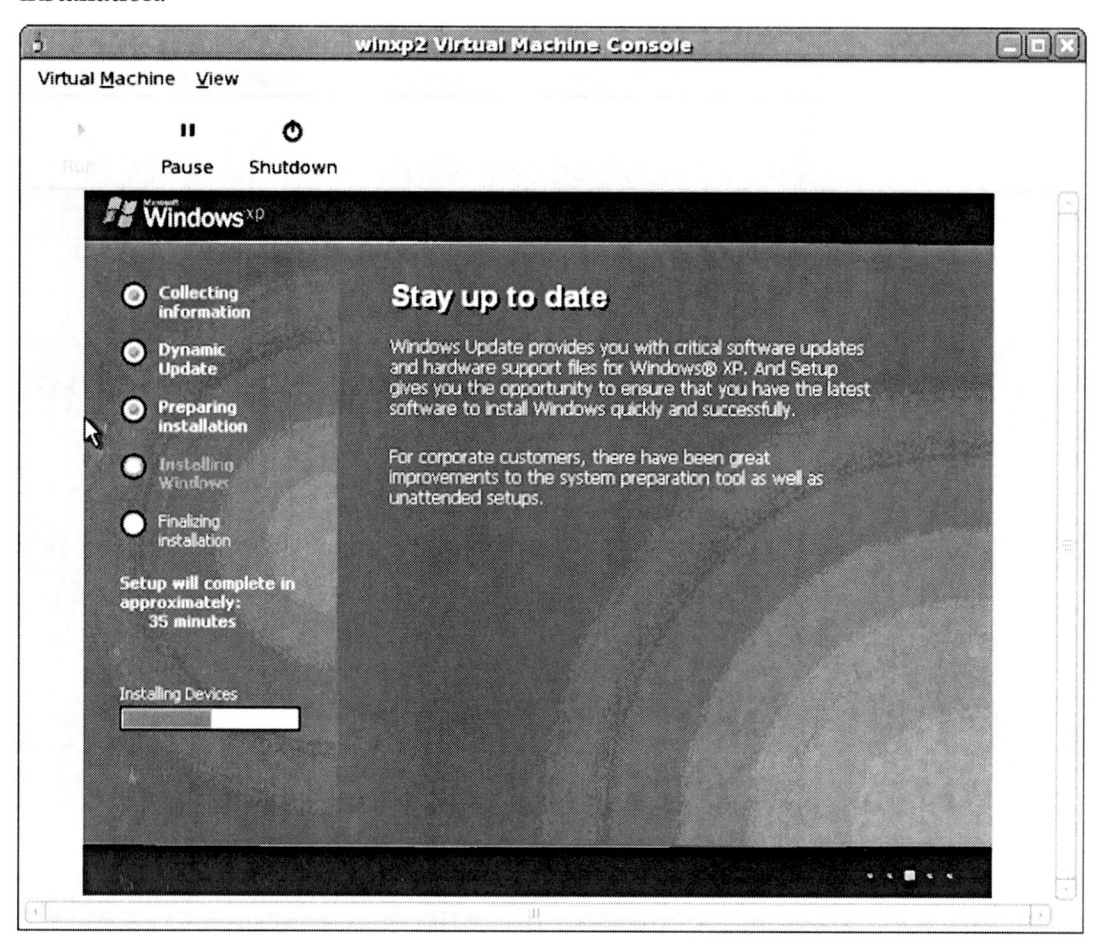

Virtualization Guide

16. If your installation seems to get stuck during the setup phase, restart the guest with `virsh reboot` *WindowsGuestName*. The will usually get the installation to continue. As you restart the virtual machine you will see a `Setup is being restarted` message:

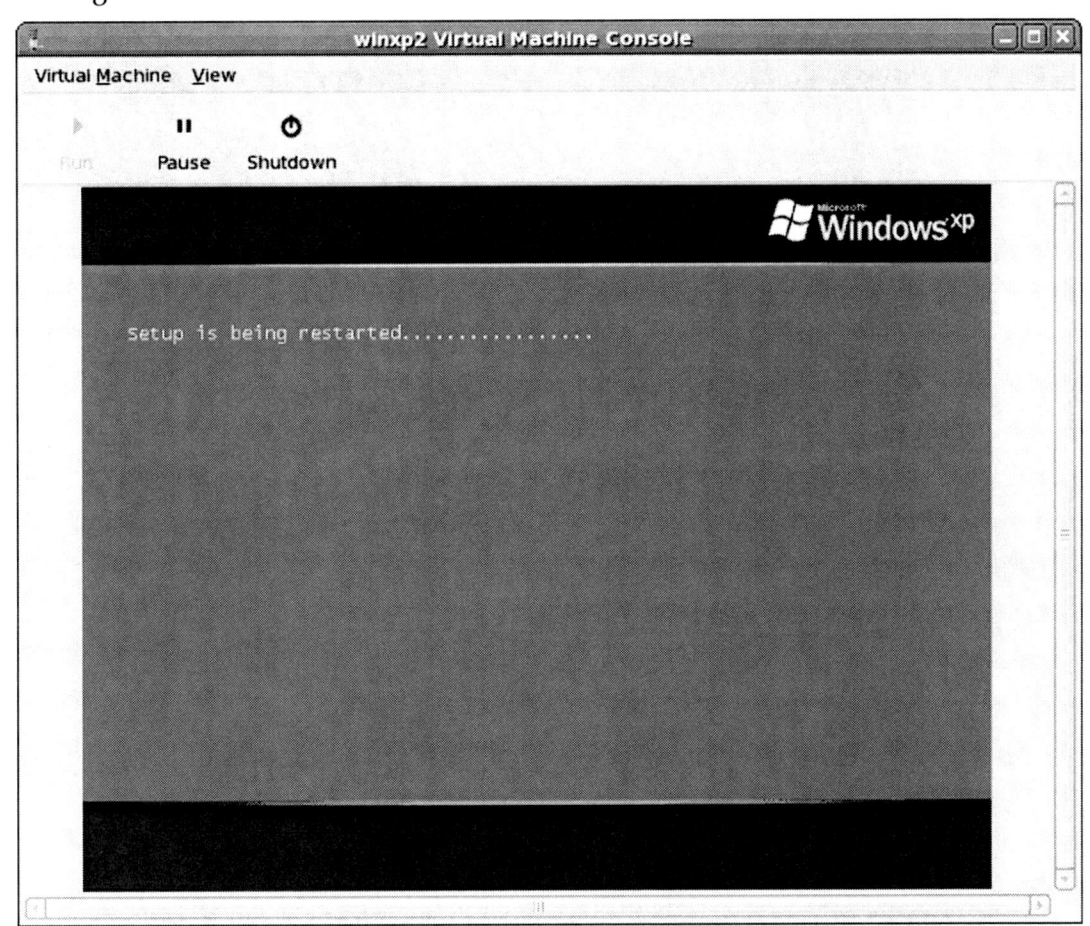

Fedora 12

17. After setup has finished you will see the Windows boot screen:

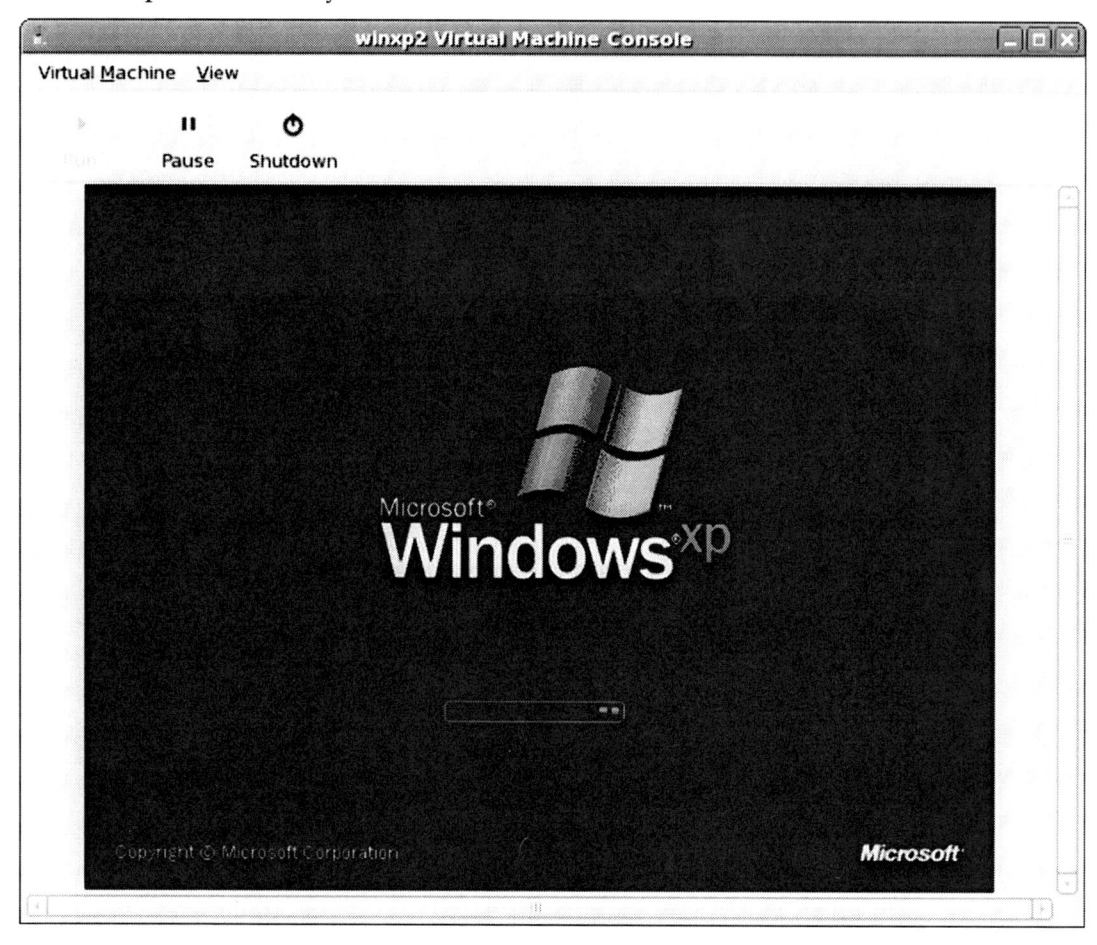

Virtualization Guide

18. Now you can continue with the standard setup of your Windows installation:

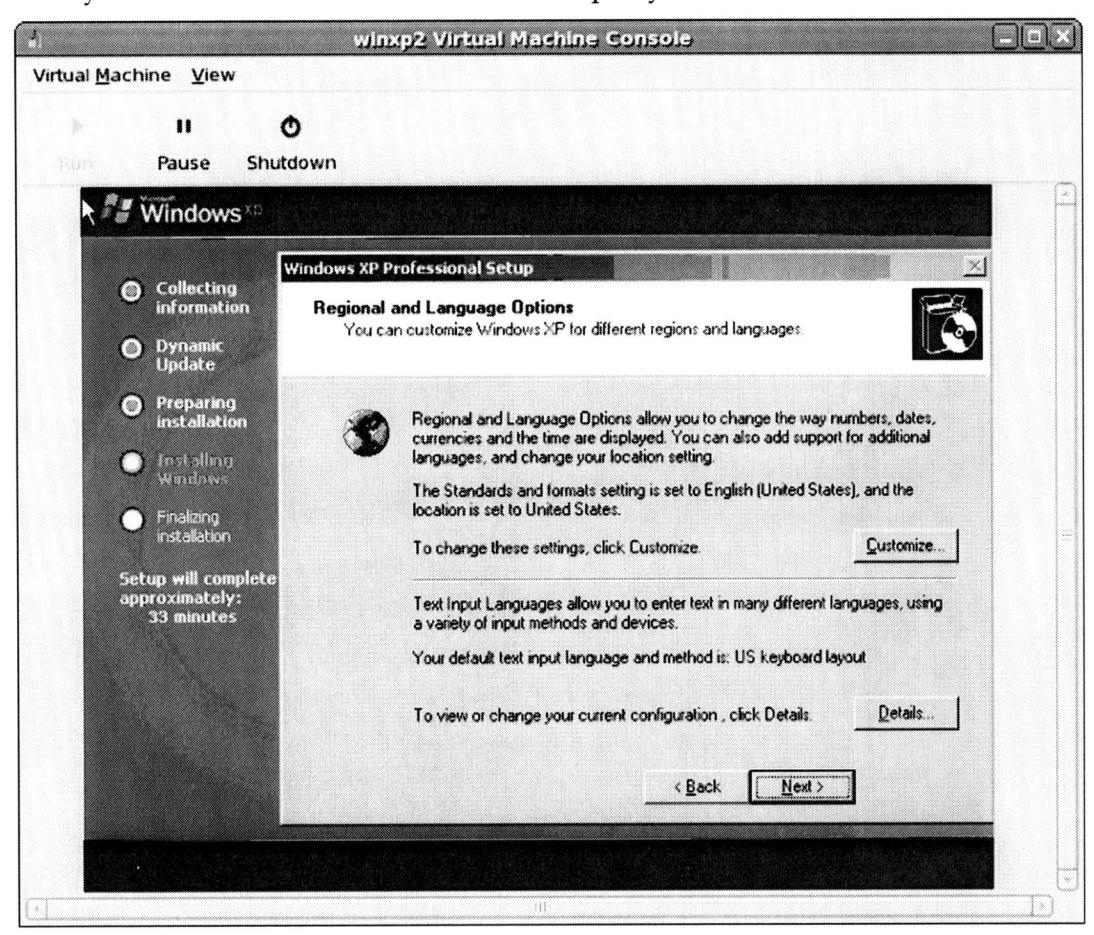

19. The setup process is complete, a Windows desktop displays.

3.4. Installing Windows Server 2003 as a fully virtualized guest

This chapter describes installing a fully virtualized Windows Server 2003 guest with the `virt-install` command. `virt-install` can be used instead of virt-manager This process is similar to the Windows XP installation covered in *Section 3.3, "Installing Windows XP as a fully virtualized guest"*.

1. Using `virt-install` for installing Windows Server 2003 as the console for the Windows guest opens the virt-viewer window promptly. An example of using the `virt-install` for installing a Windows Server 2003 guest:

   Start the installation with the `virt-install` command.
   ```
   # virt-install -hvm -s 5 -f /var/lib/libvirt/images/windows2003spi1.dsk \
   -n windows2003sp1 -cdrom=/ISOs/WIN/en_windows_server_2003_sp1.iso \
   -vnc -r 1024
   ```

Virtualization Guide

2. Once the guest boots into the installation you must quickly press **F5**. If you do not press **F5** at the right time you will need to restart the installation. Pressing **F5** allows you to select different **HAL** or **Computer Type**. Choose Standard PC as the Computer Type. This is the only non standard step required.

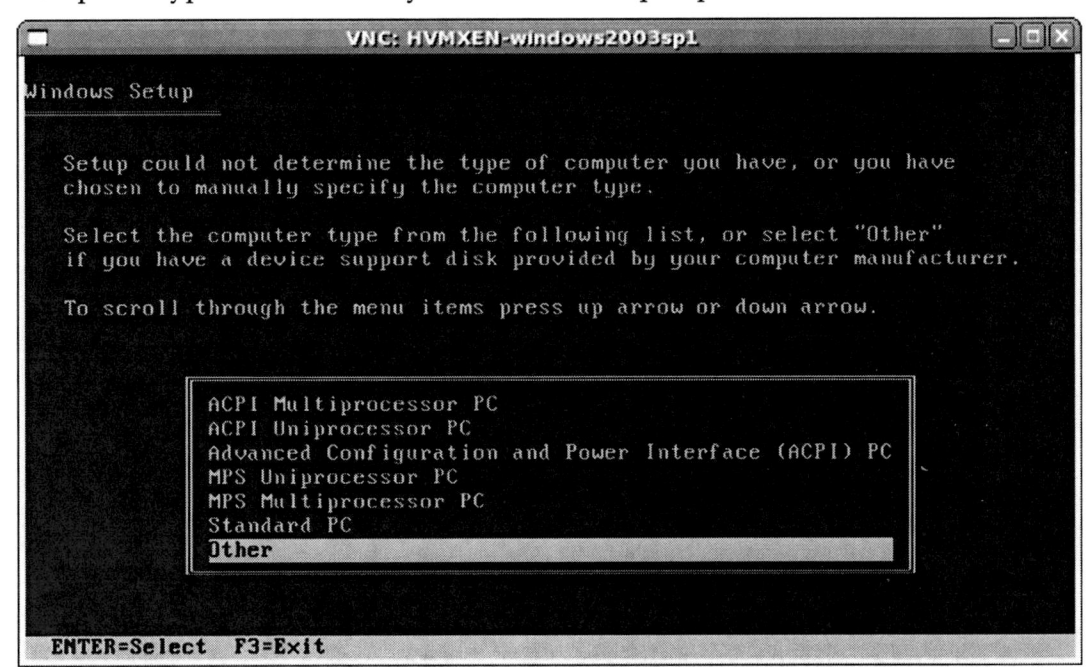

```
VNC: HVMXEN-windows2003sp1

Windows Setup

    Setup could not determine the type of computer you have, or you have
    chosen to manually specify the computer type.

    Select the computer type from the following list, or select "Other"
    if you have a device support disk provided by your computer manufacturer.

    To scroll through the menu items press up arrow or down arrow.

            ACPI Multiprocessor PC
            ACPI Uniprocessor PC
            Advanced Configuration and Power Interface (ACPI) PC
            MPS Uniprocessor PC
            MPS Multiprocessor PC
            Standard PC
            Other

ENTER=Select   F3=Exit
```

Fedora 12

3. Complete the rest of the installation.

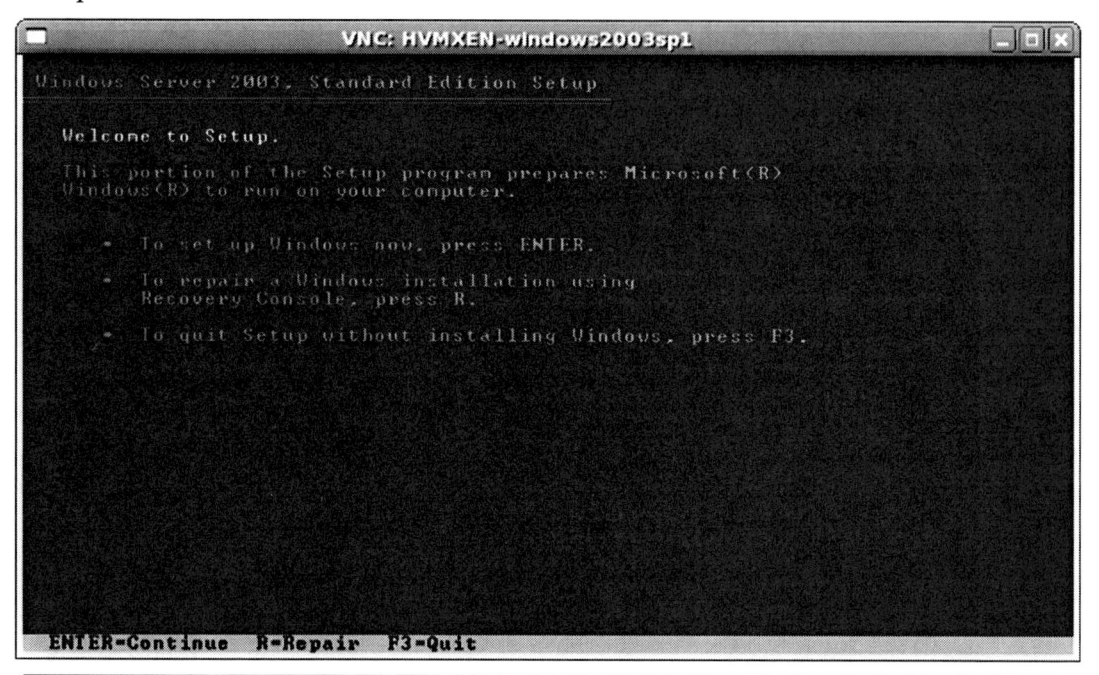

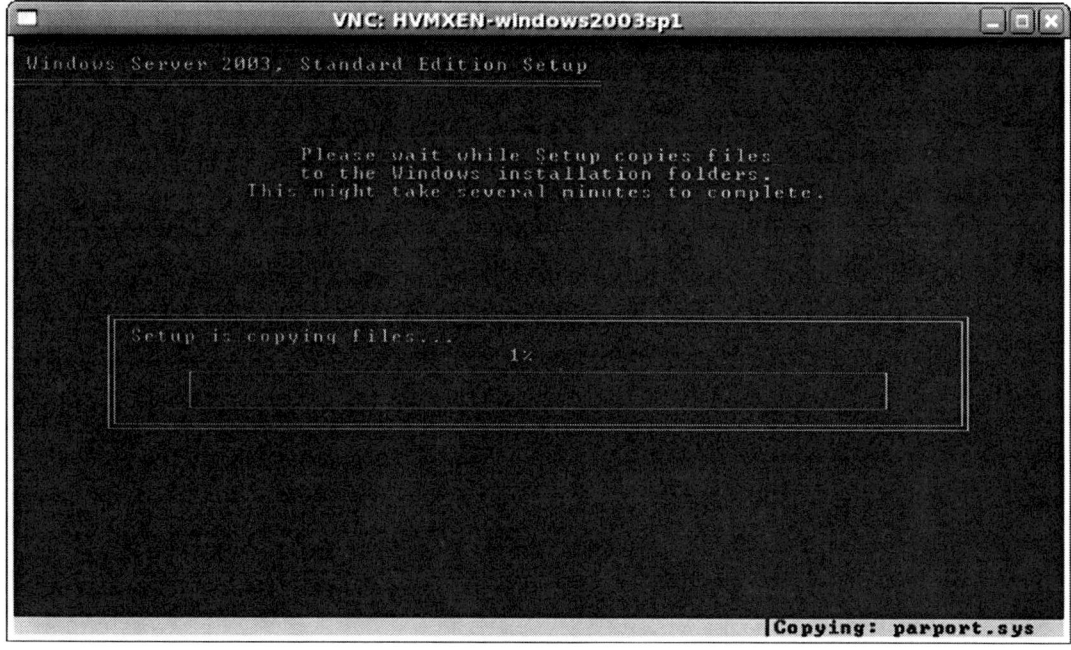

Virtualization Guide

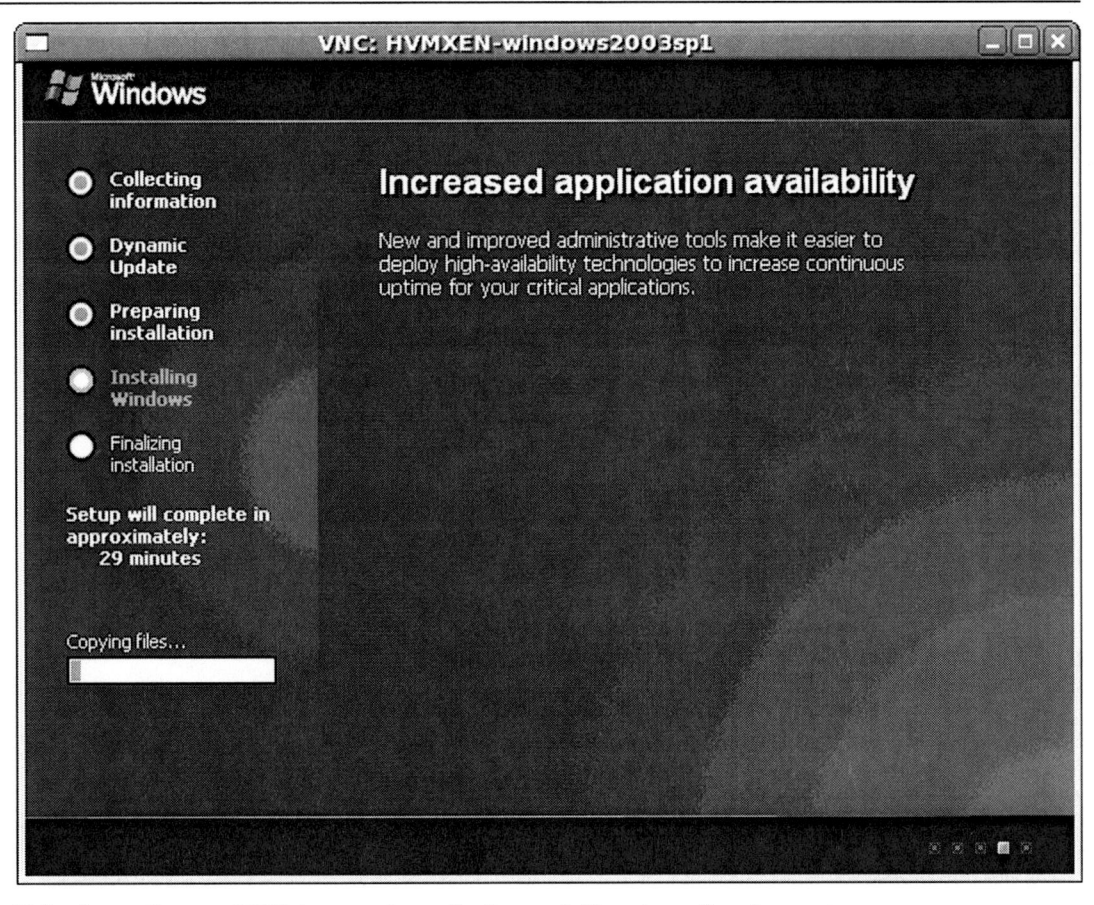

4. Windows Server 2003 is now installed as a fully virtualized guest.

3.5. Installing Windows Server 2008 as a fully virtualized guest

This section covers installing a fully virtualized Windows Server 2008 guest.

Procedure 3.4. Installing Windows Server 2008 with virt-manager

1. Open virt-manager

   Start `virt-manager`. Launch the **Virtual Machine Manager** application from the **Applications** menu and **System Tools** submenu. Alternatively, run the `virt-manager` command as root.

2. Select the hypervisor

   Select the hypervisor. If installed, select Xen or KVM. For this example, select KVM. Note that presently KVM is named `qemu`.

107

Fedora 12

Once the option is selected the **New** button becomes available. Press the **New** button.

3. Start the new virtual machine wizard

   Pressing the **New** button starts the virtual machine creation wizard.

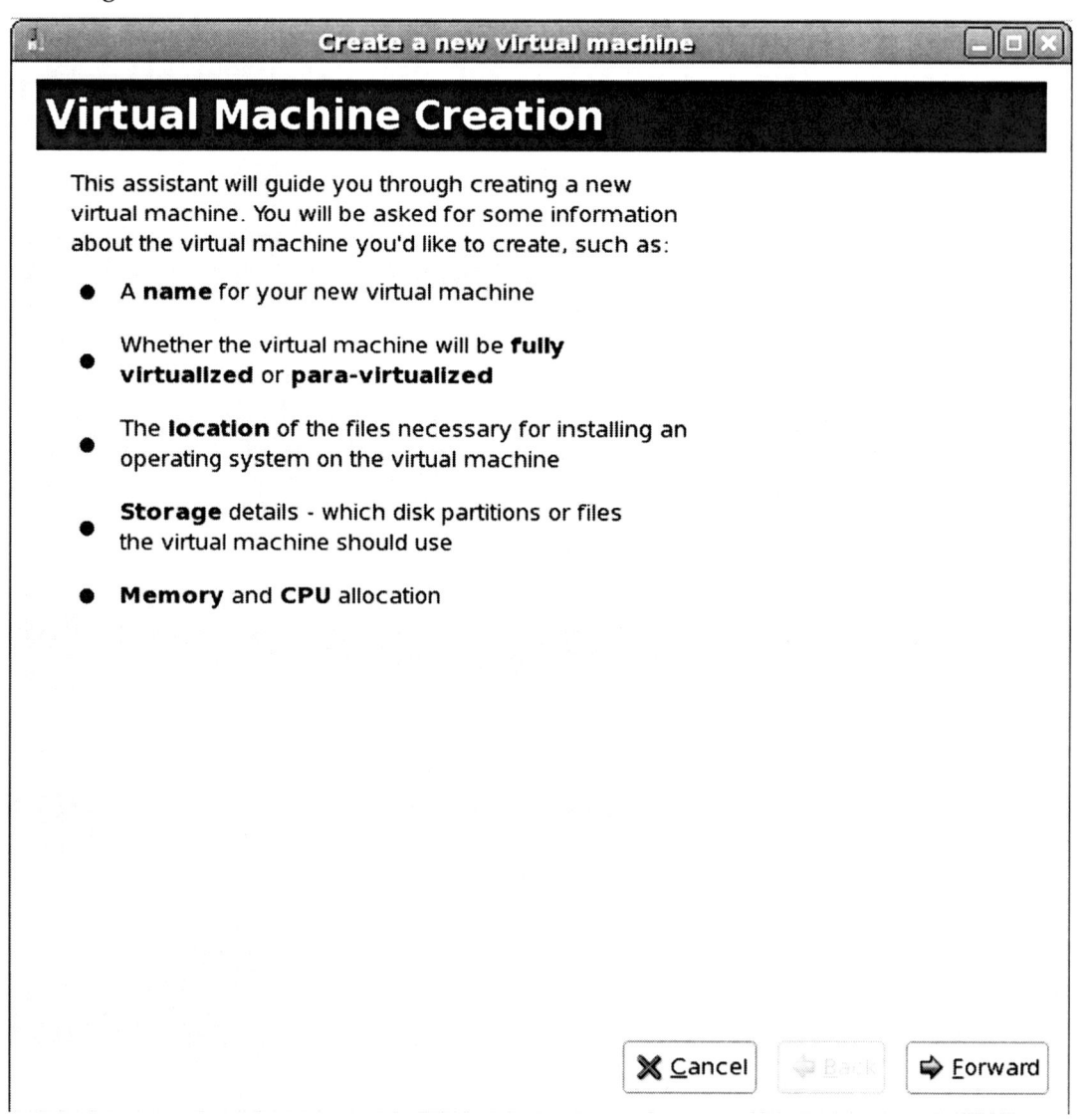

   Create a new virtual machine

   # Virtual Machine Creation

   This assistant will guide you through creating a new virtual machine. You will be asked for some information about the virtual machine you'd like to create, such as:

   - A **name** for your new virtual machine
   - Whether the virtual machine will be **fully virtualized** or **para-virtualized**
   - The **location** of the files necessary for installing an operating system on the virtual machine
   - **Storage** details - which disk partitions or files the virtual machine should use
   - **Memory** and **CPU** allocation

   [X Cancel]   [Back]   [➡ Forward]

   Press **Forward** to continue.

Virtualization Guide

4. Name the virtual machine

   Provide a name for your virtualized guest. Punctuation and whitespace characters are not permitted.

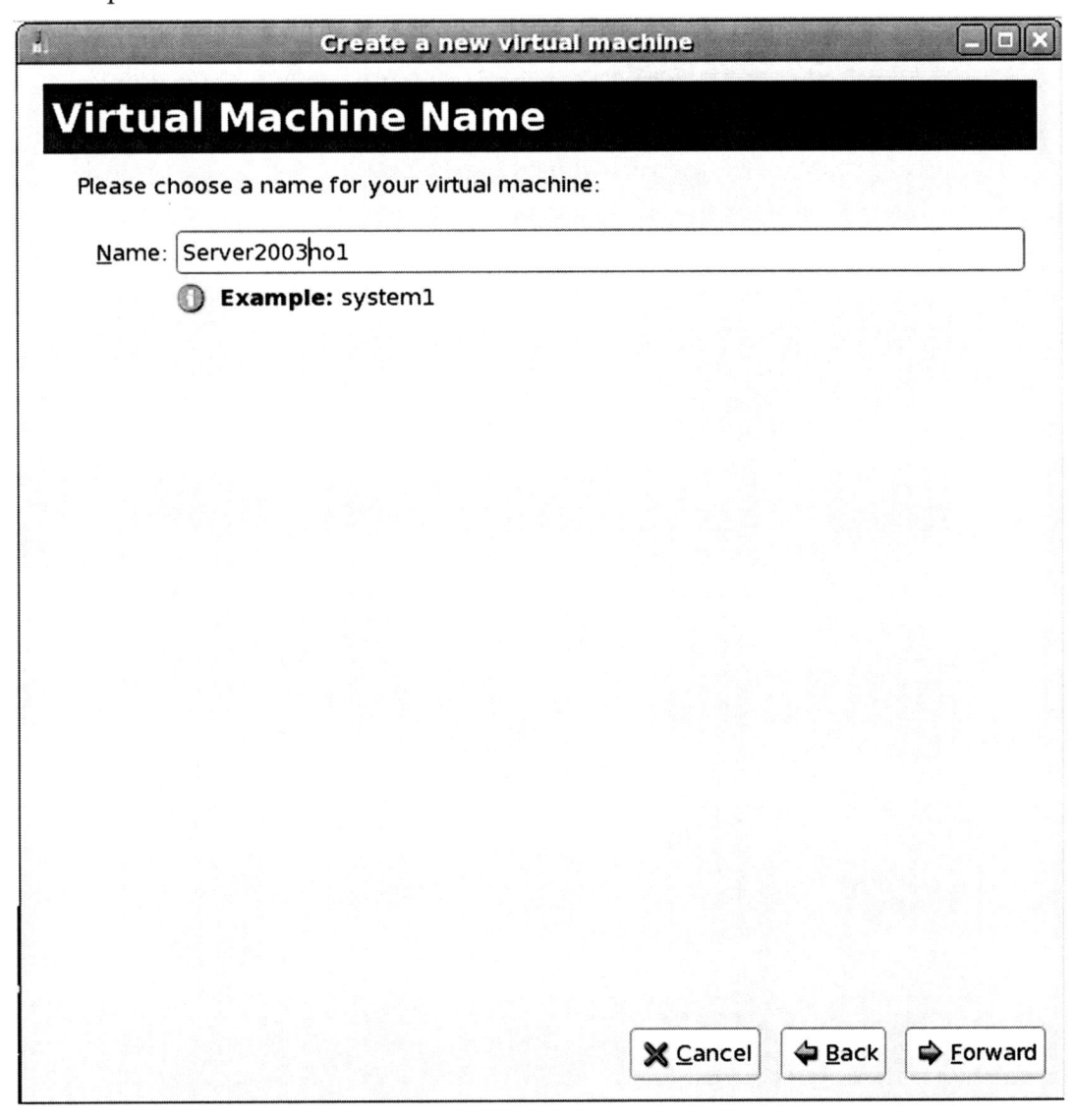

   Press **Forward** to continue.

Fedora 12

5. Choose a virtualization method

   Choose the virtualization method for the virtualized guest. Note you can only select an installed virtualization method. If you selected KVM or Xen earlier (step 2) you must use the hypervisor you selected. This example uses the KVM hypervisor.

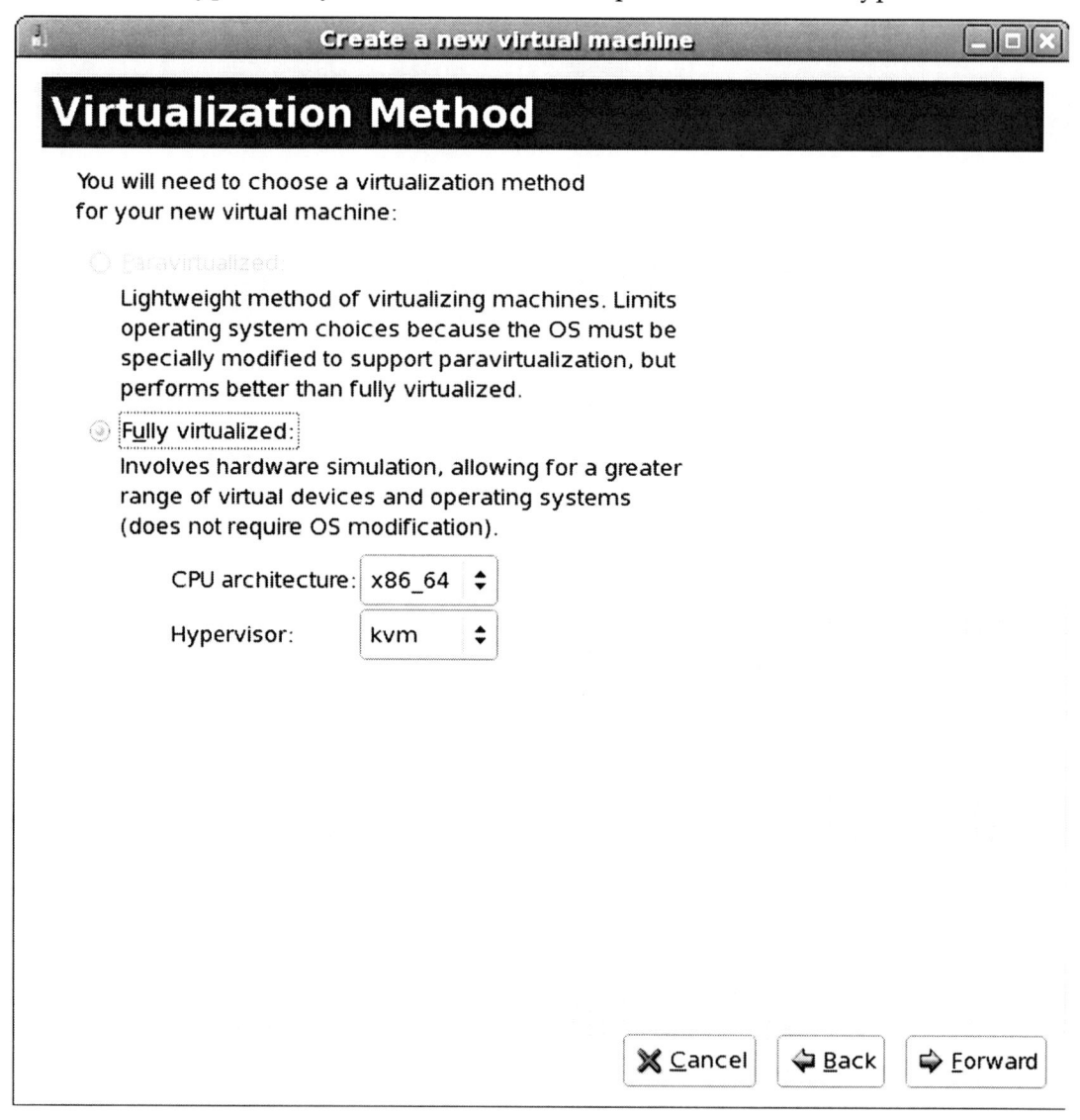

   ## Virtualization Method

   You will need to choose a virtualization method for your new virtual machine:

   ○ Paravirtualized:
   Lightweight method of virtualizing machines. Limits operating system choices because the OS must be specially modified to support paravirtualization, but performs better than fully virtualized.

   ⦿ Fully virtualized:
   Involves hardware simulation, allowing for a greater range of virtual devices and operating systems (does not require OS modification).

   CPU architecture: x86_64
   Hypervisor: kvm

   [Cancel] [Back] [Forward]

   Press **Forward** to continue.

Virtualization Guide

6. Select the installation method

    For all versions of Windows you must use **local install media**, either an ISO image or physical optical media.

    PXE may be used if you have a PXE server configured for Windows network installation. PXE Windows installation is not covered by this guide.

    Set **OS Type** to **Windows** and **OS Variant** to **Microsoft Windows 2008** as shown in the screenshot.

    ## Installation Method

    Please indicate where installation media is available for the operating system you would like to install on this virtual machine:

    - ◉ Local install media (ISO image or CDROM)
    - ○ Network install tree (HTTP, FTP, or NFS)
    - ○ Network boot (PXE)

    Please choose the operating system you will be installing on the virtual machine:

    OS Type: Windows

    OS Variant: Microsoft Windows 2008

    [✗ Cancel] [⇦ Back] [⇨ Forward]

    Press **Forward** to continue.

Fedora 12

7. Locate installation media

   Select ISO image location or CD-ROM or DVD device. This example uses an ISO file image of the Windows Server 2008 installation CD.

   1. Press the **Browse** button.
   2. Search to the location of the ISO file and select it.

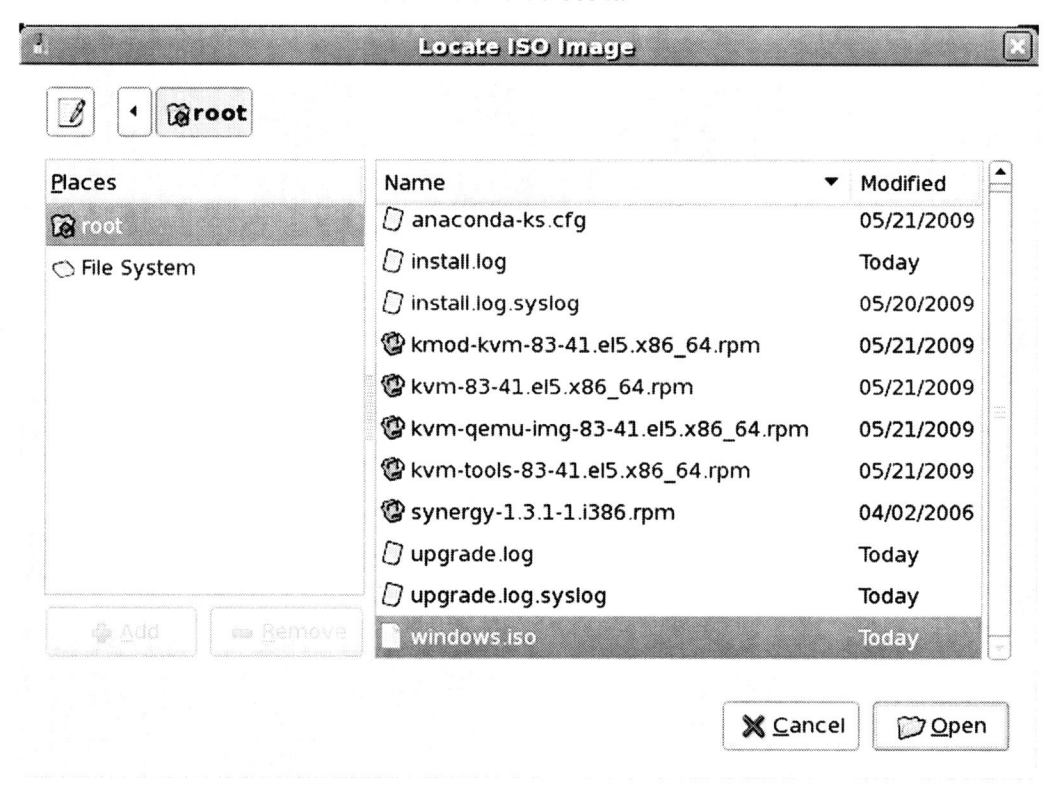

   Press **Open** to confirm your selection.

3. The file is selected and ready to install from.

Installation Media

Please indicate where installation media is available for the operating system you would like to install on this virtual machine:

- ISO image location:
  - ISO location: es/Windows2008-x64.iso [Browse...]
- CD-ROM or DVD:
  - Path to install media:

[Cancel] [Back] [Forward]

Press **Forward** to continue.

> **Image files and SELinux**
>
> For ISO image files and guest storage images, the recommended directory to use is the `/var/lib/libvirt/images/` directory. Any other location may require additional configuration for SELinux, refer to *Section 7.1, "SELinux and virtualization"* for details.

113

8. Storage setup

    Assign a physical storage device (**Block device**) or a file-based image (**File**). File-based images must be stored in the /var/lib/libvirt/images/ directory. Assign sufficient storage for your virtualized guest. Assign sufficient space for your virtualized guest and any application it requires.

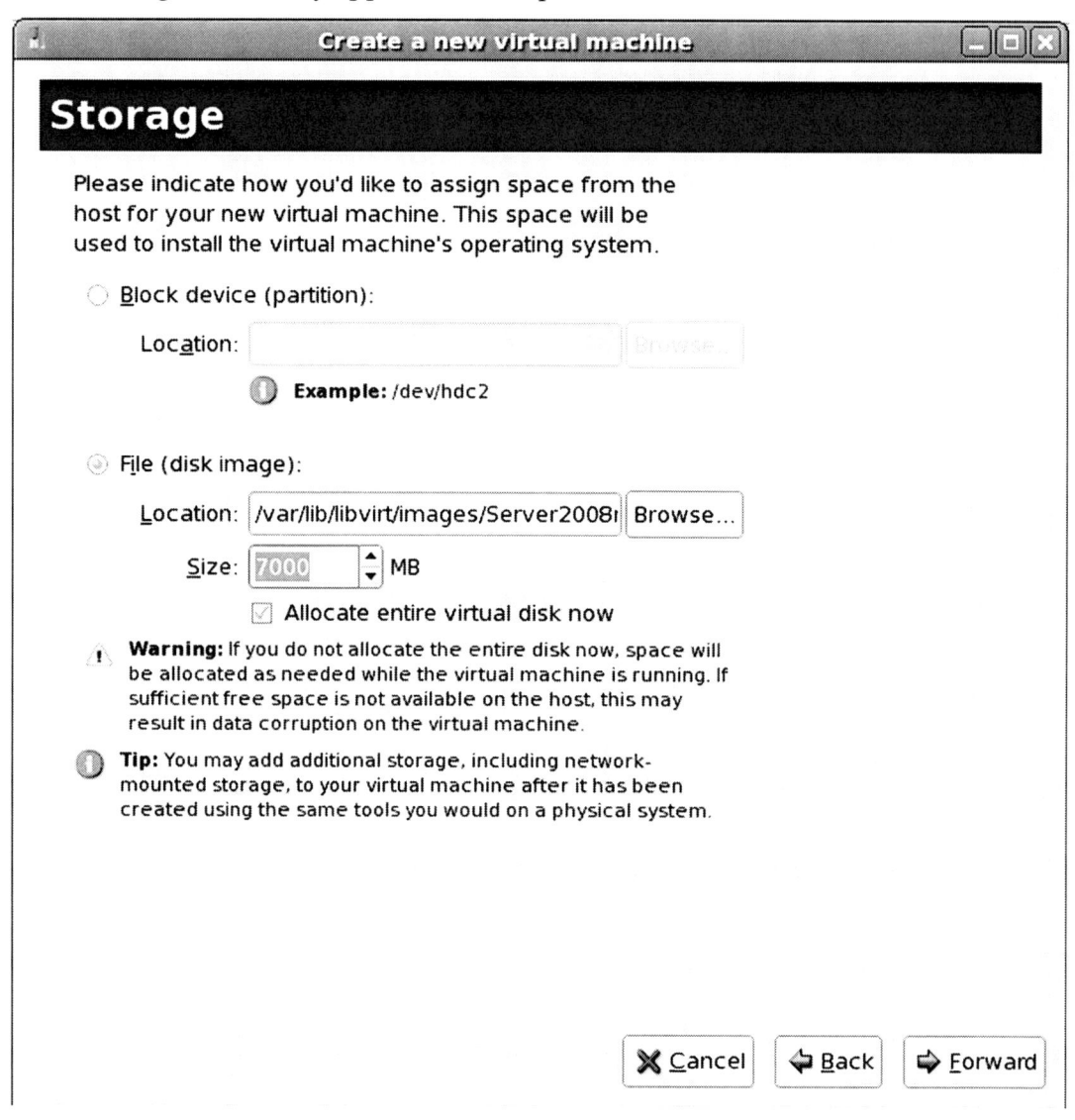

    Press **Forward** to continue.

Virtualization Guide

9. Network setup

   Select either **Virtual network** or **Shared physical device**.

   The virtual network option uses Network Address Translation (NAT) to share the default network device with the virtualized guest. Use the virtual network option for wireless networks.

   The shared physical device option uses a network bond to give the virtualized guest full access to a network device.

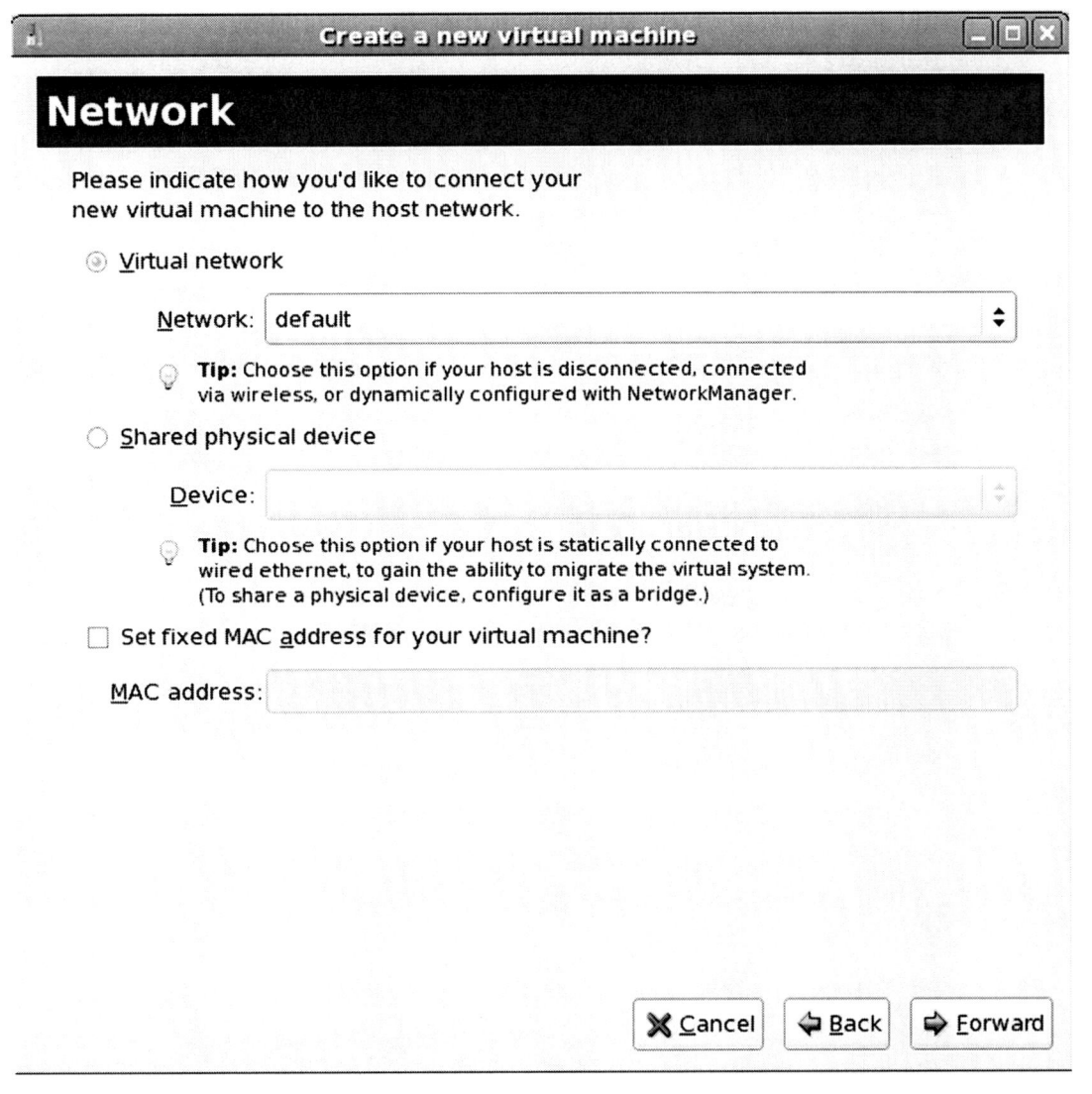

   Press **Forward** to continue.

10. Memory and CPU allocation

    The Allocate memory and CPU window displays. Choose appropriate values for the virtualized CPUs and RAM allocation. These values affect the host's and guest's performance.

    Virtualized guests require sufficient physical memory (RAM) to run efficiently and effectively. Choose a memory value which suits your guest operating system and application requirements. Windows Server 2008. Remember, guests use physical RAM. Running too many guests or leaving insufficient memory for the host system results in significant usage of virtual memory and swapping. Virtual memory is significantly slower causing degraded system performance and responsiveness. Ensure to allocate sufficient memory for all guests and the host to operate effectively.

    Assign sufficient virtual CPUs for the virtualized guest. If the guest runs a multithreaded application assign the number of virtualized CPUs it requires to run most efficiently. Do not assign more virtual CPUs than there are physical processors (or hyper-threads) available on the host system. It is possible to over allocate virtual processors, however, over allocating has a significant, negative affect on guest and host performance due to processor context switching overheads.

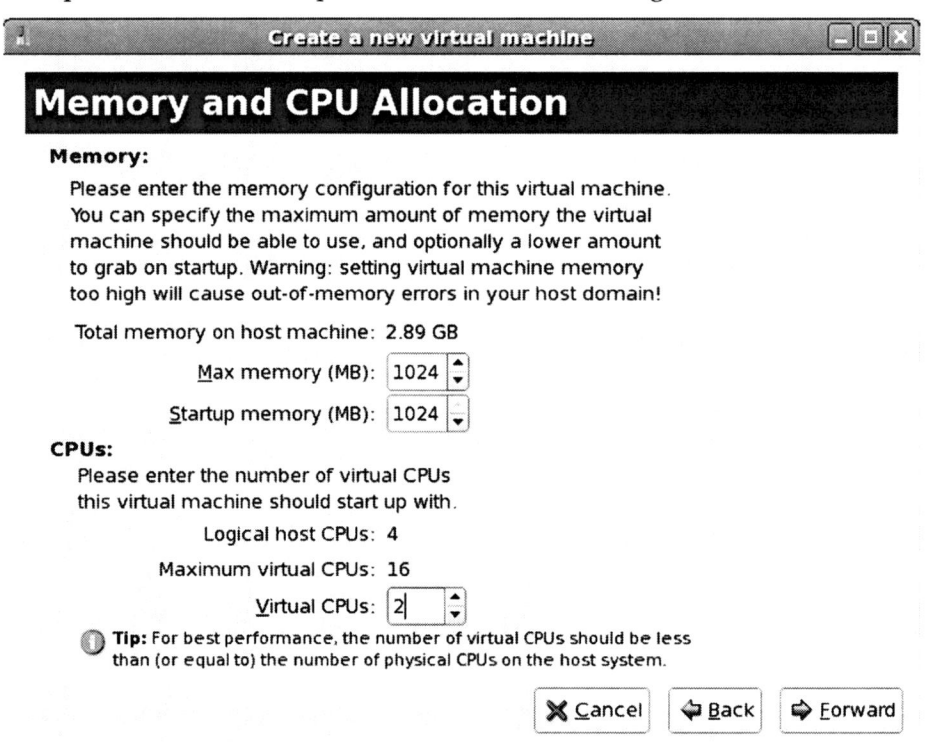

    Create a new virtual machine

    Memory and CPU Allocation

    Memory:
    Please enter the memory configuration for this virtual machine. You can specify the maximum amount of memory the virtual machine should be able to use, and optionally a lower amount to grab on startup. Warning: setting virtual machine memory too high will cause out-of-memory errors in your host domain!

    Total memory on host machine: 2.89 GB
    Max memory (MB): 1024
    Startup memory (MB): 1024

    CPUs:
    Please enter the number of virtual CPUs this virtual machine should start up with.

    Logical host CPUs: 4
    Maximum virtual CPUs: 16
    Virtual CPUs: 2

    Tip: For best performance, the number of virtual CPUs should be less than (or equal to) the number of physical CPUs on the host system.

    ✗ Cancel   ⇦ Back   ⇨ Forward

    Press **Forward** to continue.

11. Verify and start guest installation

    Verify the configuration.

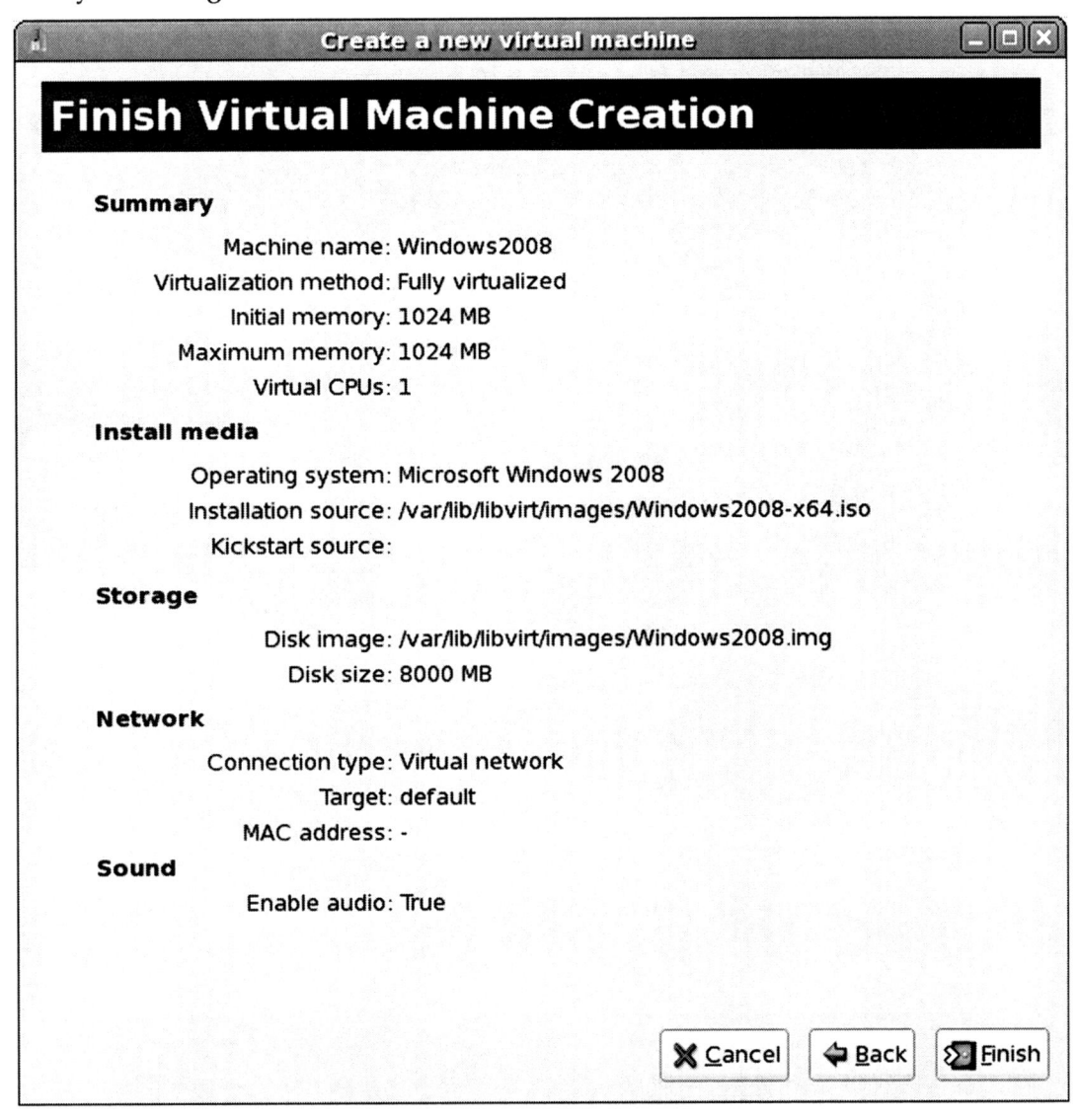

    ```
    Finish Virtual Machine Creation

    Summary
                Machine name: Windows2008
        Virtualization method: Fully virtualized
                Initial memory: 1024 MB
              Maximum memory: 1024 MB
                  Virtual CPUs: 1
    Install media
              Operating system: Microsoft Windows 2008
            Installation source: /var/lib/libvirt/images/Windows2008-x64.iso
               Kickstart source:
    Storage
                    Disk image: /var/lib/libvirt/images/Windows2008.img
                     Disk size: 8000 MB
    Network
               Connection type: Virtual network
                        Target: default
                   MAC address: -
    Sound
                  Enable audio: True
    ```

    Press **Finish** to start the guest installation procedure.

12. Installing Windows

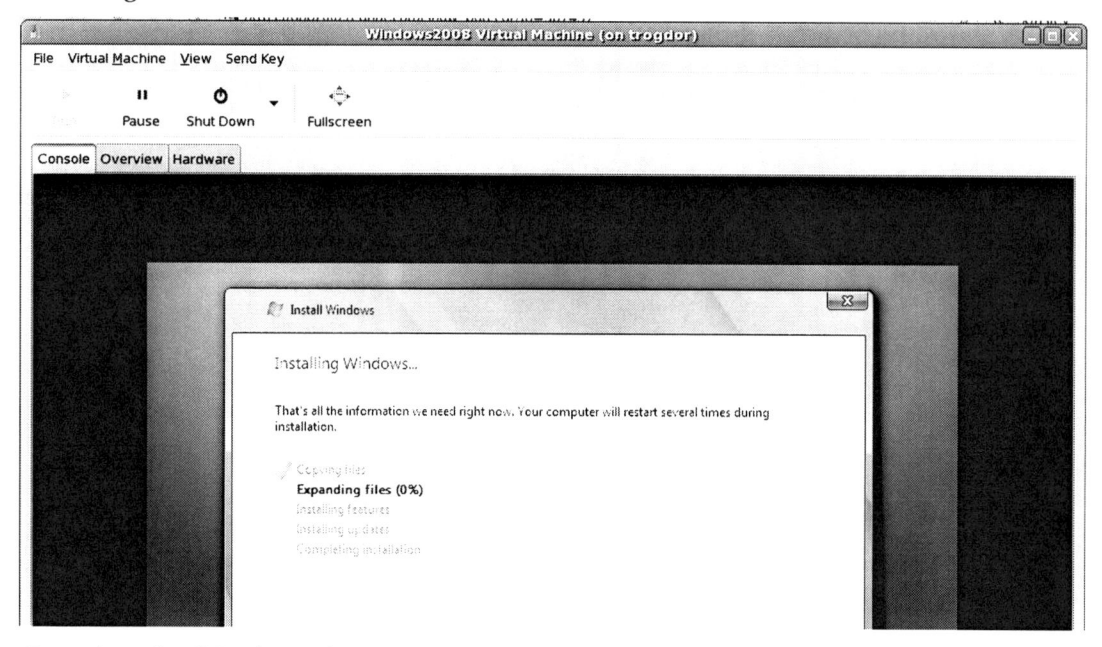

Complete the Windows Server 2008 installation sequence. The installation sequence is not covered by this guide, refer to Microsoft's *documentation*[1] for information on installing Windows.

---

[1] *http://microsoft.com/support*

Part II.
Configuration

Configuring Virtualization in Fedora

These chapters cover configuration procedures for various advanced virtualization tasks. These tasks include adding network and storage devices, enhancing security, improving performance, and using the para-virtualized drivers on fully virtualized guests.

Chapter 4.
Virtualized block devices

This chapter covers installing and configuring block devices in virtualized guests. The term block devices refers to various forms of storage devices.

4.1. Creating a virtualized floppy disk controller

Floppy disk controllers are required for a number of older operating systems, especially for installing drivers. Presently, physical floppy disk devices cannot be accessed from virtualized guests. However, creating and accessing floppy disk images from virtualized floppy drives is supported. This section covers creating a virtualized floppy device.

An image file of a floppy disk is required. Create floppy disk image files with the `dd` command. Replace /dev/fd0 with the name of a floppy device and name the disk appropriately.

```
# dd if=/dev/fd0 of=~/legacydrivers.img
```

> **Para-virtualized drivers note**
>
> The para-virtualized drivers can map physical floppy devices to fully virtualized guests.

This example uses a guest created with `virt-manager` running a fully virtualized Linux installation with an image located in /var/lib/libvirt/images/rhel5FV.img. The Xen hypervisor is used in the example.

1. Create the XML configuration file for your guest image using the `virsh` command on a running guest.
   ```
   # virsh dumpxml rhel5FV > rhel5FV.xml
   ```
   This saves the configuration settings as an XML file which can be edited to customize the operations and devices used by the guest. For more information on using the virsh XML configuration files, refer to *Chapter 18, Creating custom libvirt scripts*.

2. Create a floppy disk image for the guest.
   ```
   # dd if=/dev/zero of=/var/lib/libvirt/images/rhel5FV-floppy.img bs=512 count=2880
   ```

3. Add the content below, changing where appropriate, to your guest's configuration XML file. This example creates a guest with a floppy device as a file based virtual device.

```
<disk type='file' device='floppy'>
      <source file='/var/lib/libvirt/images/rhel5FV-floppy.img'/>
      <target dev='fda'/>
</disk>
```

4. Stop the guest.

```
# virsh stop rhel5FV
```

5. Restart the guest using the XML configuration file.

```
# virsh create rhel5FV.xml
```

The floppy device is now available in the guest and stored as an image file on the host.

4.2. Adding storage devices to guests

This section covers adding storage devices to virtualized guest. Additional storage can only be added after guests are created. The supported storage devices and protocol include:

- local hard drive partitions,
- logical volumes,
- Fibre Channel or iSCSI directly connected to the host.
- File containers residing in a file system on the host.
- **NFS** file systems mounted directly by the virtual machine.
- iSCSI storage directly accessed by the guest.
- Cluster File Systems (**GFS**).

Adding file based storage to a guest

File-based storage or file-based containers are files on the hosts file system which act as virtualized hard drives for virtualized guests. To add a file-based container perform the following steps:

1. Create an empty container file or using an existing file container (such as an ISO file).

    1. Create a sparse file using the `dd` command. Sparse files are not recommended due to data integrity and performance issues. Sparse files are created much faster and can used for testing but should not be used in production environments.

    ```
    # dd if=/dev/zero of=/var/lib/libvirt/images/FileName.img bs=1M seek=4096 count=0
    ```

121

Fedora 12

2. Non-sparse, pre-allocated files are recommended for file based storage containers. Create a non-sparse file, execute:

   ```
   # dd if=/dev/zero of=/var/lib/libvirt/images/FileName.img bs=1M
   count=4096
   ```

   Both commands create a 400MB file which can be used as additional storage for a virtualized guest.

2. Dump the configuration for the guest. In this example the guest is called *Guest1* and the file is saved in the users home directory.

   ```
   # virsh dumpxml Guest1 > ~/Guest1.xml
   ```

3. Open the configuration file (*Guest1.xml* in this example) in a text editor. Find the entries starting with "disk=". This entry resembles:

   ```
   >disk type='file' device='disk'<
           >driver name='tap' type='aio'/<
           >source file='/var/lib/libvirt/images/Guest1.img'/<
           >target dev='xvda'/<
   >/disk<
   ```

4. Add the additional storage by modifying the end of disk= entry. Ensure you specify a device name for the virtual block device which is not used already in the configuration file. The following example entry adds file, named FileName.img, as a file based storage container:

   ```
   >disk type='file' device='disk'<
           >driver name='tap' type='aio'/<
           >source file='/var/lib/libvirt/images/Guest1.img'/<
           >target dev='xvda'/<
   >/disk<
   >disk type='file' device='disk'<
           >driver name='tap' type='aio'/<
          >source file='/var/lib/libvirt/images/FileName.img'/<
           >target dev='hda'/<
   >/disk<
   ```

5. Restart the guest from the updated configuration file.

   ```
   # virsh create Guest1.xml
   ```

6. The following steps are Linux guest specific. Other operating systems handle new storage devices in different ways. For non Linux systems refer to your guest operating systems documentation.

   The guest now uses the file FileName.img as the device called /dev/hdb. This device requires formatting from the guest. On the guest, partition the device into one primary partition for the entire device then format the device.

1. Press *n* for a new partition.

   ```
   # fdisk /dev/hdb
   Command (m for help):
   ```

2. Press *p* for a primary partition.

   ```
   Command action
      e   extended
      p   primary partition (1-4)
   ```

3. Choose an available partition number. In this example the first partition is chosen by entering *1*.

   ```
   Partition number (1-4): 1
   ```

4. Enter the default first cylinder by pressing *Enter*.

   ```
   First cylinder (1-400, default 1):
   ```

5. Select the size of the partition. In this example the entire disk is allocated by pressing *Enter*.

   ```
   Last cylinder or +size or +sizeM or +sizeK (2-400, default 400):
   ```

6. Set the type of partition by pressing *t*.

   ```
   Command (m for help): t
   ```

7. Choose the partition you created in the previous steps. In this example it's partition *1*.

   ```
   Partition number (1-4): 1
   ```

8. Enter *83* for a Linux partition.

   ```
   Hex code (type L to list codes): 83
   ```

9. write changes to disk and quit.

   ```
   Command (m for help): w
   Command (m for help): q
   ```

10. Format the new partition with the ext3 file system.

    ```
    # mke2fs -j /dev/hdb
    ```

7. Mount the disk on the guest.

   ```
   # mount /dev/hdb1 /myfiles
   ```

The guest now has an additional virtualized file-based storage device.

Adding hard drives and other block devices to a guest

System administrators use additional hard drives for to provide more storage space or to separate system data from user data. This procedure, *Procedure 4.1, "Adding physical block devices to virtualized guests"*, describes how to add a hard drive on the host to a virtualized guest.

The procedure works for all physical block devices, this includes CD-ROM, DVD and floppy devices.

Procedure 4.1. Adding physical block devices to virtualized guests

1. Physically attach the hard disk device to the host. Configure the host if the drive is not accessible by default.

2. Configure the device with `multipath` and persistence on the host if required.

3. Use the `virsh attach` command. Replace: `myguest` with your guest's name, `/dev/hdb1` with the device to add, and `hdc` with the location for the device on the guest. The `hdc` must be an unused device name. Use the `hd*` notation for Windows guests as well, the guest will recognize the device correctly.

   Append the `--type hdd` parameter to the command for CD-ROM or DVD devices.

   Append the `--type floppy` parameter to the command for floppy devices.

   ```
   # virsh attach-disk myguest /dev/hdb1 hdc --driver tap --mode readonly
   ```

4. The guest now has a new hard disk device called `/dev/hdb` on Linux or `D: drive`, or similar, on Windows. This device may require formatting.

4.3. Configuring persistent storage

This section is for systems with external or networked storage; that is, Fibre Channel or iSCSI based storage devices. It is recommended that those systems have persistent device names configured for your hosts. This assists live migration as well as providing consistent device names and storage for multiple virtualized systems.

Universally Unique Identifiers(UUIDs) are a standardized method for identifying computers and devices in distributed computing environments. This sections uses UUIDs to identify iSCSI or Fibre Channel LUNs. UUIDs persist after restarts, disconnection and device swaps. The UUID is similar to a label on the device.

Systems which are not running `multipath` must use *Single path configuration* below. Systems running `multipath` can use *Multiple path configuration* below.

Virtualization Guide

Single path configuration

This procedure implements *LUN* (see page 241) device persistence using `udev`. Only use this procedure for hosts which are not using `multipath`.

1. Edit the `/etc/scsi_id.config` file.

    1. Ensure the `options=-b` is line commented out.
    ```
    # options=-b
    ```
    2. Add the following line:
    ```
    options=-g
    ```
    This option configures `udev` to assume all attached SCSI devices return a UUID.

2. To display the UUID for a given device run the `scsi_id -g -s /block/sd*` command. For example:
   ```
   # scsi_id -g -s /block/sd*
   3600a0b800013275100000015427b625e
   ```
   The output may vary from the example above. The output displays the UUID of the device `/dev/sdc`.

3. Verify the UUID output by the `scsi_id -g -s /block/sd*` command is identical from computer which accesses the device.

4. Create a rule to name the device. Create a file named `20-names.rules` in the `/etc/udev/rules.d` directory. Add new rules to this file. All rules are added to the same file using the same format. Rules follow this format:
   ```
   KERNEL="sd*", BUS="scsi", PROGRAM="/sbin/scsi_id -g -s", RESULT=UUID,
   NAME=devicename
   ```
   Replace *UUID* and *devicename* with the UUID retrieved above, and a name for the device. This is a rule for the example above:
   ```
   KERNEL="sd*", BUS="scsi", PROGRAM="/sbin/scsi_id -g -s",
   RESULT="3600a0b800013275100000015427b625e", NAME="rack4row16"
   ```
   The `udev` daemon now searches all devices named `/dev/sd*` for the UUID in the rule. Once a matching device is connected to the system the device is assigned the name from the rule. In the a device with a UUID of 3600a0b800013275100000015427b625e would appear as `/dev/rack4row16`.

5. Append this line to `/etc/rc.local`:
   ```
   /sbin/start_udev
   ```

6. Copy the changes in the `/etc/scsi_id.config`, `/etc/udev/rules.d/20-names.rules`, and `/etc/rc.local` files to all relevant hosts.
   ```
   /sbin/start_udev
   ```

125

Networked storage devices with configured rules now have persistent names on all hosts where the files were updated This means you can migrate guests between hosts using the shared storage and the guests can access the storage devices in their configuration files.

Multiple path configuration

The `multipath` package is used for systems with more than one physical path from the computer to storage devices. `multipath` provides fault tolerance, fail-over and enhanced performance for network storage devices attached to Linux systems.

Implementing LUN persistence in a `multipath` environment requires defined alias names for your multipath devices. Each storage device has a UUID which acts as a key for the aliased names. Identify a device's UUID using the `scsi_id` command.

```
# scsi_id -g -s /block/sdc
```

The multipath devices will be created in the `/dev/mpath` directory. In the example below 4 devices are defined in `/etc/multipath.conf`:

```
multipaths {
    multipath {
    wwid            3600805f30015987000000000768a0019
    alias           oramp1
    }
    multipath {
    wwid            3600805f30015987000000000d643001a
    alias           oramp2
    }
    mulitpath {
    wwid            3600805f3001598700000000086fc001b
    alias           oramp3
    }
    mulitpath {
    wwid            3600805f30015987000000000984001c
    alias           oramp4
    }
}
```

This configuration will create 4 LUNs named `/dev/mpath/oramp1`, `/dev/mpath/oramp2`, `/dev/mpath/oramp3` and `/dev/mpath/oramp4`. Once entered, the mapping of the devices' WWID to their new names are now persistent after rebooting.

4.4. Add a virtualized CD-ROM or DVD device to a guest

To attach an ISO file to a guest while the guest is online use `virsh` with the `attach-disk` parameter.

```
# virsh attach-disk [domain-id] [source] [target] --driver file --type
cdrom --mode readonly
```

Virtualization Guide

The `source` and `target` parameters are paths for the files and devices, on the host and guest respectively. The `source` parameter can be a path to an ISO file or the device from the `/dev` directory.

Chapter 5.
Shared storage and virtualization

This chapter covers using shared, networked storage with virtualization on Fedora.

The following methods are supported for virtualization:

- Fibre Channel
- iSCSI
- NFS
- GFS2

Networked storage is essential for live and offline guest migrations. You cannot migrate guests without shared storage.

5.1. Using iSCSI for storing guests

This section covers using iSCSI-based devices to store virtualized guests.

5.2. Using NFS for storing guests

This section covers using NFS to store virtualized guests.

5.3. Using GFS2 for storing guests

This section covers using the fedora Global File System 2 (GFS2) to store virtualized guests.

Chapter 6.
Server best practices

The following tasks and tips can assist you with securing and ensuring reliability of your Fedora server host (dom0).

- Run SELinux in enforcing mode. You can do this by executing the command below.
  ```
  # setenforce 1
  ```
- Remove or disable any unnecessary services such as `AutoFS`, `NFS`, `FTP`, `HTTP`, `NIS`, `telnetd`, `sendmail` and so on.
- Only add the minimum number of user accounts needed for platform management on the server and remove unnecessary user accounts.
- Avoid running any unessential applications on your host. Running applications on the host may impact virtual machine performance and can affect server stability. Any application which may crash the server will also cause all virtual machines on the server to go down.
- Use a central location for virtual machine installations and images. Virtual machine images should be stored under `/var/lib/libvirt/images/`. If you are using a different directory for your virtual machine images make sure you add the directory to your SELinux policy and relabel it before starting the installation.
- Installation sources, trees, and images should be stored in a central location, usually the location of your `vsftpd` server.

Chapter 7.
Security for virtualization

When deploying virtualization technologies on your corporate infrastructure, you must ensure that the host cannot be compromised. The host, in the Xen hypervisor, is a privileged domain that handles system management and manages all virtual machines. If the host is insecure, all other domains in the system are vulnerable. There are several ways to enhance security on systems using virtualization. You or your organization should create a *Deployment Plan* containing the operating specifications and specifies which services are needed on your virtualized guests and host servers as well as what support is required for these services. Here are a few security issues to consider while developing a deployment plan:

- Run only necessary services on hosts. The fewer processes and services running on the host, the higher the level of security and performance.
- Enable *SELinux* on the hypervisor. Read *Section 7.1, "SELinux and virtualization"* for more information on using SELinux and virtualization.
- Use a firewall to restrict traffic to dom0. You can setup a firewall with default-reject rules that will help secure attacks on dom0. It is also important to limit network facing services.
- Do not allow normal users to access dom0. If you do permit normal users dom0 access, you run the risk of rendering dom0 vulnerable. Remember, dom0 is privileged, and granting unprivileged accounts may compromise the level of security.

7.1. SELinux and virtualization

Security Enhanced Linux was developed by the NSA with assistance from the Linux community to provide stronger security for Linux. SELinux limits an attackers abilities and works to prevent many common security exploits such as buffer overflow attacks and privilege escalation. It is because of these benefits that Fedora recommends all Linux systems should run with SELinux enabled and in enforcing mode.

SELinux prevents guest images from loading if SELinux is enabled and the images are not in the correct directory. SELinux requires that all guest images are stored in `/var/lib/libvirt/images`.

Virtualization Guide

Adding LVM based storage with SELinux in enforcing mode

The following section is an example of adding a logical volume to a virtualized guest with SELinux enabled. These instructions also work for hard drive partitions.

Procedure 7.1.
Creating and mounting a logical volume on a virtualized guest with SELinux enabled

1. Create a logical volume. This example creates a 5 gigabyte logical volume named *NewVolumeName* on the volume group named *volumegroup*.

   `# lvcreate -n NewVolumeName -L 5G volumegroup`

2. Format the *NewVolumeName* logical volume with a file system that supports extended attributes, such as ext3.

   `# mke2fs -j /dev/volumegroup/NewVolumeName`

3. Create a new directory for mounting the new logical volume. This directory can be anywhere on your file system. It is advised not to put it in important system directories (/etc, /var, /sys) or in home directories (/home or /root). This example uses a directory called /virtstorage

   `# mkdir /virtstorage`

4. Mount the logical volume.

   `# mount /dev/volumegroup/NewVolumeName /virtstorage`

5. Set the correct SELinux type for the Xen folder.

   `semanage fcontext -a -t xen_image_t "/virtualization(/.*)?"`

   Alternatively, set the correct SELinux type for a KVM folder.

   `semanage fcontext -a -t virt_image_t "/virtualization(/.*)?"`

   If the targeted policy is used (targeted is the default policy) the command appends a line to the /etc/selinux/targeted/contexts/files/file_contexts.local file which makes the change persistent. The appended line may resemble this:

   `/virtstorage(/.*)?    system_u:object_r:xen_image_t:s0`

6. Run the command to change the type of the mount point (/virtstorage) and all files under it to xen_image_t (restorecon and setfiles read the files in /etc/selinux/targeted/contexts/files/).

   `# restorecon -R -v /virtualization`

131

7.2. SELinux considerations

This sections contains things to you must consider when you implement SELinux into your virtualization deployment. When you deploy system changes or add devices, you must update your SELinux policy accordingly. To configure an LVM volume for a guest, you must modify the SELinux context for the respective underlying block device and volume group.

```
# semanage fcontext -a -t xen_image _t -f -b /dev/sda2
# restorecon /dev/sda2
```

The Boolean parameter `xend_disable_t` can set the `xend` to unconfined mode after restarting the daemon. It is better to disable protection for a single daemon than the whole system. It is advisable that you should not re-label directories as `xen_image_t` that you will use elsewhere.

Chapter 8.
Network Configuration

This page provides an introduction to the common networking configurations used by libvirt based applications. This information applies to all hypervisors, whether Xen, KVM or another. For additional information consult the libvirt network architecture docs.

The two common setups are "virtual network" or "shared physical device". The former is identical across all distributions and available out-of-the-box. The latter needs distribution specific manual configuration.

8.1. Network address translation (NAT) with libvirt

One of the most common methods for sharing network connections is to use Network address translation (NAT) forwarding (also know as virtual networks).

Host configuration

Every standard `libvirt` installation provides NAT based connectivity to virtual machines out of the box. This is the so called 'default virtual network'. Verify that it is available with the `virsh net-list --all` command.

```
# virsh net-list --all
Name                 State      Autostart
-----------------------------------------
default              active     yes
```

If it is missing, the example XML configuration file can be reloaded and activated:

```
# virsh net-define /usr/share/libvirt/networks/default.xml
```

The default network is defined from `/usr/share/libvirt/networks/default.xml`

Mark the default network to automatically start:

```
# virsh net-autostart default
Network default marked as autostarted
```

Start the default network:

```
# virsh net-start default
Network default started
```

133

Once the `libvirt` default network is running, you will see an isolated bridge device. This device does *not* have any physical interfaces added, since it uses NAT and IP forwarding to connect to outside world. Do not add new interfaces.

```
# brctl show
bridge name     bridge id               STP enabled     interfaces
virbr0          8000.000000000000       yes
```

`libvirt` adds `iptables` rules which allow traffic to and from guests attached to the `virbr0` device in the `INPUT`, `FORWARD`, `OUTPUT` and `POSTROUTING` chains. `libvirt` then attempts to enable the `ip_forward` parameter. Some other applications may disable `ip_forward`, so the best option is to add the following to `/etc/sysctl.conf`.

```
net.ipv4.ip_forward = 1
```

Guest configuration

Once the host configuration is complete, a guest can be connected to the virtual network based on its name. To connect a guest to the 'default' virtual network, the following XML can be used in the guest:

```
<interface type='network'>
  <source network='default'/>
</interface>
```

> **Note**
>
> Defining a MAC address is optional. A MAC address is automatically generated if omitted. Manually setting the MAC address is useful in certain situations.
>
> ```
> <interface type='network'>
>   <source network='default'/>
>   <mac address='00:16:3e:1a:b3:4a'/>
> </interface>
> ```

8.2. Bridged networking with libvirt

Bridged networking (also known as physical device sharing) is used for dedicating a physical device to a virtual machine. Bridging is often used for more advanced setups and on servers with multiple network interfaces.

Disable Xen network scripts

If your system was using a Xen bridge, it is recommended to disable the default Xen network bridge by editing `/etc/xen/xend-config.sxp` and changing the line:

```
(network-script network-bridge)
```

To:

```
(network-script /bin/true)
```

Virtualization Guide

Disable NetworkManager

NetworkManager does not support bridging. NetworkManager must be disabled to use the older network scripts networking.

```
# chkconfig NetworkManager off
# chkconfig network on
# service NetworkManager stop
# service network start
```

> **Note**
>
> Instead of turning off NetworkManager, you can add "`NM_CONTROLLED=no`" to the `ifcfg-*` scripts used in the examples.

Creating network initscripts

Create or edit the following two network configuration files. This step can be repeated (with different names) for additional network bridges.

Change to the `/etc/sysconfig/network-scripts` directory:

```
# cd /etc/sysconfig/network-scripts
```

Open the network script for the device you are adding to the bridge. In this example, `ifcfg-eth0` defines the physical network interface which is set as part of a bridge:

```
DEVICE=eth0
# change the hardware address to match the hardware address your NIC uses
HWADDR=00:16:76:D6:C9:45
ONBOOT=yes
BRIDGE=br0
```

> **Note**
>
> You can configure the device's Maximum Transfer Unit (MTU) by appending an *MTU* variable to the end of the configuration file.
>
> ```
> MTU=9000
> ```

Create a new network script in the `/etc/sysconfig/network-scripts` directory called `ifcfg-br0` or similar. The `br0` is the name of the bridge, this can be anything as long as the name of the file is the same as the DEVICE parameter.

```
DEVICE=br0
TYPE=Bridge
BOOTPROTO=dhcp
ONBOOT=yes
DELAY=0
```

Fedora 12

> **Warning**
>
> The line, `TYPE=Bridge`, is case-sensitive. It must have uppercase 'B' and lower case 'ridge'.

After configuring, restart networking or reboot.

```
# service network restart
```

Configure `iptables` to allow all traffic to be forwarded across the bridge.

```
# iptables -I FORWARD -m physdev --physdev-is-bridged -j ACCEPT
# service iptables save
# service iptables restart
```

> **Disable iptables on bridges**
>
> Alternatively, prevent bridged traffic from being processed by `iptables` rules. In /etc/sysctl.conf append the following lines:
>
> ```
> net.bridge.bridge-nf-call-ip6tables = 0
> net.bridge.bridge-nf-call-iptables = 0
> net.bridge.bridge-nf-call-arptables = 0
> ```
>
> Reload the kernel parameters configured with `sysctl`

```
# sysctl -p /etc/sysctl.conf
```

Restart the `libvirt` daemon.

```
# service libvirtd reload
```

You should now have a "shared physical device", which guests can be attached and have full LAN access. Verify your new bridge:

```
# brctl show
bridge name     bridge id               STP enabled     interfaces
virbr0          8000.000000000000       yes
br0             8000.000e0cb30550       no              eth0
```

Note, the bridge is completely independent of the `virbr0` bridge. Do *not* attempt to attach a physical device to `virbr0`. The `virbr0` bridge is only for Network Address Translation (NAT) connectivity.

Chapter 9.
KVM Para-virtualized Drivers

Para-virtualized drivers are available for virtualized Windows guests running on KVM hosts. These para-virtualized drivers are included in the virtio package. The virtio package supports block (storage) devices and network interface controllers.

Para-virtualized drivers enhance the performance of fully virtualized guests. With the para-virtualized drivers guest I/O latency decreases and throughput increases to near bare-metal levels. It is recommended to use the para-virtualized drivers for fully virtualized guests running I/O heavy tasks and applications.

The KVM para-virtualized drivers are automatically loaded and installed on newer versions of Fedora. Those Fedora versions detect and install the drivers so additional installation steps are not required.

As with the KVM module, the virtio drivers are only available on hosts running newer versions of Fedora.

> **Note**
>
> There are only 28 PCI slots available for additional devices per guest. Every para-virtualized network or block device uses one slot. Each guest can use up to 28 additional devices made up of any combination of para-virtualized network, para-virtualized disk devices, or other PCI devices using VTd.

The following Microsoft Windows versions have supported KVM para-virtualized drivers:

- Windows XP,
- Windows Server 2003,
- Windows Vista, and
- Windows Server 2008.

9.1. Installing the KVM Windows para-virtualized drivers

This section covers the installation process for the KVM Windows para-virtualized drivers. The KVM para-virtualized drivers can be loaded during the Windows installation or installed after the guest is installed.

You can install the para-virtualized drivers on your guest by one of the following methods:

- hosting the installation files on a network accessible to the guest,
- using a virtualized CD-ROM device of the driver installation disk .iso file, or
- using a virtualized floppy device to install the drivers during boot time (for Windows guests).

This guide describes installation from the para-virtualized installer disk as a virtualized CD-ROM device.

1. Download the drivers

    The drivers are available from Microsoft (*windowsservercatalog.com*).

    The virtio-win package installs a CD-ROM image, `virtio-win.iso`, in the `/usr/share/virtio-win/` directory.

2. Install the para-virtualized drivers

    It is recommended to install the drivers on the guest before attaching or modifying a device to use the para-virtualized drivers.

    For block devices storing root file systems or other block devices required for booting the guest, the drivers must be installed before the device is modified. If the drivers are not installed on the guest and the driver is set to the virtio driver the guest will not boot.

Mounting the image with virt-manager

Follow *Procedure 9.1, "Using `virt-manager` to mount a CD-ROM image for a Windows guest"* to add a CD-ROM image with `virt-manager`.

Procedure 9.1. Using virt-manager to mount a CD-ROM image for a Windows guest

1. Open `virt-manager`, select your virtualized guest from the list of virtual machines and press the **Details** button.
2. Click the **Add** button in the **Details** panel.

3. This opens a wizard for adding the new device. Select **Storage device** from the drop down menu, then click **Forward**.

> **Adding new virtual hardware**
>
> This assistant will guide you through adding a new piece of virtual hardware. First select what type of hardware you wish to add:
>
> Hardware type: Storage device
>
> ✗ Cancel   Back   ➡ Forward

Fedora 12

4. Choose the **File (disk image)** option and set the file location of the para-virtualized drivers .iso file. The location of the .iso files is /usr/share/xenpv-win if you used yum to install the para-virtualized driver packages.

   If the drivers are stored physical CD, use the **Normal Disk Partition** option.

   Set the **Device type** to **IDE cdrom** and click **Forward** to proceed.

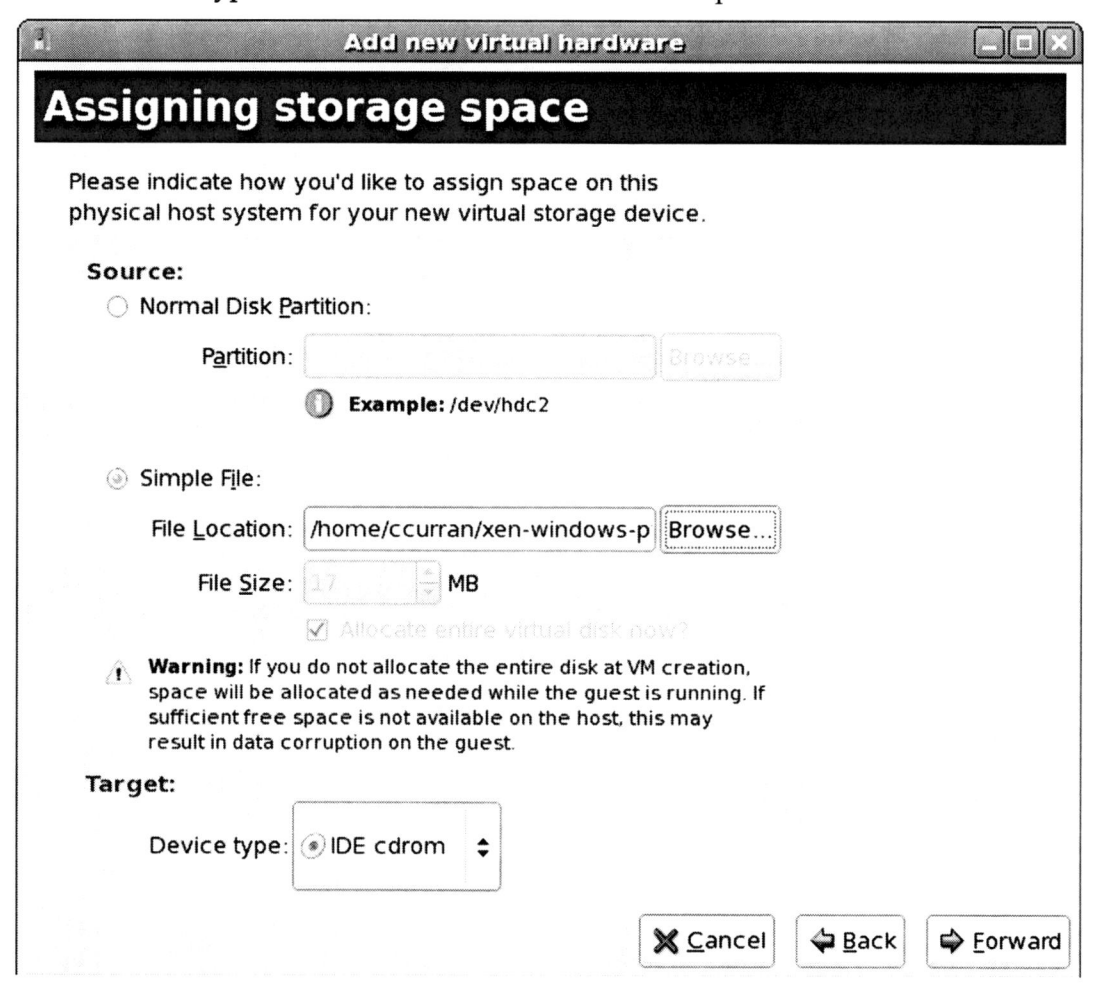

140

Virtualization Guide

5. The disk has been assigned and is available for the guest once the guest is started. Click **Finish** to close the wizard or back if you made a mistake.

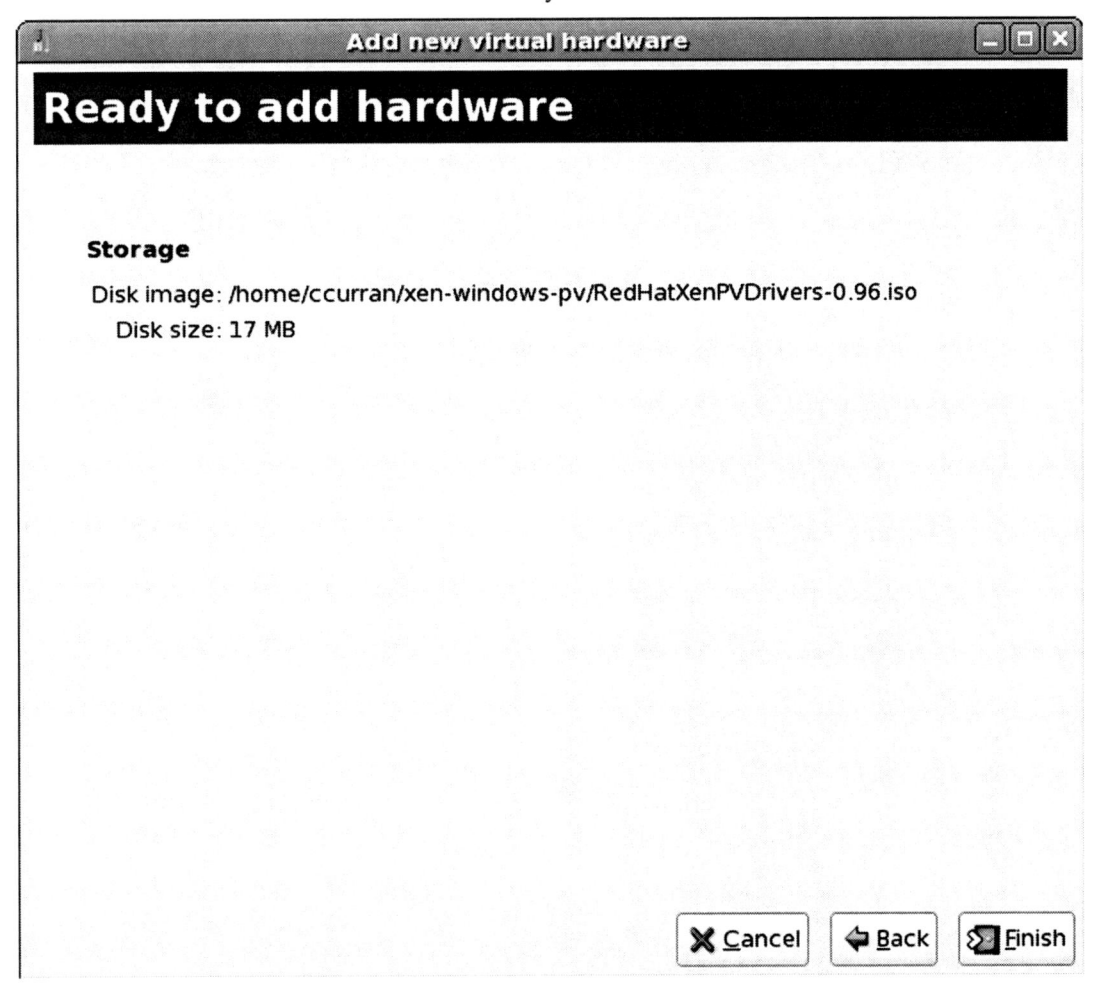

Add new virtual hardware

Ready to add hardware

Storage
Disk image: /home/ccurran/xen-windows-pv/RedHatXenPVDrivers-0.96.iso
Disk size: 17 MB

[Cancel] [Back] [Finish]

Installing with a virtualized floppy disk

This procedure covers installing the para-virtualized drivers during a Windows installation.

- Upon installing the Windows VM for the first time using the run-once menu attach `viostor.vfd` as a floppy

    1. Windows Server 2003

        When windows prompts to press F6 for third party drivers, do so and follow the onscreen instructions.

141

2. Windows Server 2008

   When the installer prompts you for the driver, click on "Load Driver", point the installer to drive A: and pick the driver that suits your OS and bittage.

Using KVM para-virtualized drivers for existing devices

Modify an existing hard disk device attached to the guest to use the `virtio` driver instead of virtualized IDE driver. This example edits libvirt configuration files. Alternatively, `virt-manager`, `virsh attach-disk` or `virsh attach-interface` can add a new device using the para-virtualized drivers *Using KVM para-virtualized drivers for new devices* (see below).

1. Below is a file-based block device using the virtualized IDE driver. This is a typical entry for a virtualized guest not using the para-virtualized drivers.
   ```
   <disk type='file' device='disk'>
      <source file='/var/lib/libvirt/images/disk1.img'/>
      <target dev='hda' bus='ide'/>
   </disk>
   ```

2. Change the entry to use the para-virtualized device by modifying the **bus=** entry to `virtio`.
   ```
   <disk type='file' device='disk'>
      <source file='/var/lib/libvirt/images/disk1.img'/>
      <target dev='hda' bus='virtio'/>
   </disk>
   ```

Using KVM para-virtualized drivers for new devices

This procedure covers creating new devices using the KVM para-virtualized drivers with `virt-manager`.

Alternatively, the `virsh attach-disk` or `virsh attach-interface` commands can be used to attach devices using the para-virtualized drivers.

> **⚠ Install the drivers first**
>
> Ensure the drivers have been installed on the Windows guest before proceeding to install new devices. If the drivers are unavailable the device will not be recognized and will not work.

1. Open the virtualized guest by double clicking on the name of the guest in `virt-manager`.
2. Open the **Hardware** tab.
3. Press the **Add Hardware** button.
4. In the Adding Virtual Hardware tab select **Storage** or **Network** for the type of device.

Virtualization Guide

1. **New disk devices**

   Select the storage device or file based image. Select **Virtio Disk** as the **Device type** and press **Forward**.

Fedora 12

2. **New network devices**

   Select **Virtual network** or **Shared physical device**. Select **virtio** as the **Device type** and press **Forward**.

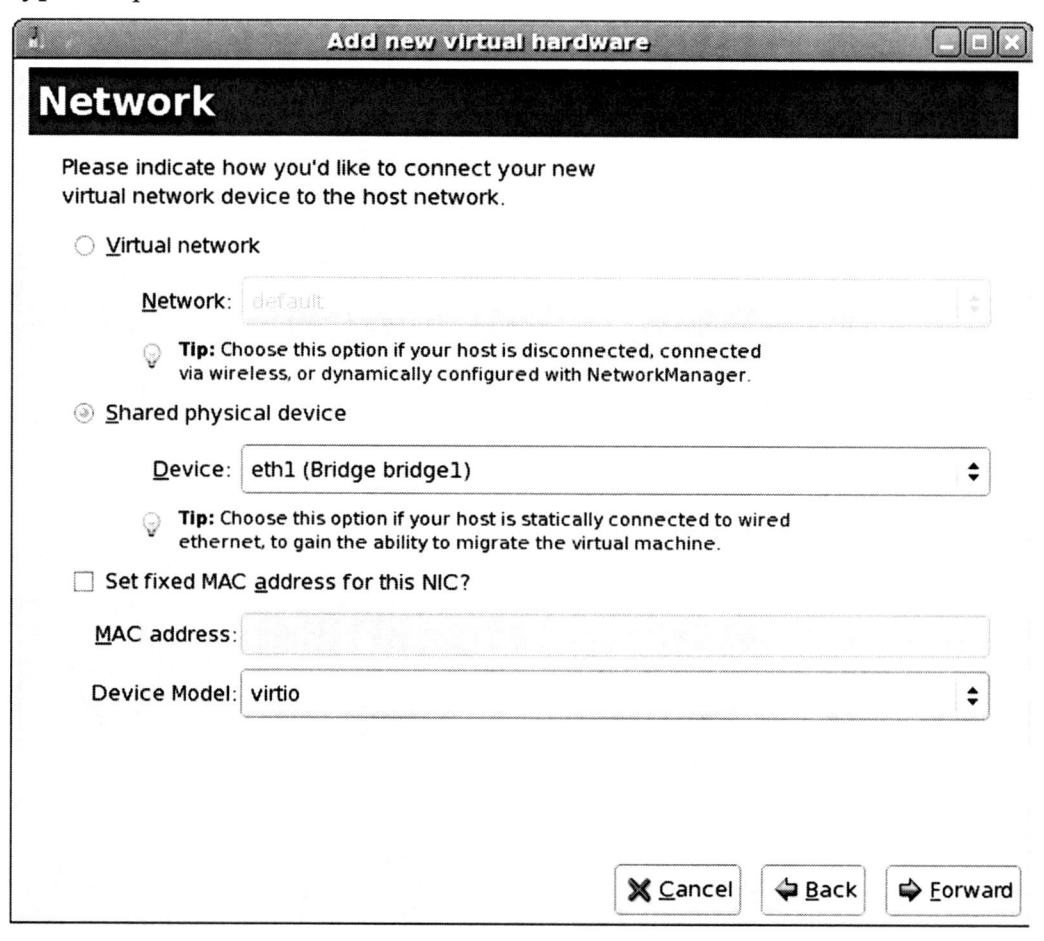

Virtualization Guide

5. Press **Finish** to save the device.

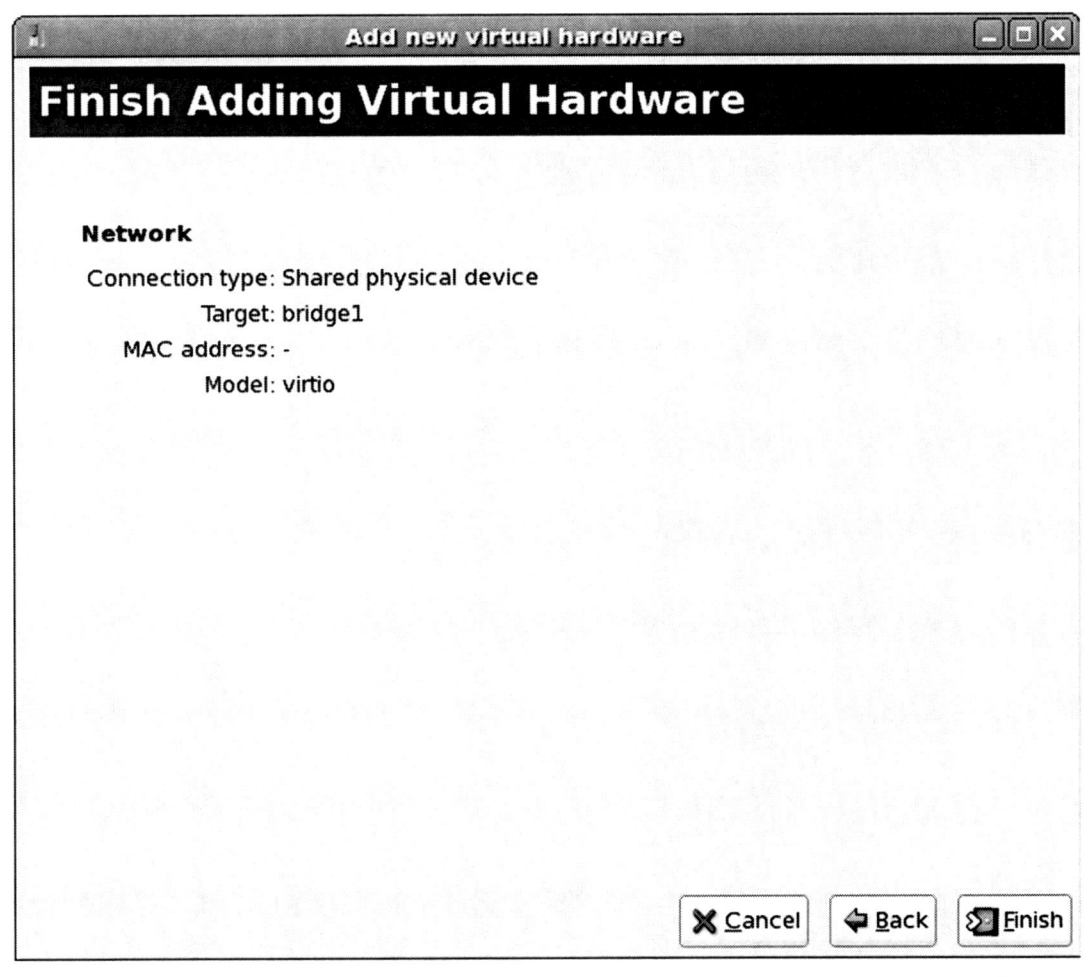

   ![Add new virtual hardware - Finish Adding Virtual Hardware dialog showing Network connection type: Shared physical device, Target: bridge1, MAC address: -, Model: virtio, with Cancel, Back, and Finish buttons]

6. Reboot the guest. The device may to be recognized by the Windows guest until it restarts.

Part III.
Administration

Administering virtualized systems

These chapters contain information for administering host and virtualized guests using tools included in Fedora.

Chapter 10.
Managing guests with xend

The **xend** node control daemon performs certain system management functions that relate to virtual machines. This daemon controls the virtualized resources, and **xend** must be running to interact with virtual machines. Before you start **xend**, you must specify the operating parameters by editing the **xend** configuration file `/etc/xen/xend-config.sxp`. Here are the parameters you can enable or disable in the `xend-config.sxp` configuration file:

Item	Description
(console-limit)	Determines the console server's memory buffer limit xend_unix_server and assigns values on a per domain basis.
(min-mem)	Determines the minimum number of megabytes that is reserved for domain0 (if you enter 0, the value does not change).
(dom0-cpus)	Determines the number of CPUs in use by domain0 (at least 1 CPU is assigned by default).
(enable-dump)	Determines that a crash occurs then enables a dump (the default is 0).
(external-migration-tool)	Determines the script or application that handles external device migration. Scripts must reside in `etc/xen/scripts/external-device-migrate`.
(logfile)	Determines the location of the log file (default is `/var/log/xend.log`).
(loglevel)	Filters out the log mode values: DEBUG, INFO, WARNING, ERROR, or CRITICAL (default is DEBUG).
(network-script)	Determines the script that enables the networking environment (scripts must reside in `etc/xen/scripts` directory).
(xend-http-server)	Enables the http stream packet management server (the default is no).
(xend-unix-server)	Enables the unix domain socket server, which is a socket server is a communications endpoint that handles low level network connections and accepts or rejects incoming connections. The default value is set to yes.
(xend-relocation-server)	Enables the relocation server for cross-machine migrations (the default is no).
(xend-unix-path)	Determines the location where the `xend-unix-server` command outputs data (default is `var/lib/xend/xend-socket`)
(xend-port)	Determines the port that the http management server uses (the default is 8000).
(xend-relocation-port)	Determines the port that the relocation server uses (the default is 8002).

Fedora 12

Item	Description
(xend-relocation-address)	Determines the host addresses allowed for migration. The default value is the value of xend-address.
(xend-address)	Determines the address that the domain socket server binds to. The default value allows all connections.

Table 10.1. xend configuration parameters

After setting these operating parameters, you should verify that xend is running and if not, initialize the daemon. At the command prompt, you can start the **xend** daemon by entering the following:

```
service xend start
```

You can use **xend** to stop the daemon:

```
service xend stop
```

This stops the daemon from running.

You can use **xend** to restart the daemon:

```
service xend restart
```

The daemon starts once again.

You check the status of the **xend** daemon.

```
service xend status
```

The output displays the daemon's status.

> **Enabling xend at boot time**
>
> Use the chkconfig command to add the xend to the initscript.
> ```
> chkconfig --level 345 xend
> ```
> The the xend will now start at runlevels 3, 4 and 5.

Chapter 11.
KVM guest timing management

KVM uses the constant Time Stamp Counter (TSC) feature of many modern CPUs. Some CPUs do not have a constant Time Stamp Counter which will affect the way guests running on KVM keep time. Guest's running without accurate timekeeping can have serious affects on some networked applications as your guest will run faster or slower than the actual time.

Guests can have several problems caused by inaccurate clocks and counters:

- Clocks can fall out of synchronization with the actual time which invalidates sessions and affects networks.
- Guests with slower clocks may have issues migrating.
- Guests may stop or crash.

These problems exist on other virtualization platforms and timing should always be tested.

> **NTP**
>
> The Network Time Protocol (NTP) daemon should be running on the host and the guests. Enable the `ntpd` service:
> ```
> # service ntpd start
> ```
> Add the ntpd service to the default startup sequence:
> ```
> # chkconfig ntpd on
> ```
> Using the `ntpd` service should minimize the affects of clock skew in all cases.

Determining if your CPU has the constant Time Stamp Counter

Your CPU has a constant Time Stamp Counter if the `constant_tsc` flag is present. To determine if your CPU has the `constant_tsc` flag run the following command:

```
$ cat /proc/cpuinfo | grep constant_tsc
```

If any output is given your CPU has the `constant_tsc` bit. If no output is given follow the instructions below.

Fedora 12

Configuring hosts without a constant Time Stamp Counter

Systems without constant time stamp counters require additional configuration. Power management features interfere with accurate time keeping and must be disabled for guests to accurately keep time with KVM.

> **Note**
>
> These instructions are for AMD revision F cpus only.

If the CPU lacks the `constant_tsc` bit, disable all power management features (*BZ#513138*[1]). Each system has several timers it uses to keep time. The TSC is not stable on the host, which is sometimes caused by `cpufreq` changes, deep C state, or migration to a host with a faster TSC. To stop deep C states, which cam stop the TSC, add "`processor.max_cstate=1`" to the kernel boot options in grub on the host:

```
term Fedora (vmlinuz-2.6.29.6-217.2.3.fc11)
        root (hd0,0)
    kernel /vmlinuz-vmlinuz-2.6.29.6-217.2.3.fc11 ro
root=/dev/VolGroup00/LogVol00 rhgb quiet processor.max_cstate=1
```

Disable `cpufreq` (only necessary on hosts without the `constant_tsc`) by editing the `/etc/sysconfig/cpuspeed` configuration file and change the `MIN_SPEED` and `MAX_SPEED` variables to the highest frequency available. Valid limits can be found in the `/sys/devices/system/cpu/cpu*/cpufreq/scaling_available_frequencies` files.

Using the para-virtualized clock with Red Hat Enterprise Linux guests

For certain Red Hat Enterprise Linux guests, additional kernel parameters are required. These parameters can be set by appending them to the end of the /kernel line in the /boot/grub/grub.conf file of the guest.

The table below lists versions of Red Hat Enterprise Linux and the parameters required for guests on systems without a constant Time Stamp Counter.

Red Hat Enterprise Linux	Additional guest kernel parameters
5.4 AMD64/Intel 64 with the para-virtualized clock	Additional parameters are not required
5.4 AMD64/Intel 64 without the para-virtualized clock	divider=10 notsc lpj=n
5.4 x86 with the para-virtualized clock	Additional parameters are not required
5.4 x86 without the para-virtualized clock	divider=10 clocksource=acpi_pm lpj=n
5.3 AMD64/Intel 64	divider=10 notsc
5.3 x86	divider=10 clocksource=acpi_pm

---

[1] *https://bugzilla.redhat.com/show_bug.cgi?id=513138*

Red Hat Enterprise Linux	Additional guest kernel parameters
4.8 AMD64/Intel 64	notsc divider=10
4.8 x86	clock=pmtmr divider=10
3.9 AMD64/Intel 64	Additional parameters are not required
3.9 x86	Additional parameters are not required

Using the para-virtualized clock with Windows guests

Enable the para-virtualized clock on Window guests by editing the boot parameters. Windows boot settings are stored in the boot.ini file. To enable the para-virtualized clock add the following line:

```
/use pmtimer
```

For more information on Windows boot settings and the pmtimer option, refer to *Available switch options for the Windows XP and the Windows Server 2003 Boot.ini files*[2].

---

[2] *http://support.microsoft.com/kb/833721*

Chapter 12.
KVM live migration

This chapter covers migrating guests running on a KVM hypervisor to another KVM host.

Migration is name for the process of moving a virtualized guest from one host to another. Migration is a key feature of virtualization as software is completely separated from hardware. Migration is useful for:

- Load balancing - guests can be moved to hosts with lower usage when a host becomes overloaded.
- Hardware failover - when hardware devices on the host start to fail, guests can be safely relocated so the host can be powered down and repaired.
- Energy saving - guests can be redistributed to other hosts and host systems powered off to save energy and cut costs in low usage periods.
- Geographic migration - guests can be moved to another location for lower latency or in serious circumstances.

Migrations can be performed live or offline. To migrate guests the storage must be shared. Migration works by sending the guests memory to the destination host. The shared storage stores the guest's default file system. The file system image is not sent over the network from the source host to the destination host.

An offline migration suspends the guest then moves an image of the guests memory to the destination host. The guest is resumed on the destination host and the memory the guest used on the source host is freed.

The time an offline migration takes depends network bandwidth and latency. A guest with 2GB of memory should take an average of ten or so seconds on a 1 Gbit Ethernet link.

A live migration keeps the guest running on the source host and begins moving the memory without stopping the guest. All modified memory pages are monitored for changes and sent to the destination while the image is sent. The memory is updated with the changed pages. The process continues until the amount of pause time allowed for the guest equals the predicted time for the final few pages to be transfer. KVM estimates that and attempts to transfer the maximum amount of pages from the source to the destination until we predict than the amount of remaining pages can be transferred in configured time while the VM is paused. The registers are loaded on the new host and the guest is then resumed on the destination host. If the guest is cannot be merged (which happens when guests are under extreme loads) the guest is paused and then an offline migration is started instead.

The time an offline migration takes depends network bandwidth and latency. If the network is in heavy use or a low bandwidth the migration will take much longer.

12.1. Live migration requirements

Migrating guests requires the following:

Migration requirements

- A virtualized guest installed on shared networked storage using one of the following protocols:
    - Fibre Channel
    - iSCSI
    - NFS
    - GFS2
- Two or more Fedora systems of the same version with the same updates.
- Both system must have the appropriate ports open.
- Both systems must have identical network configurations. All bridging and network configurations must be exactly the same on both hosts.
- Shared storage must mount at the same location on source and destination systems. The mounted directory name must be identical.

Configuring network storage

Configure shared storage and install a guest on the shared storage. For shared storage instructions, refer to *Chapter 5, Shared storage and virtualization*.

Alternatively, use the NFS example in *Section 12.2, "Share storage example: NFS for a simple migration"*.

12.2. Share storage example: NFS for a simple migration

This example uses NFS to share guest images with other KVM hosts. This example is not practical for large installations, this example is only for demonstrating migration techniques and small deployments. Do not use this example for migrating or running more than a few virtualized guests.

For advanced and more robust shared storage instructions, refer to *Chapter 5, Shared storage and virtualization*

1. Export your libvirt image directory

   Add the default image directory to the `/etc/exports` file:

   `/var/lib/libvirt/images *.bne.redhat.com(rw,no_root_squash,async)`

   Change the hosts parameter as required for your environment.

2. Start NFS

   1. Install the NFS packages if they are not yet installed:

      `# yum install nfs`

   2. Open the ports for NFS in `iptables` and add NFS to the `/etc/hosts.allow` file.

   3. Start the NFS service:

      `# service nfs start`

3. Mount the shared storage on the destination

   On the destination system, mount the `/var/lib/libvirt/images` directory:

   `# mount sourceURL:/var/lib/libvirt/images /var/lib/libvirt/images`

> **Locations must be the same on source and destination**
>
> Whichever directory is chosen for the guests must exactly the same on host and guest. This applies to all types of shared storage. The directory must be the same or the migration will fail.

12.3. Live KVM migration with virsh

A guest can be migrated to another host with the `virsh` command. The `migrate` command accepts parameters in the following format:

`# virsh migrate --live GuestName DestinationURL`

The `GuestName` parameter represents the name of the guest which you want to migrate.

The `DestinationURL` parameter is the URL or hostname of the destination system. The destination system must run the same version of Fedora, be using the same hypervisor and have `libvirt` running.

Once the command is entered you will be prompted for the root password of the destination system.

Virtualization Guide

Example: live migration with virsh

This example migrates from `test1.bne.redhat.com` to `test2.bne.redhat.com`. Change the host names for your environment. This example migrates a virtual machine named `CentOS4test`.

This example assumes you have fully configured shared storage and meet all the prerequisites (see section *Migration requirements* – page 153).

1. Verify the guest is running

   From the source system, `test1.bne.redhat.com`, verify `CentOS4test` is running:
   ```
   [root@test1 ~]# virsh list
   Id Name                 State
   ----------------------------------
    10 CentOS4             running
   ```

2. Migrate the guest

   Execute the following command to live migrate the guest to the destination, `test2.bne.redhat.com`. Append `/system` to the end of the destination URL to tell libvirt that you need full access.
   ```
   # virsh migrate --live CentOS4test
   qemu+ssh://test2.bne.redhat.com/system
   ```
   Once the command is entered you will be prompted for the root password of the destination system.

3. Wait

   The migration may take some time depending on load and the size of the guest. `virsh` only reports errors. The guest continues to run on the source host until fully migrated.

4. Verify the guest has arrived at the destination host

   From the destination system, `test2.bne.redhat.com`, verify `CentOS4test` is running:
   ```
   [root@test2 ~]# virsh list
   Id Name                 State
   ----------------------------------
    10 CentOS4             running
   ```

The live migration is now complete.

> **Other networking methods**
>
> libvirt supports a variety of networking methods including TLS/SSL, unix sockets, SSH, and unecrypted TCP. Refer to *Chapter 13, Remote management of virtualized guests* for more information on using other methods.

12.4. Migrating with virt-manager

This section covers migrating KVM based guests with `virt-manager`.

1. Connect to the source and target hosts. On the **File** menu, click **Add Connection**, the **Add Connection** window appears.

    Enter the following details:

    - **Hypervisor**: Select **QEMU**.
    - **Connection**: Select the connection type.
    - **Hostname**: Enter the hostname.

    Click **Connect**.

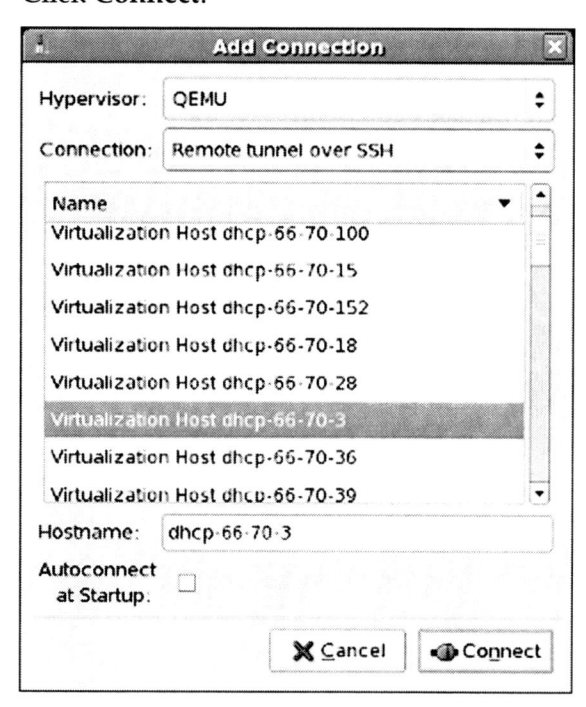

Virtualization Guide

The Virtual Machine Manager displays a list of connected hosts.

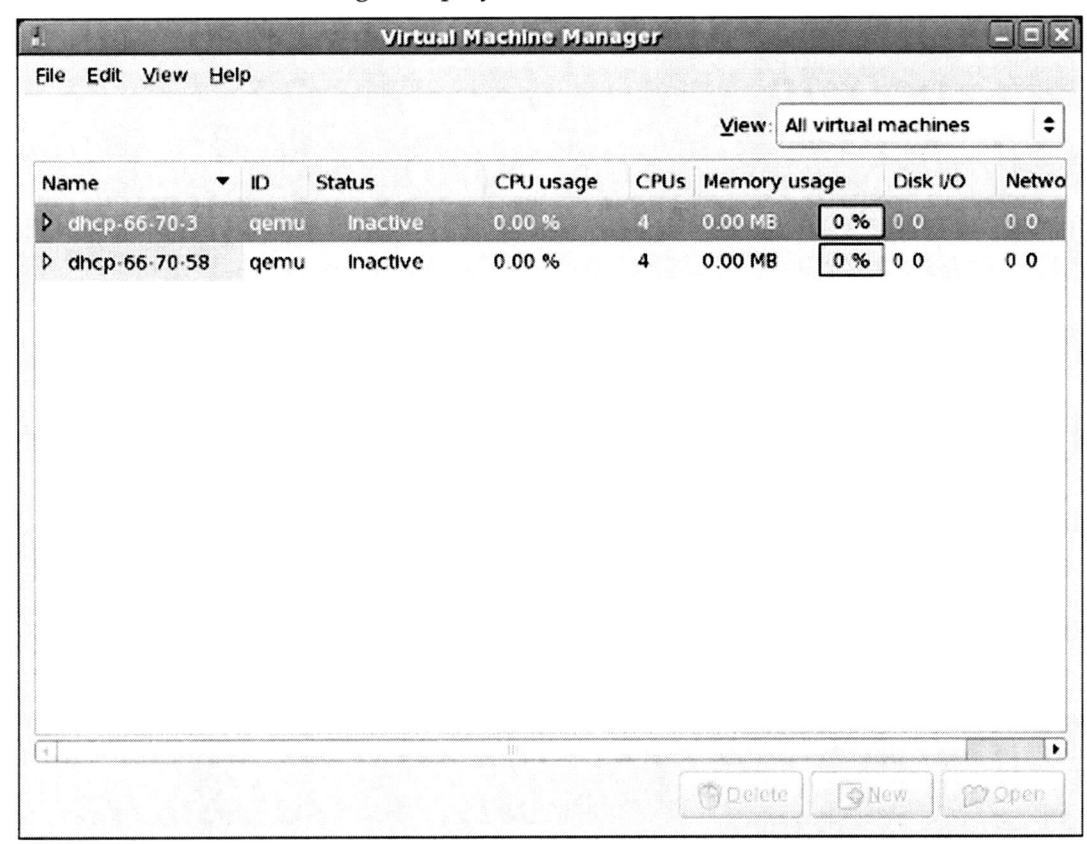

Fedora 12

2. Add a storage pool with the same NFS to the source and target hosts.

   On the **Edit** menu, click **Host Details**, the Host Details window appears.

   Click the **Storage** tab.

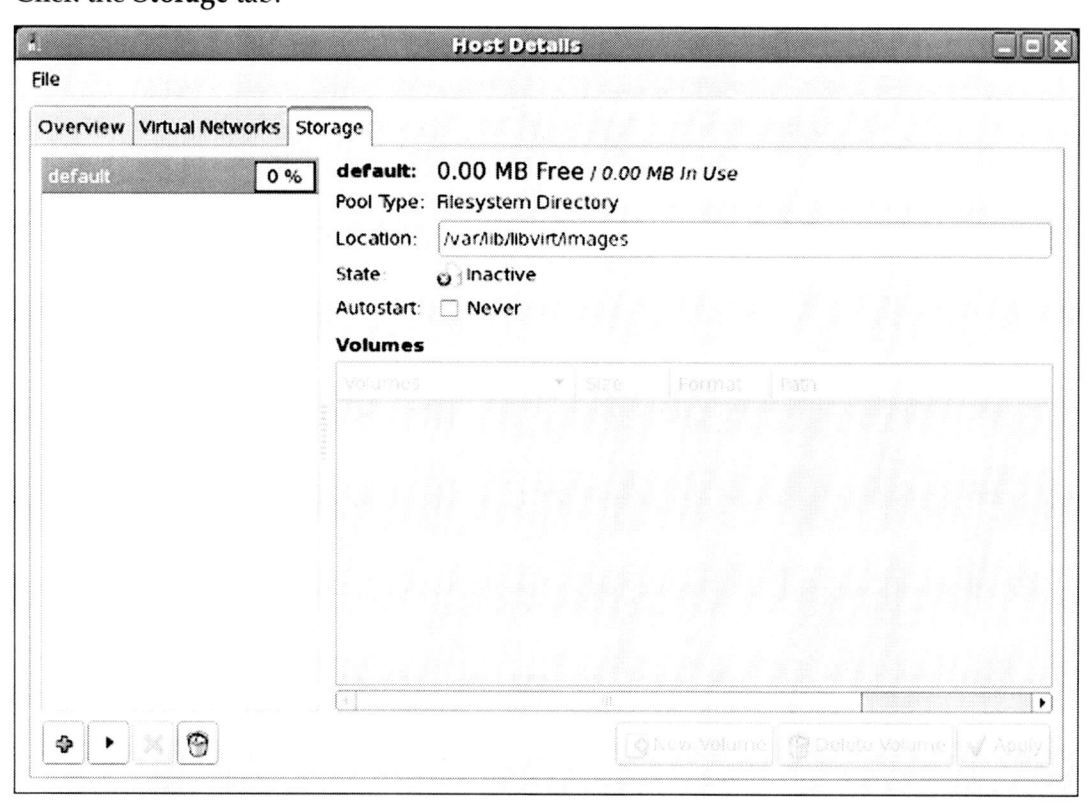

3. Add a new storage pool. In the lower left corner of the window, click the **+** button. The Add a New Storage Pool window appears.

   Enter the following details:

   - **Name**: Enter the name of the storage pool.
   - **Type**: Select **netfs: Network Exported Directory**.

   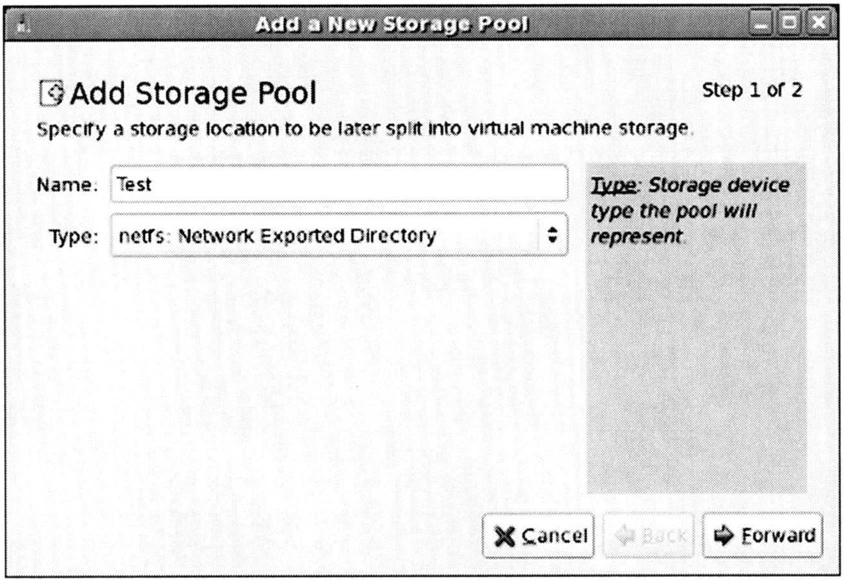
   Add a New Storage Pool
Add Storage Pool
Step 1 of 2
Specify a storage location to be later split into virtual machine storage.
Name: Test
Type: netfs: Network Exported Directory
Type: Storage device type the pool will represent
Cancel
Back
Forward

   Click **Forward**.

Fedora 12

4. Enter the following details:

    - **Format**: Select the storage type. This must be NFS or iSCSI for live migrations.
    - **Host Name**: Enter the IP address or fully-qualified domain name of the storage server.

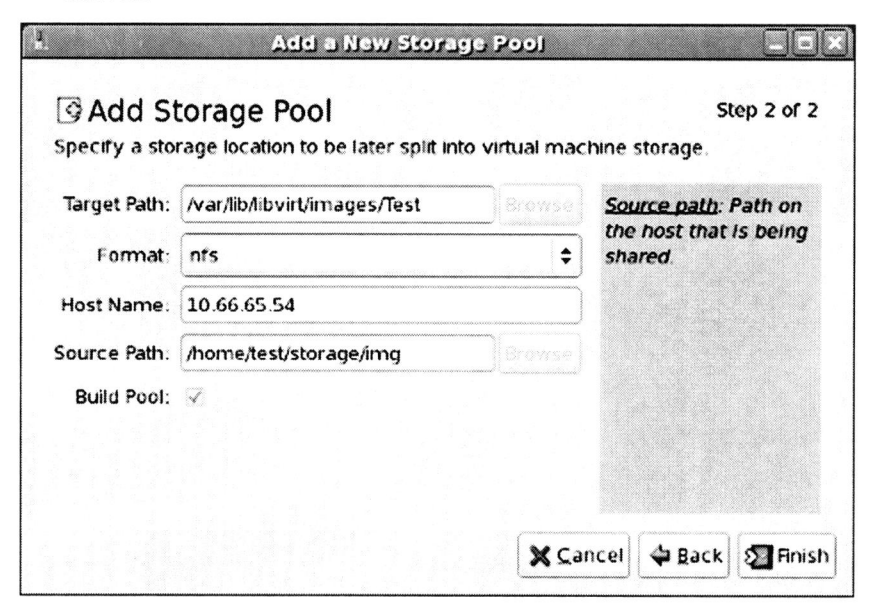

Click **Finish**.

Virtualization Guide

5. Create a new volume in the shared storage pool, click **New Volume**.

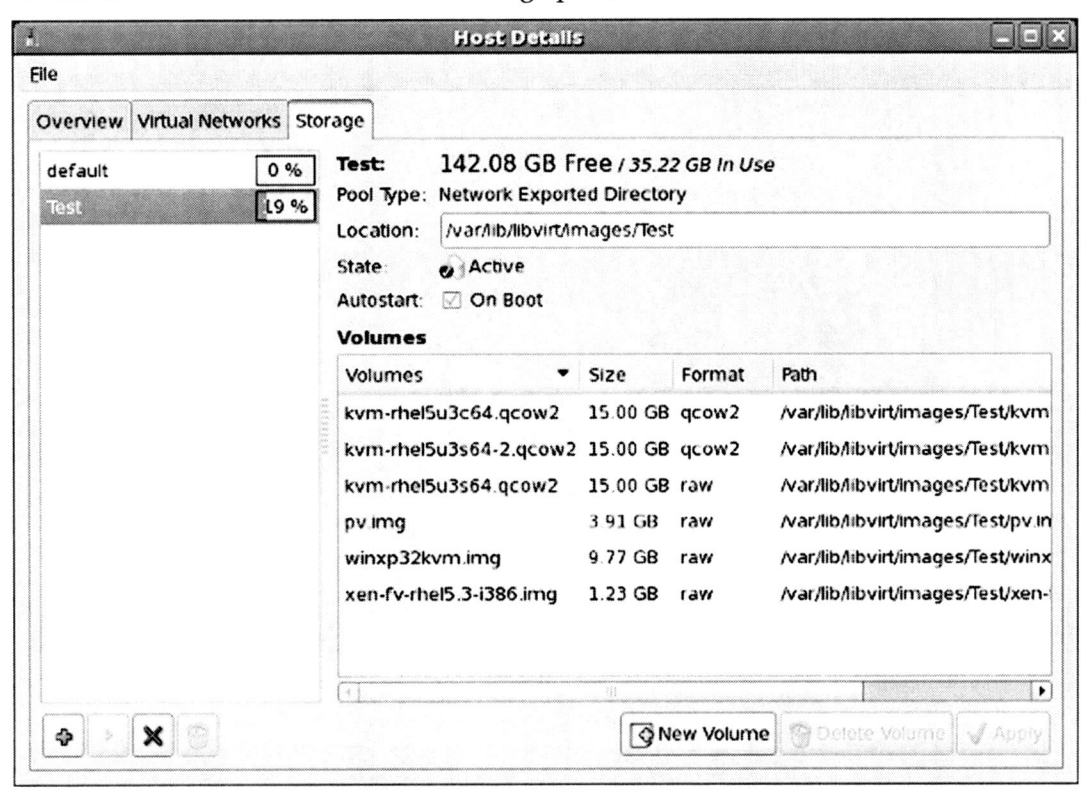

6. Enter the details, then click **Create Volume**.

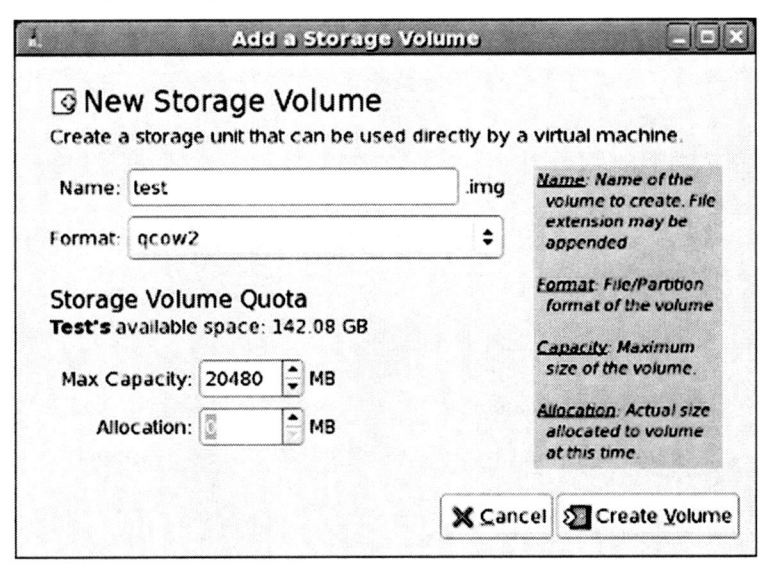

Fedora 12

7. Create a virtual machine with the new volume, then run the virtual machine.

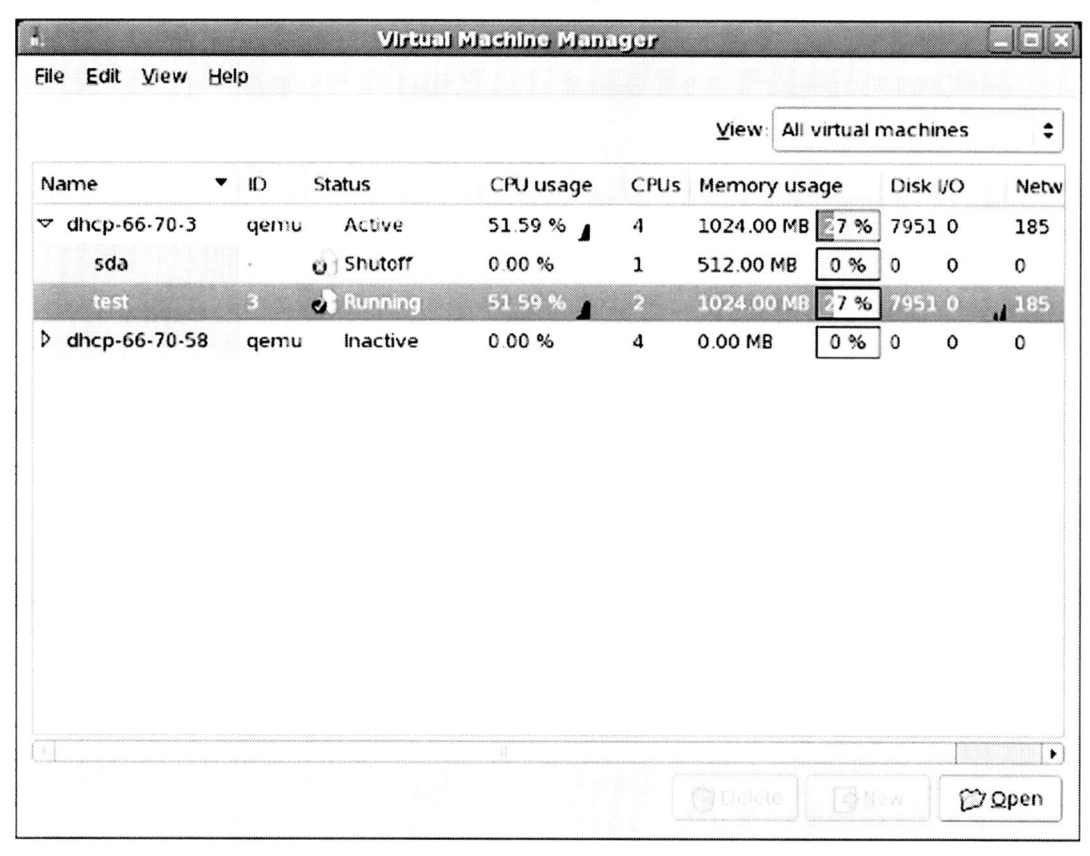

Name	ID	Status	CPU usage	CPUs	Memory usage		Disk I/O		Netw
▽ dhcp-66-70-3	qemu	Active	51.59 %	4	1024.00 MB	7 %	7951	0	185
sda	-	Shutoff	0.00 %	1	512.00 MB	0 %	0	0	0
test	3	Running	51.59 %	2	1024.00 MB	7 %	7951	0	185
▷ dhcp-66-70-58	qemu	Inactive	0.00 %	4	0.00 MB	0 %	0	0	0

The Virtual Machine window appears.

Fedora 12

8. In the Virtual Machine Manager window, right-click on the virtual machine, select **Migrate**, then click the migration location.

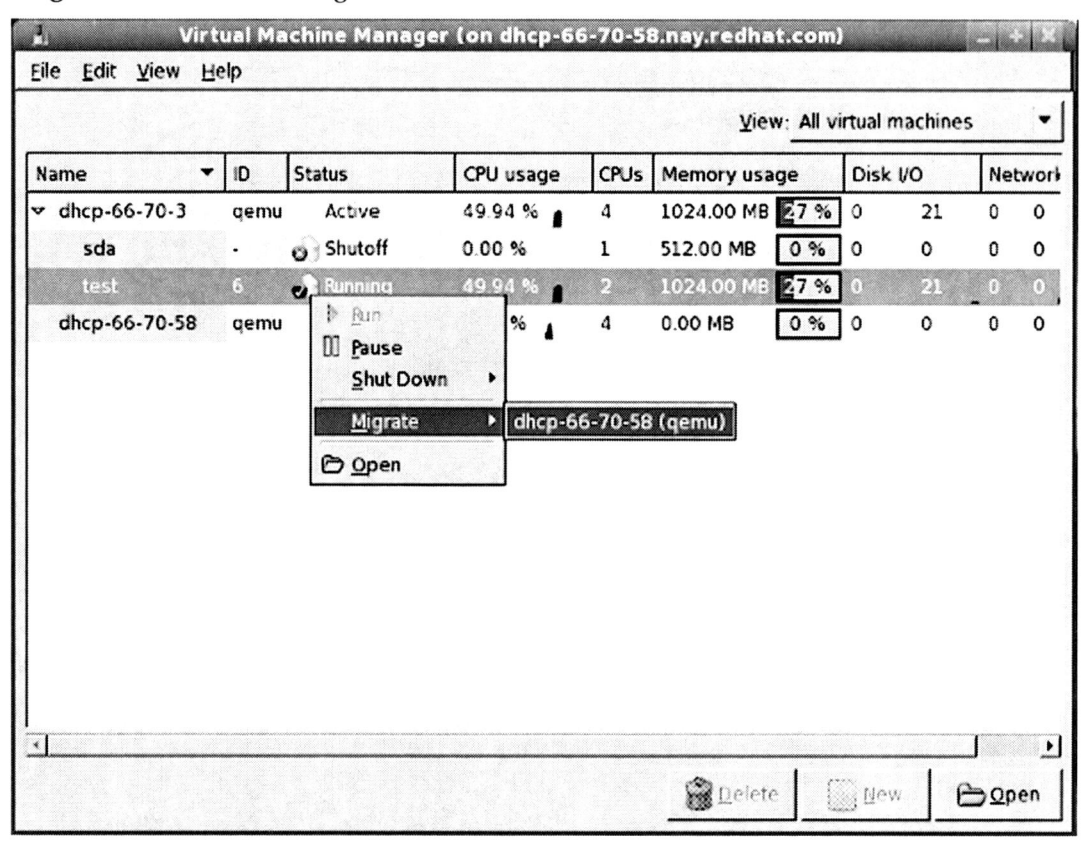

9. Click **Yes** to confirm migration.

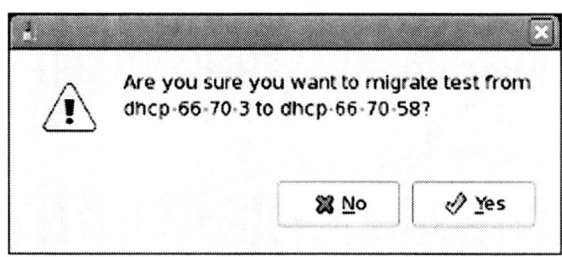

Virtualization Guide

The Virtual Machine Manger displays the virtual machine in its new location.

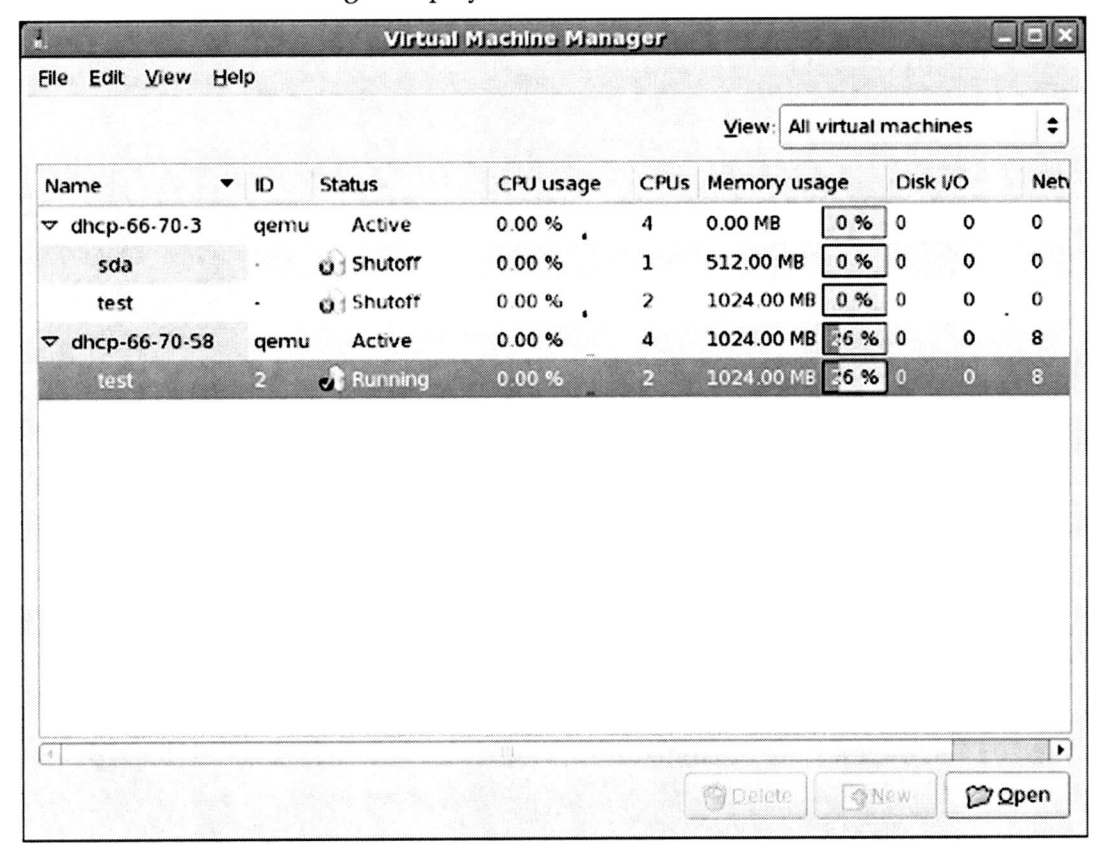

Name	ID	Status	CPU usage	CPUs	Memory usage		Disk I/O	Net
▽ dhcp-66-70-3	qemu	Active	0.00 %	4	0.00 MB	0 %	0	0	0
sda	-	Shutoff	0.00 %	1	512.00 MB	0 %	0	0	0
test	-	Shutoff	0.00 %	2	1024.00 MB	0 %	0	0	0
▽ dhcp-66-70-58	qemu	Active	0.00 %	4	1024.00 MB	6 %	0	0	8
test	2	Running	0.00 %	2	1024.00 MB	6 %	0	0	8

Fedora 12

The Virtual Machine window displays the new virtual machine location.

Chapter 13.
Remote management of virtualized guests

This section explains how to remotely manage your virtualized guests using ssh or TLS and SSL.

13.1. Remote management with SSH

The ssh package provides an encrypted network protocol which can securely send management functions to remote virtualization servers. The method described uses the libvirt management connection securely tunneled over an SSH connection to manage the remote machines. All the authentication is done using SSH public key cryptography and passwords or passphrases gathered by your local SSH agent. In addition the VNC console for each guest virtual machine is tunneled over SSH.

SSH is usually configured by default so you probably already have SSH keys setup and no extra firewall rules needed to access the management service or VNC console.

Be aware of the issues with using SSH for remotely managing your virtual machines, including:

- you require root log in access to the remote machine for managing virtual machines,
- the initial connection setup process may be slow,
- there is no standard or trivial way to revoke a user's key on all hosts or guests, and
- ssh does not scale well with larger numbers of remote machines.

Configuring SSH access for virt-manager

The following instructions assume you are starting from scratch and do not already have SSH keys set up.

1. You need a public key pair on the machine virt-manager is used. If ssh is already configured you can skip this command.
   ```
   $ ssh-keygen -t rsa
   ```
2. To permit remote log in, virt-manager needs a copy of the public key on each remote machine running libvirt. Copy the file $HOME/.ssh/id_rsa.pub from the machine you want to use for remote management using the scp command:
   ```
   $ scp $HOME/.ssh/id_rsa.pub root@somehost:/root/key-dan.pub
   ```

3. After the file has copied, use ssh to connect to the remote machines as root and add the file that you copied to the list of authorized keys. If the root user on the remote host does not already have an list of authorized keys, make sure the file permissions are correctly set

```
$ ssh root@somehost
# mkdir /root/.ssh
# chmod go-rwx /root/.ssh
# cat /root/key-dan.pub >> /root/.ssh/authorized_keys
# chmod go-rw /root/.ssh/authorized_keys
```

The libvirt daemon (libvirtd)

The libvirt daemon provide an interface for managing virtual machines. You should use the libvirtd daemon installed and running on every remote host that you need to manage. Using the Fedora kernel-xen package requires a speci TODO

```
$ ssh root@somehost
# chkconfig libvirtd on
# service libvirtd start
```

After libvirtd and SSH are configured you should be able to remotely access and manage your virtual machines. You should also be able to access your guests with VNC at this point.

13.2. Remote management over TLS and SSL

You can manage virtual machines using TLS and SSL. TLS and SSL provides greater scalability but is more complicated than ssh (refer to Section 13.1, "Remote management with SSH"). TLS and SSL is the same technology used by web browsers for secure connections. The libvirt management connection opens a TCP port for incoming connections, which is securely encrypted and authenticated based on x509 certificates. In addition the VNC console for each guest virtual machine will be setup to use TLS with x509 certificate authentication.

This method does not require shell accounts on the remote machines being managed. However, extra firewall rules are needed to access the management service or VNC console. Certificate revocation lists can revoke users' access.

Steps to setup TLS/SSL access for virt-manager

The following short guide assuming you are starting from scratch and you do not have any TLS/SSL certificate knowledge. If you are lucky enough to have a certificate management server you can probably skip the first steps.

libvirt server setup

> For more information on creating certificates, refer to the libvirt website, *http://libvirt.org/remote.html*.

Virtualization Guide

Xen VNC Server

The Xen VNC server can have TLS enabled by editing the configuration file, /etc/xen/xend-config.sxp. Remove the commenting on the (vnc-tls 1) configuration parameter in the configuration file.

The /etc/xen/vnc directory needs the following 3 files:

- ca-cert.pem - The CA certificate
- server-cert.pem - The Server certificate signed by the CA
- server-key.pem - The server private key

This provides encryption of the data channel. It might be appropriate to require that clients present their own x509 certificate as a form of authentication. To enable this remove the commenting on the (vnc-x509-verify 1) parameter.

virt-manager and virsh client setup

The setup for clients is slightly inconsistent at this time. To enable the libvirt management API over TLS, the CA and client certificates must be placed in /etc/pki. For details on this consult http://libvirt.org/remote.html

In the virt-manager user interface, use the 'SSL/TLS' transport mechanism option when connecting to a host.

For virsh, the URI has the following format:

- qemu://hostname.guestname/system for KVM.
- xen://hostname.guestname/ for Xen.

To enable SSL and TLS for VNC, it is necessary to put the certificate authority and client certificates into $HOME/.pki, that is the following three files:

- CA or ca-cert.pem - The CA certificate.
- libvirt-vnc or clientcert.pem - The client certificate signed by the CA.
- libvirt-vnc or clientkey.pem - The client private key.

13.3. Transport modes

For remote management, libvirt supports the following transport modes:

Transport Layer Security (TLS)

Transport Layer Security TLS 1.0 (SSL 3.1) authenticated and encrypted TCP/IP socket, usually listening on a public port number. To use this you will need to generate client and server certificates. The standard port is 16514.

UNIX sockets

Unix domain sockets are only accessible on the local machine. Sockets are not encrypted, and use UNIX permissions or SELinux for authentication. The standard socket names are /var/run/libvirt/libvirt-sock and /var/run/libvirt/libvirt-sock-ro (for read-only connections).

SSH

Transported over an Secure Shell protocol (SSH) connection. Requires Netcat (the nc package) installed. The libvirt daemon (libvirtd) must be running on the remote machine. Port 22 must be open for SSH access. You should use some sort of ssh key management (for example, the ssh-agent utility) or you will be prompted for a password.

ext

The ext parameter is used for any external program which can make a connection to the remote machine by means outside the scope of libvirt. This usually covers third-party, unsupported security applications.

tcp

Unencrypted TCP/IP socket. Not recommended for production use, this is normally disabled, but an administrator can enable it for testing or use over a trusted network. The default port is 16509.

The default transport, if no other is specified, is tls.

Remote URIs

A Uniform Resource Identifier (URI) is used by virsh and libvirt to connect to a remote host. URIs can also be used with the --connect parameter for the virsh command to execute single commands or migrations on remote hosts.

libvirt URIs take the general form (content in square brackets, "[]", represents optional functions):

```
driver[+transport]://[username@][hostname][:port]/[path][?extraparameters]
```

Either the transport method or the hostname must be provided in order to distinguish this from a local URI.

Examples of remote management parameters

- Connect to a remote Xen hypervisor on the host named towada, using SSH transport and the SSH username ccurran.
    ```
    xen+ssh://ccurran@towada/
    ```

Virtualization Guide

- Connect to a remote Xen hypervisor on the host named towada using TLS.
  `xen://towada/`
- Connect to a remote Xen hypervisor on host towada using TLS. The *no_verify=1* tells libvirt not to verify the server's certificate.
  `xen://towada/?no_verify=1`
- Connect to a remote KVM hypervisor on host towada using SSH.
  `qemu+ssh://towada/system`

Testing examples

- Connect to the local KVM hypervisor with a non-standard UNIX socket. The full path to the Unix socket is supplied explicitly in this case.
  `qemu+unix:///system?socket=/opt/libvirt/run/libvirt/libvirt-sock`
- Connect to the libvirt daemon with an unencrypted TCP/IP connection to the server with the IP address 10.1.1.10 on port 5000. This uses the test driver with default settings.
  `test+tcp://10.1.1.10:5000/default`

Extra URI parameters

Extra parameters can be appended to remote URIs. The table below *Table 13.1, "Extra URI parameters"* covers the recognized parameters. All other parameters are ignored. Note that parameter values must be URI-escaped (that is, a question mark (?) is appended before the parameter and special characters are converted into the URI format).

Name	Transport mode	Description	Example usage
name	all modes	The name passed to the remote virConnectOpen function. The name is normally formed by removing transport, hostname, port number, username and extra parameters from the remote URI, but in certain very complex cases it may be better to supply the name explicitly.	name=qemu:///system
command	ssh and ext	The external command. For ext transport this is required. For ssh the default is ssh. The PATH is searched for the command.	command=/opt/openssh/bin/ssh
socket	unix and ssh	The path to the UNIX domain socket, which overrides the default. For ssh transport, this is passed to the remote netcat command (see netcat).	socket=/opt/libvirt/run/libvirt/libvirt-sock
netcat	ssh	The name of the netcat command on the remote machine. The default is nc. For ssh	netcat=/opt/netcat/bin/nc

171

Fedora 12

Name	Transport mode	Description	Example usage
		transport, libvirt constructs an ssh command which looks like: command -p port [-l username] hostname netcat -U socket where port, username, hostname can be specified as part of the remote URI, and command, netcat and socket come from extra parameters (or sensible defaults).	
no_verify	tls	If set to a non-zero value, this disables client checks of the server's certificate. Note that to disable server checks of the client's certificate or IP address you must change the libvirtd configuration.	no_verify=1
no_tty	ssh	If set to a non-zero value, this stops ssh from asking for a password if it cannot log in to the remote machine automatically (for using ssh-agent or similar). Use this when you do not have access to a terminal - for example in graphical programs which use libvirt.	no_tty=1

Table 13.1. Extra URI parameters

Part IV.
Virtualization Reference Guide

Virtualization commands, system tools, applications and additional systems reference

These chapters provide detailed descriptions of virtualization commands, system tools, and applications included in Fedora. These chapters are designed for users requiring information on advanced functionality and other features.

Chapter 14.
Virtualization tools

The following is a list of tools for virtualization administration, debugging and networking tools that are useful for systems running Xen.

System Administration Tools

- vmstat
- iostat
- lsof

  ```
  # lsof -i :5900
  xen-vncfb 10635  root  5u  IPv4 218738 TCP grumble.boston.redhat.com:5900 (LISTEN)
  ```

- qemu-img

Advanced Debugging Tools

- systemTap
- crash
- xen-gdbserver
- sysrq
- sysrq t
- sysrq w
- sysrq c

Networking

brtcl

```
# brctl show
bridge name   bridge id          STP enabled   interfaces
xenbr0        8000.feffffffffff  no            vif13.0
                                               pdummy0
                                               vif0.0

# brctl showmacs xenbr0
port no  mac addr              is local?   aging timer
  1      fe:ff:ff:ff:ff:ff     yes         0.00
```

```
# brctl showstp xenbr0
xenbr0
bridge id                8000.feffffffffff
designated root          8000.feffffffffff
root port                0                       path cost                0
max age                  20.00                   bridge max age           20.00
hello time               2.00                    bridge hello time        2.00
forward delay            0.00                    bridge forward delay     0.00
aging time               300.01
hello timer              1.43                    tcn timer                0.00
topology change timer    0.00                    gc timer                 0.02
flags

vif13.0 (3)
port id                  8003                    state                    forwarding
designated root          8000.feffffffffff       path cost                100
designated bridge        8000.feffffffffff       message age timer        0.00
designated port          8003                    forward delay timer      0.00
designated cost          0                       hold timer               0.43
flags

pdummy0 (2)
port id                  8002                    state                    forwarding
designated root          8000.feffffffffff       path cost                100
designated bridge        8000.feffffffffff       message age timer        0.00
designated port          8002                    forward delay timer      0.00
designated cost          0                       hold timer               0.43
flags

vif0.0 (1)
port id                  8001                    state                    forwarding
designated root          8000.feffffffffff       path cost                100
designated bridge        8000.feffffffffff       message age timer        0.00
designated port          8001                    forward delay timer      0.00
designated cost          0                       hold timer               0.43
flags
```

- ifconfig
- tcpdump

KVM tools

- ps
- pstree
- top
- kvmtrace
- kvm_stat

Xen tools

- xentop
- xm dmesg
- xm log

Chapter 15.
Managing guests with virsh

virsh is a command line interface tool for managing guests and the hypervisor.

The virsh tool is built on the libvirt management API and operates as an alternative to the xm command and the graphical guest Manager (virt-manager). virsh can be used in read-only mode by unprivileged users. You can use virsh to execute scripts for the guest machines.

virsh command quick reference

The following tables provide a quick reference for all virsh command line options.

Command	Description
`help`	Prints basic help information.
`list`	Lists all guests.
`dumpxml`	Outputs the XML configuration file for the guest.
`create`	Creates a guest from an XML configuration file and starts the new guest.
`start`	Starts an inactive guest.
`destroy`	Forces a guest to stop.
`define`	Outputs an XML configuration file for a guest.
`domid`	Displays the guest's ID.
`domuuid`	Displays the guest's UUID.
`dominfo`	Displays guest information.
`domname`	Displays the guest's name.
`domstate`	Displays the state of a guest.
`quit`	Quits the interactive terminal.
`reboot`	Reboots a guest.
`restore`	Restores a previously saved guest stored in a file.
`resume`	Resumes a paused guest.
`save`	Save the present state of a guest to a file.
`shutdown`	Gracefully shuts down a guest.

Command	Description
`suspend`	Pauses a guest.
`undefine`	Deletes all files associated with a guest.
`migrate`	Migrates a guest to another host.

Table 15.1. Guest management commands

The following virsh command options to manage guest and hypervisor resources:

Command	Description
`setmem`	Sets the allocated memory for a guest.
`setmaxmem`	Sets maximum memory limit for the hypervisor.
`setvcpus`	Changes number of virtual CPUs assigned to a guest.
`vcpuinfo`	Displays virtual CPU information about a guest.
`vcpupin`	Controls the virtual CPU affinity of a guest.
`domblkstat`	Displays block device statistics for a running guest.
`domifstat`	Displays network interface statistics for a running guest.
`attach-device`	Attach a device to a guest, using a device definition in an XML file.
`attach-disk`	Attaches a new disk device to a guest.
`attach-interface`	Attaches a new network interface to a guest.
`detach-device`	Detach a device from a guest, takes the same kind of XML descriptions as command `attach-device`.
`detach-disk`	Detach a disk device from a guest.
`detach-interface`	Detach a network interface from a guest.

Table 15.2. Resource management options

These are miscellaneous virsh options:

Command	Description
`version`	Displays the version of `virsh`
`nodeinfo`	Outputs information about the hypervisor

Table 15.3. Miscellaneous options

Connecting to the hypervisor

Connect to a hypervisor session with virsh:

```
# virsh connect {hostname OR URL}
```

Where <name> is the machine name of the hypervisor. To initiate a read-only connection, append the above command with -readonly.

Fedora 12

Creating a virtual machine XML dump (configuration file)

Output a guest's XML configuration file with virsh:

```
# virsh dumpxml {domain-id, domain-name or domain-uuid}
```

This command outputs the guest's XML configuration file to standard out (stdout). You can save the data by piping the output to a file. An example of piping the output to a file called *guest.xml*:

```
# virsh dumpxml GuestID > guest.xml
```

This file guest.xml can recreate the guest (refer to Editing a guest's configuration file. You can edit this XML configuration file to configure additional devices or to deploy additional guests. Refer to Section 18.1, "Using XML configuration files with virsh" for more information on modifying files created with virsh dumpxml.

An example of virsh dumpxml output:

```
# virsh dumpxml r5b2-mySQL01
<domain type='xen' id='13'>
    <name>r5b2-mySQL01</name>
    <uuid>4a4c59a7ee3fc78196e4288f2862f011</uuid>
    <bootloader>/usr/bin/pygrub</bootloader>
    <os>
        <type>linux</type>
        <kernel>/var/lib/libvirt/vmlinuz.2dgnU_</kernel>
    <initrd>/var/lib/libvirt/initrd.UQafMw</initrd>
        <cmdline>ro root=/dev/VolGroup00/LogVol00 rhgb quiet</cmdline>
    </os>
    <memory>512000</memory>
    <vcpu>1</vcpu>
    <on_poweroff>destroy</on_poweroff>
    <on_reboot>restart</on_reboot>
    <on_crash>restart</on_crash>
    <devices>
        <interface type='bridge'>
            <source bridge='xenbr0'/>
            <mac address='00:16:3e:49:1d:11'/>
            <script path='vif-bridge'/>
        </interface>
        <graphics type='vnc' port='5900'/>
        <console tty='/dev/pts/4'/>
    </devices>
</domain>
```

Creating a guest from a configuration file

Guests can be created from XML configuration files. You can copy existing XML from previously created guests or use the dumpxml option (refer to Creating a virtual machine XML dump (configuration file)). To create a guest with virsh from an XML file:

```
# virsh create configuration_file.xml
```

Editing a guest's configuration file

Instead of using the dumpxml option (refer to Creating a virtual machine XML dump (configuration file)) guests can be edited either while they run or while they are offline. The virsh edit command provides this functionality. For example, to edit the guest named *softwaretesting*:

```
# virsh edit softwaretesting
```

This opens a text editor. The default text editor is the $EDITOR shell parameter (set to vi by default).

Suspending a guest

Suspend a guest with virsh:

```
# virsh suspend {domain-id, domain-name or domain-uuid}
```

When a guest is in a suspended state, it consumes system RAM but not processor resources. Disk and network I/O does not occur while the guest is suspended. This operation is immediate and the guest can be restarted with the resume (Resuming a guest) option.

Resuming a guest

Restore a suspended guest with virsh using the resume option:

```
# virsh resume {domain-id, domain-name or domain-uuid}
```

This operation is immediate and the guest parameters are preserved for suspend and resume operations.

Save a guest

Save the current state of a guest to a file using the virsh command:

```
# virsh save {domain-name, domain-id or domain-uuid} filename
```

This stops the guest you specify and saves the data to a file, which may take some time given the amount of memory in use by your guest. You can restore the state of the guest with the restore (Restore a guest) option. Save is similar to pause, instead of just pausing a guest the present state of the guest is saved.

Restore a guest

Restore a guest previously saved with the virsh save command (Save a guest) using virsh:

```
# virsh restore filename
```

This restarts the saved guest, which may take some time. The guest's name and UUID are preserved but are allocated for a new id.

Fedora 12

Shut down a guest

Shut down a guest using the virsh command:

```
# virsh shutdown {domain-id, domain-name or domain-uuid}
```

You can control the behavior of the rebooting guest by modifying the on_shutdown parameter in the guest's configuration file file.

Rebooting a guest

Reboot a guest using virsh command:

```
#virsh reboot {domain-id, domain-name or domain-uuid}
```

You can control the behavior of the rebooting guest by modifying the on_reboot parameter in the guest's configuration file file.

Forcing a guest to stop

Force a guest to stop with the virsh command:

```
# virsh destroy {domain-id, domain-name or domain-uuid}
```

This command does an immediate ungraceful shutdown and stops the specified guest. Using virsh destroy can corrupt guest file systems . Use the destroy option only when the guest is unresponsive. For para-virtualized guests, use the shutdown option(Shut down a guest) instead.

Getting the domain ID of a guest

To get the domain ID of a guest:

```
# virsh domid {domain-name or domain-uuid}
```

Getting the domain name of a guest

To get the domain name of a guest:

```
# virsh domname {domain-id or domain-uuid}
```

Getting the UUID of a guest

To get the Universally Unique Identifier (UUID) for a guest:

```
# virsh domuuid {domain-id or domain-name}
```

An example of virsh domuuid output:

```
# virsh domuuid r5b2-mySQL01
4a4c59a7-ee3f-c781-96e4-288f2862f011
```

Displaying guest Information

Using virsh with the guest's domain ID, domain name or UUID you can display information on the specified guest:

```
# virsh dominfo {domain-id, domain-name or domain-uuid}
```

This is an example of virsh dominfo output:

```
# virsh dominfo r5b2-mySQL01
id:             13
name:           r5b2-mysql01
uuid:           4a4c59a7-ee3f-c781-96e4-288f2862f011
os type:        linux
state:          blocked
cpu(s):         1
cpu time:       11.0s
max memory:     512000 kb
used memory:    512000 kb
```

Displaying host information

To display information about the host:

```
# virsh nodeinfo
```

An example of virsh nodeinfo output:

```
# virsh nodeinfo
CPU model               x86_64
CPU (s)                 8
CPU frequency           2895 Mhz
CPU socket(s)           2
Core(s) per socket      2
Threads per core:       2
Numa cell(s)            1
Memory size:            1046528 kb
```

This displays the node information and the machines that support the virtualization process.

Displaying the guests

To display the guest list and their current states with virsh:

```
# virsh list
```

Other options available include:

the --inactive option to list inactive guests (that is, guests that have been defined but are not currently active), and

the --all option lists all guests. For example:

Fedora 12

```
# virsh list --all
 Id Name                      State
----------------------------------
  0 Domain-0                  running
  1 Domain202                 paused
  2 Domain010                 inactive
  3 Domain9600                crashed
```

The output from virsh list is categorized as one of the six states (listed below).

- The running state refers to guests which are currently active on a CPU.
- Guests listed as blocked are blocked, and are not running or runnable. This is caused by a guest waiting on I/O (a traditional wait state) or guests in a sleep mode.
- The paused state lists domains that are paused. This occurs if an administrator uses the pause button in virt-manager, xm pause or virsh suspend. When a guest is paused it consumes memory and other resources but it is ineligible for scheduling and CPU resources from the hypervisor.
- The shutdown state is for guests in the process of shutting down. The guest is sent a shutdown signal and should be in the process of stopping its operations gracefully. This may not work with all guest operating systems; some operating systems do not respond to these signals.
- Domains in the dying state are in is in process of dying, which is a state where the domain has not completely shut-down or crashed.
- crashed guests have failed while running and are no longer running. This state can only occur if the guest has been configured not to restart on crash.

Displaying virtual CPU information

To display virtual CPU information from a guest with virsh:

```
# virsh vcpuinfo {domain-id, domain-name or domain-uuid}
```

An example of virsh vcpuinfo output:

```
# virsh vcpuinfo r5b2-mySQL01
VCPU:           0
CPU:            0
State:          blocked
CPU time:       0.0s
CPU Affinity:   yy
```

Configuring virtual CPU affinity

To configure the affinity of virtual CPUs with physical CPUs:

```
# virsh vcpupin {domain-id, domain-name or domain-uuid} vcpu, cpulist
```

Where vcpu is the virtual VCPU number and cpulist lists the physical number of CPUs.

Virtualization Guide

Configuring virtual CPU count

To modify the number of CPUs assigned to a guest with virsh:

```
# virsh setvcpus {domain-name, domain-id or domain-uuid} count
```

The new *count* value cannot exceed the count above the amount specified when the guest was created.

Configuring memory allocation

To modify a guest's memory allocation with virsh :

```
# virsh setmem {domain-id or domain-name} count
```

You must specify the count in kilobytes. The new count value cannot exceed the amount you specified when you created the guest. Values lower than 64 MB are unlikely to work with most guest operating systems. A higher maximum memory value will not affect the an active guest unless the new value is lower which will shrink the available memory usage.

Displaying guest block device information

Use virsh domblkstat to display block device statistics for a running guest.

```
# virsh domblkstat GuestName block-device
```

Displaying guest network device information

Use virsh domifstat to display network interface statistics for a running guest.

```
# virsh domifstat GuestName interface-device
```

Migrating guests with virsh

A guest can be migrated to another host with virsh. Migrate domain to another host. Add --live for live migration. The migrate command accepts parameters in the following format:

```
# virsh migrate --live GuestName DestinationURL
```

The *--live* parameter is optional. Add the *--live* parameter for live migrations.

The *GuestName* parameter represents the name of the guest which you want to migrate.

The *DestinationURL* parameter is the URL or hostname of the destination system. The destination system must run the same version of Fedora, be using the same hypervisor and have libvirt running.

Once the command is entered you will be prompted for the root password of the destination system.

Fedora 12

Managing virtual networks

This section covers managing virtual networks with the virsh command. To list virtual networks:

```
# virsh net-list
```

This command generates output similar to:

```
# virsh net-list
Name                 State      Autostart
-----------------------------------------
default              active     yes
vnet1                active     yes
vnet2                active     yes
```

To view network information for a specific virtual network:

```
# virsh net-dumpxml NetworkName
```

This displays information about a specified virtual network in XML format:

```
# virsh net-dumpxml vnet1
<network>
  <name>vnet1</name>
  <uuid>98361b46-1581-acb7-1643-85a412626e70</uuid>
  <forward dev='eth0'/>
  <bridge name='vnet0' stp='on' forwardDelay='0' />
  <ip address='192.168.100.1' netmask='255.255.255.0'>
    <dhcp>
      <range start='192.168.100.128' end='192.168.100.254' />
    </dhcp>
  </ip>
</network>
```

Other virsh commands used in managing virtual networks are:

- virsh net-autostart *network-name* — Autostart a network specified as *network-name*.
- virsh net-create *XMLfile* — generates and starts a new network using an existing XML file.
- virsh net-define *XMLfile* — generates a new network device from an existing XML file without starting it.
- virsh net-destroy *network-name* — destroy a network specified as *network-name*.
- virsh net-name *networkUUID* — convert a specified *networkUUID* to a network name.
- virsh net-uuid *network-name* — convert a specified *network-name* to a network UUID.
- virsh net-start *nameOfInactiveNetwork* — starts an inactive network.
- virsh net-undefine *nameOfInactiveNetwork* — removes the definition of an inactive network.

Chapter 16.
Managing guests with the Virtual Machine Manager (virt-manager)

This section describes the Virtual Machine Manager (virt-manager) windows, dialog boxes, and various GUI controls.

virt-manager provides a graphical view of hypervisors and guest on your system and on remote machines. You can use virt-manager to define both para-virtualized and fully virtualized guests. virt-manager can perform virtualization management tasks, including:

- assigning memory,
- assigning virtual CPUs,
- monitoring operational performance,
- saving and restoring, pausing and resuming, and shutting down and starting virtualized guests,
- links to the textual and graphical consoles, and
- live and offline migrations.

16.1. The open connection window

This window appears first and prompts the user to choose a hypervisor session. Non-privileged users can initiate a read-only session. Root users can start a session with full blown read-write status. For normal use, select the Local Xen host option or QEMU (for KVM).

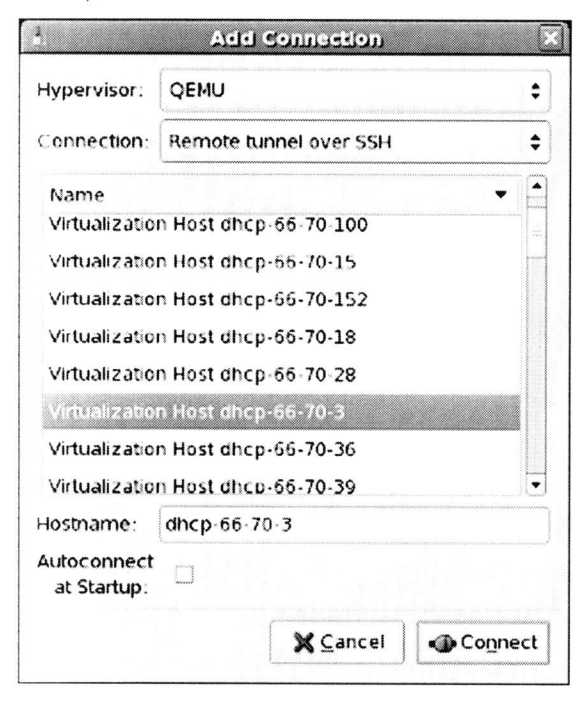

Figure 16.1. Virtual Machine Manager connection window

Virtualization Guide

16.2. The Virtual Machine Manager main window

This main window displays all the running virtual machines and resources currently allocated to them (including domain0). You can decide which fields to display. Double-clicking on the desired virtual machine brings up the respective console for that particular machine. Selecting a virtual machine and double-click the Details button to display the Details window for that machine. You can also access the File menu to create a new virtual machine.

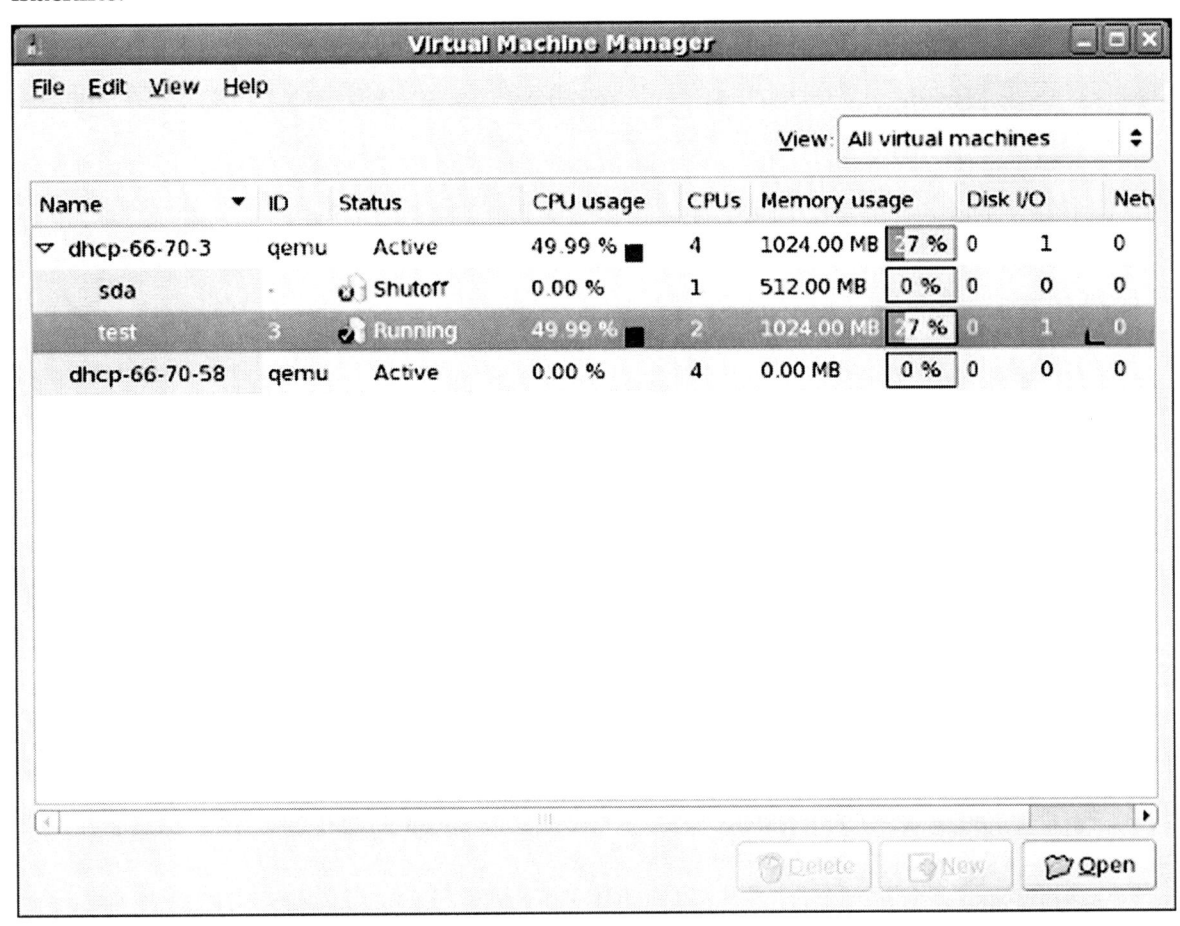

Figure 16.2. Virtual Machine Manager main window

187

Fedora 12

16.3. The Virtual Machine Manager details window

This window displays graphs and statistics of a guest's live resource utilization data available from virt-manager. The UUID field displays the globally unique identifier for the virtual machines.

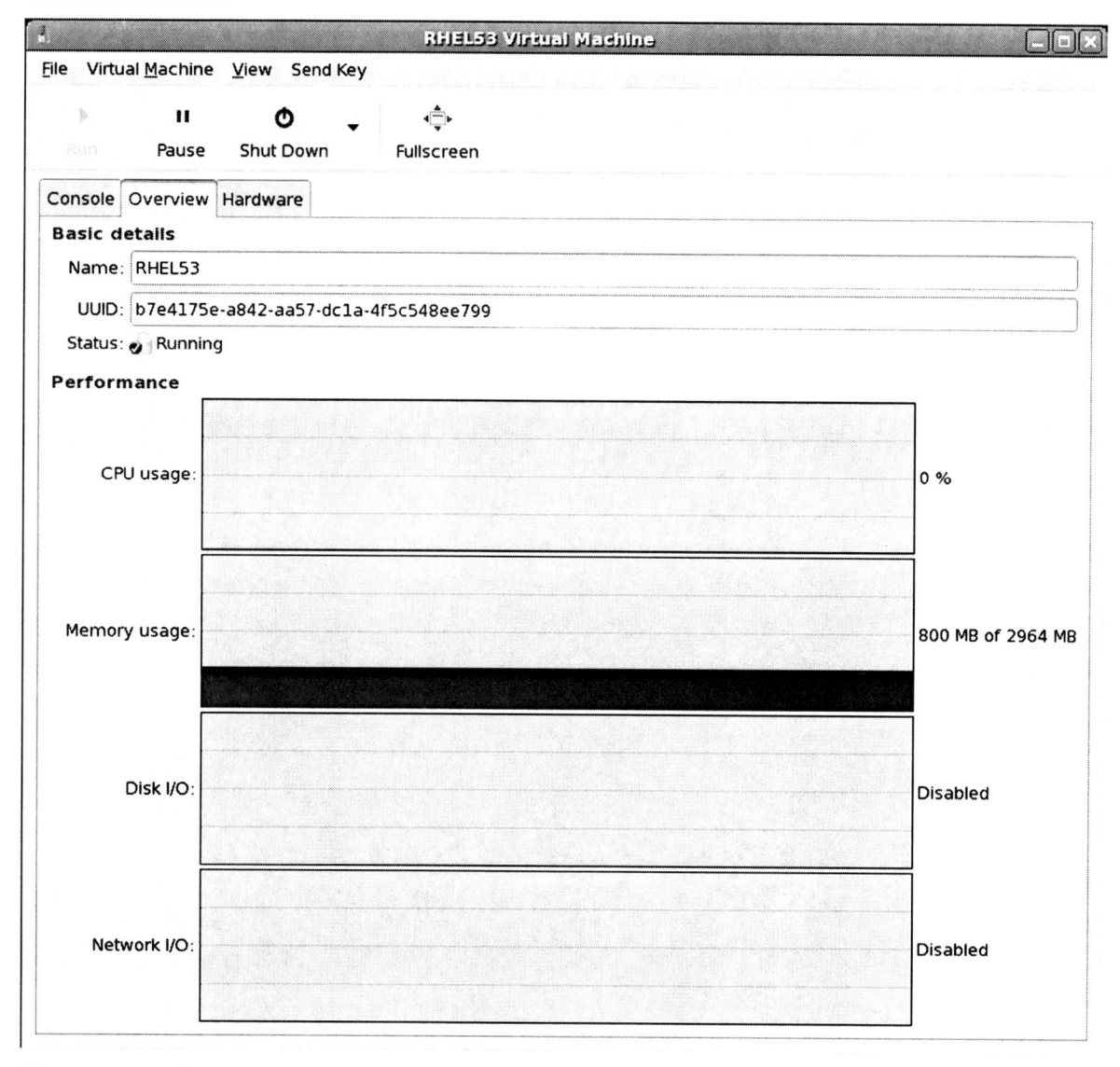

Figure 16.3. virt-manager details window

16.4. Virtual Machine graphical console

This window displays a virtual machine's graphical console. Para-virtualized and fully virtualized guests use different techniques to export their local virtual framebuffers, but both technologies use VNC to make them available to the Virtual Machine Manager's console window. If your virtual machine is set to require authentication, the Virtual Machine Graphical console prompts you for a password before the display appears.

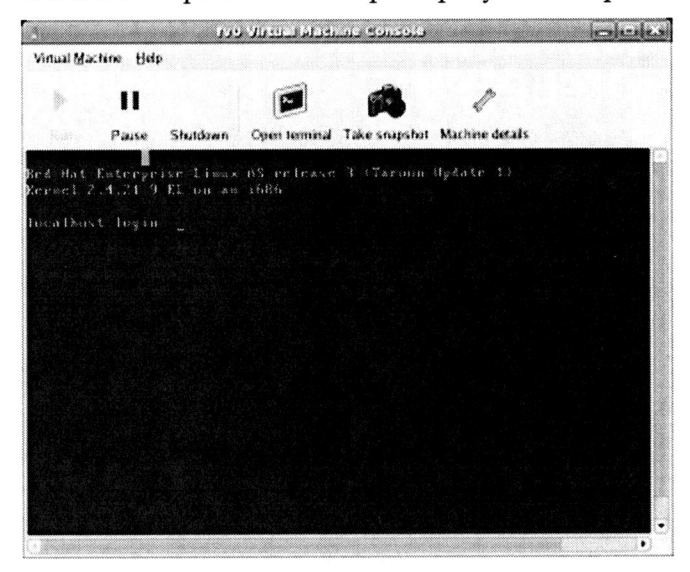

Figure 16.4. Graphical console window

> **A note on security and VNC**
>
> VNC is considered insecure by many security experts, however, several changes have been made to enable the secure usage of VNC for virtualization on Fedora. The guest machines only listen to the local host (dom0)'s loopback address (127.0.0.1). This ensures only those with shell privileges on the host can access virt-manager and the virtual machine through VNC.
>
> Remote administration can be performed following the instructions in *Chapter 13, Remote management of virtualized guests*. TLS can provide enterprise level security for managing guest and host systems.

Your local desktop can intercept key combinations (for example, Ctrl+Alt+F11) to prevent them from being sent to the guest machine. You can use virt-managersticky key' capability to send these sequences. You must press any modifier key (Ctrl or Alt) 3 times and the key you specify gets treated as active until the next non-modifier key is pressed. Then you can send Ctrl-Alt-F11 to the guest by entering the key sequence 'Ctrl Ctrl Ctrl Alt+F1'.

Fedora 12

16.5. Starting virt-manager

To start virt-manager session open the Applications menu, then the System Tools menu and select Virtual Machine Manager (virt-manager).

The virt-manager main window appears.

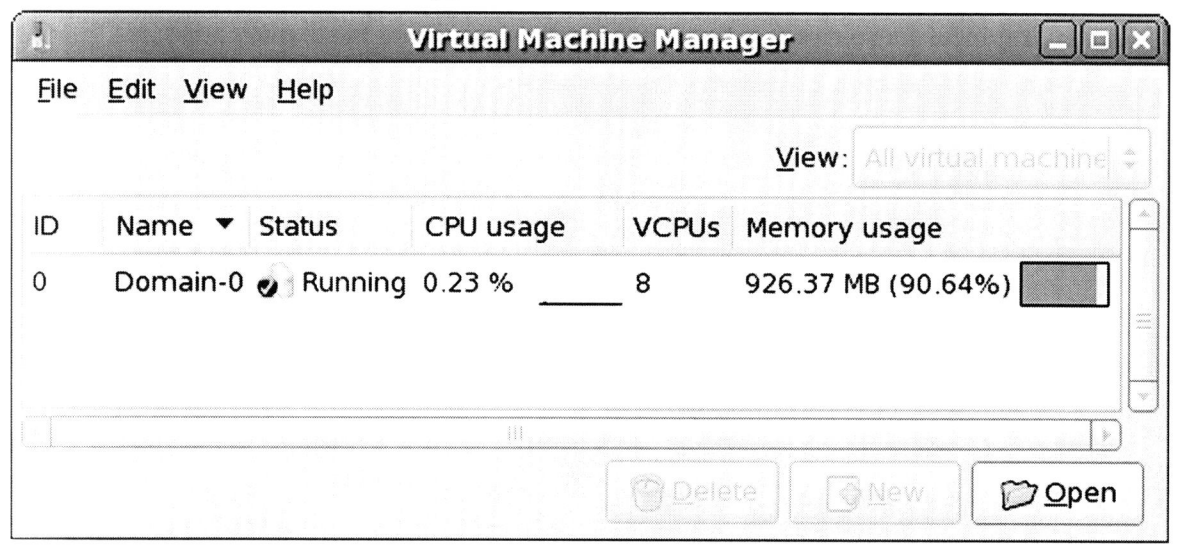

Figure 16.5. Starting virt-manager

Alternatively, virt-manager can be started remotely using ssh as demonstrated in the following command:

```
ssh -X host's address[remotehost]# virt-manager
```

Using ssh to manage virtual machines and hosts is discussed further in *Section 13.1, "Remote management with SSH"*.

16.6. Restoring a saved machine

After you start the Virtual Machine Manager, all virtual machines on your system are displayed in the main window. Domain0 is your host system. If there are no machines present, this means that currently there are no machines running on the system.

To restore a previously saved session:

Virtualization Guide

1. From the File menu, select Restore a saved machine.

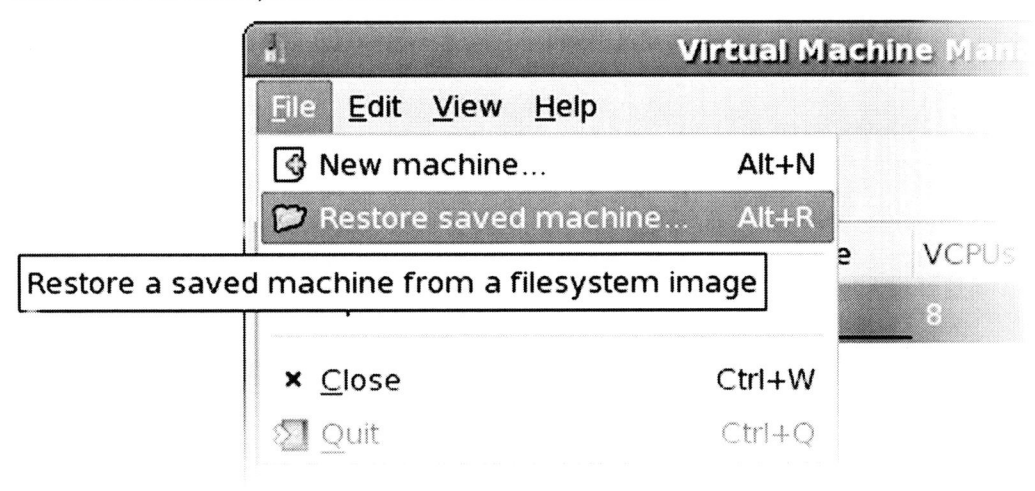

Figure 16.6. Restoring a virtual machine

2. The Restore Virtual Machine main window appears.
3. Navigate to correct directory and select the saved session file.
4. Click Open.

The saved virtual system appears in the Virtual Machine Manager main window.

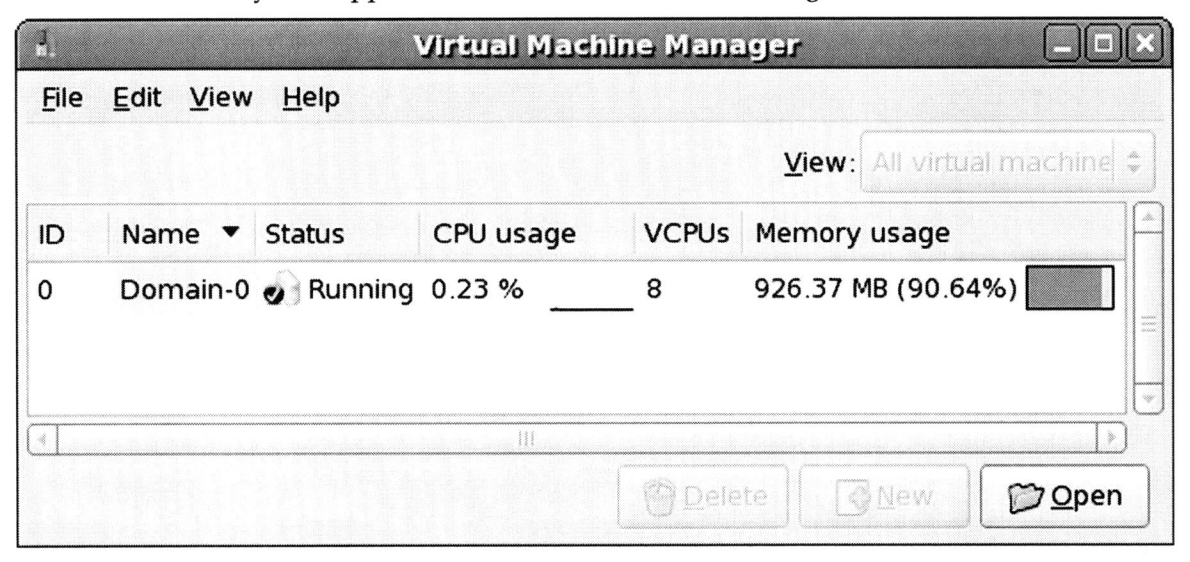

Figure 16.7. A restored virtual machine manager session

191

Fedora 12

16.7. Displaying guest details

You can use the Virtual Machine Monitor to view activity data information for any virtual machines on your system.

To view a virtual system's details:

1. In the Virtual Machine Manager main window, highlight the virtual machine that you want to view.

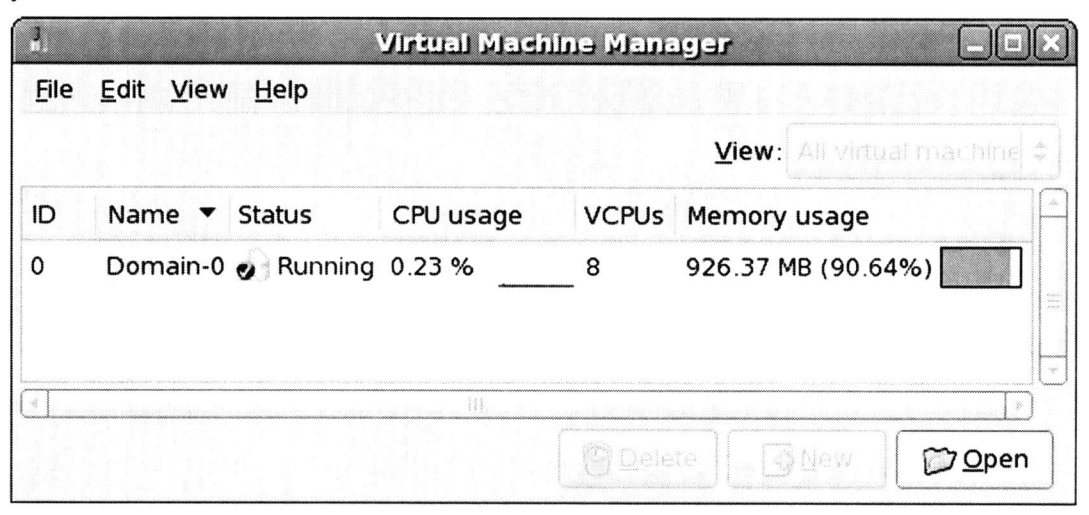

Figure 16.8. Selecting a virtual machine to display

Virtualization Guide

2. From the Virtual Machine Manager Edit menu, select Machine Details (or click the Details button on the bottom of the Virtual Machine Manager main window).

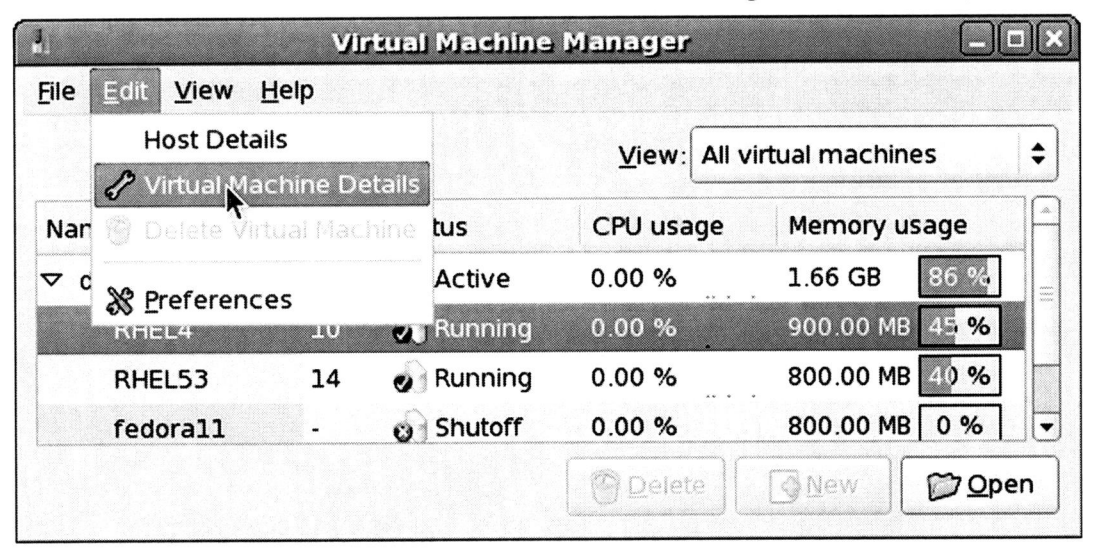

Figure 16.9. Displaying virtual machine details menu

Fedora 12

The Virtual Machine Details Overview window appears. This window summarizes CPU and memory usage for the domains you specified.

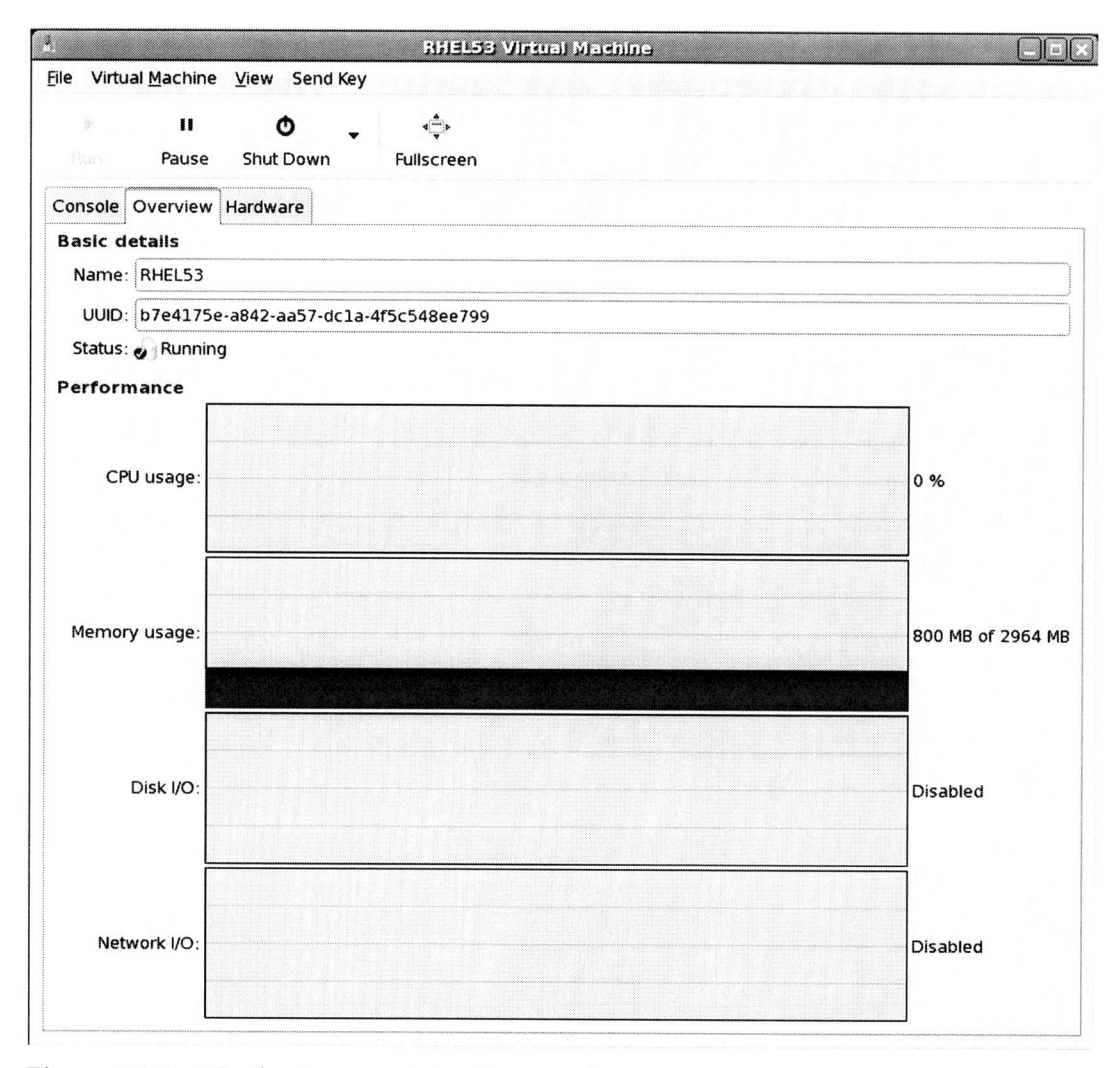

Figure 16.10. Displaying guest details overview

3. On the Virtual Machine Details window, click the Hardwaretab.

The Virtual Machine Details Hardware window appears.

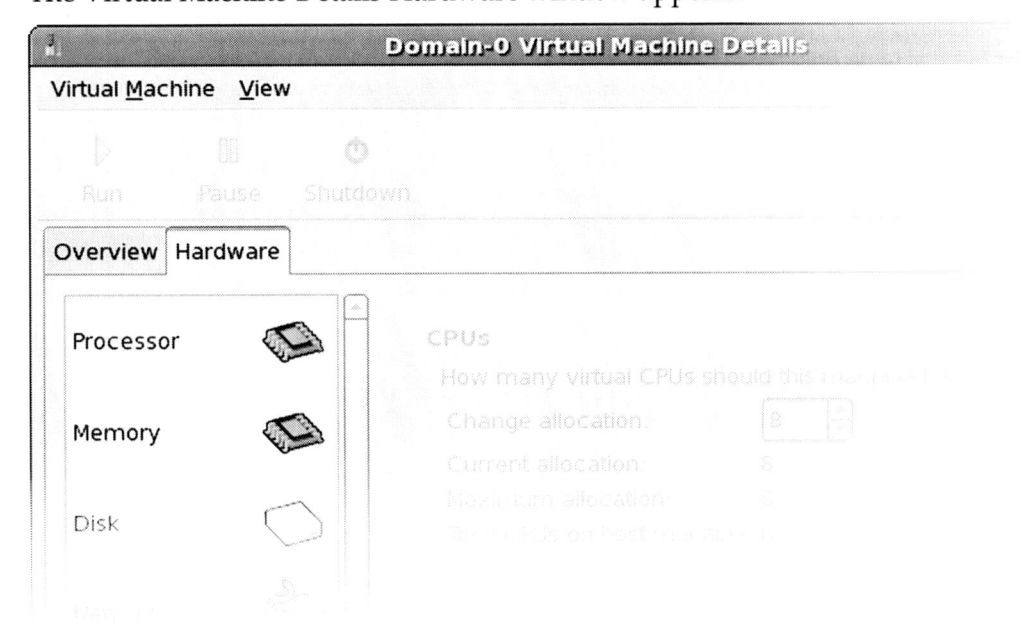

Figure 16.11. Displaying guest hardware details

Fedora 12

4. On the Hardware tab, click on Processor to view or change the current processor allocation.

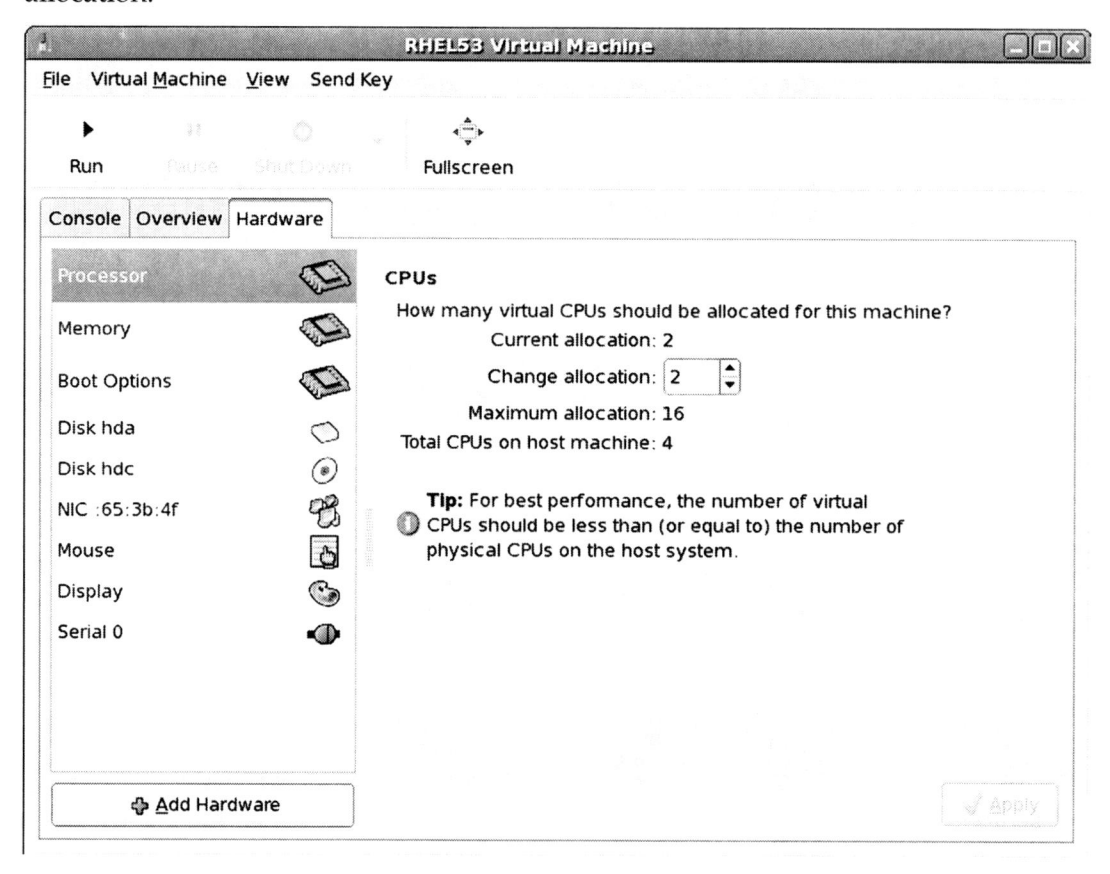

Figure 16.12. Processor allocation panel

Virtualization Guide

5. On the Hardware tab, click on Memory to view or change the current RAM memory allocation.

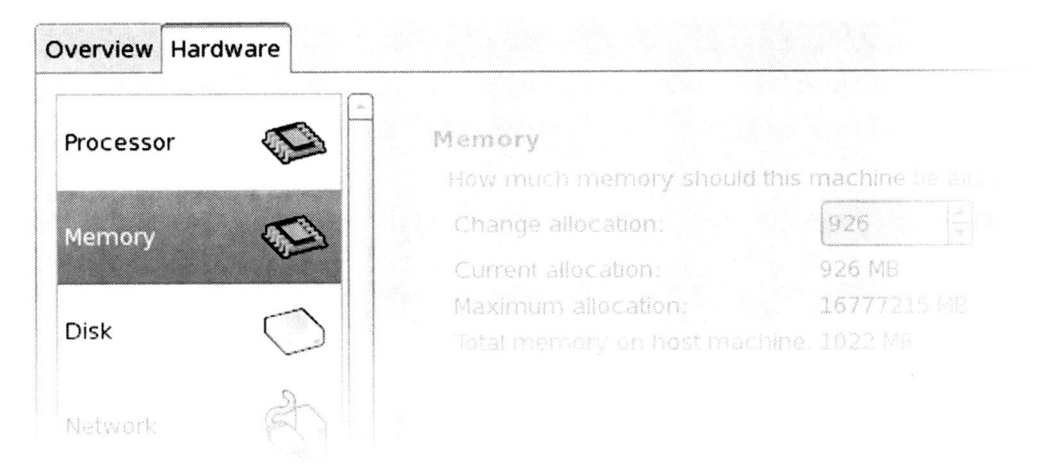

Figure 16.13. Displaying memory allocation

6. On the Hardware tab, click on Disk to view or change the current hard disk configuration.

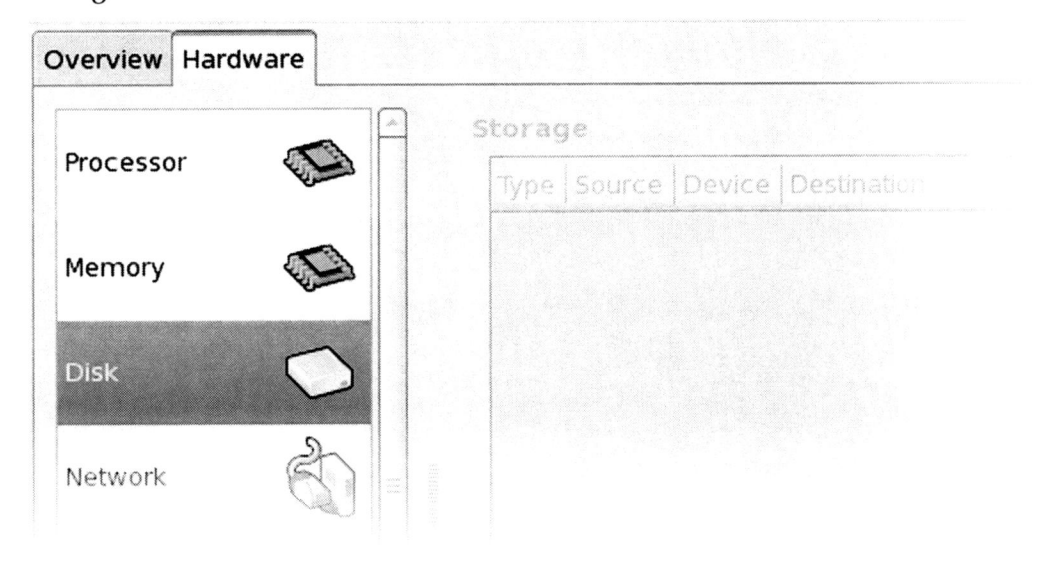

Figure 16.14. Displaying disk configuration

197

Fedora 12

7. On the Hardware tab, click on Network to view or change the current network configuration.

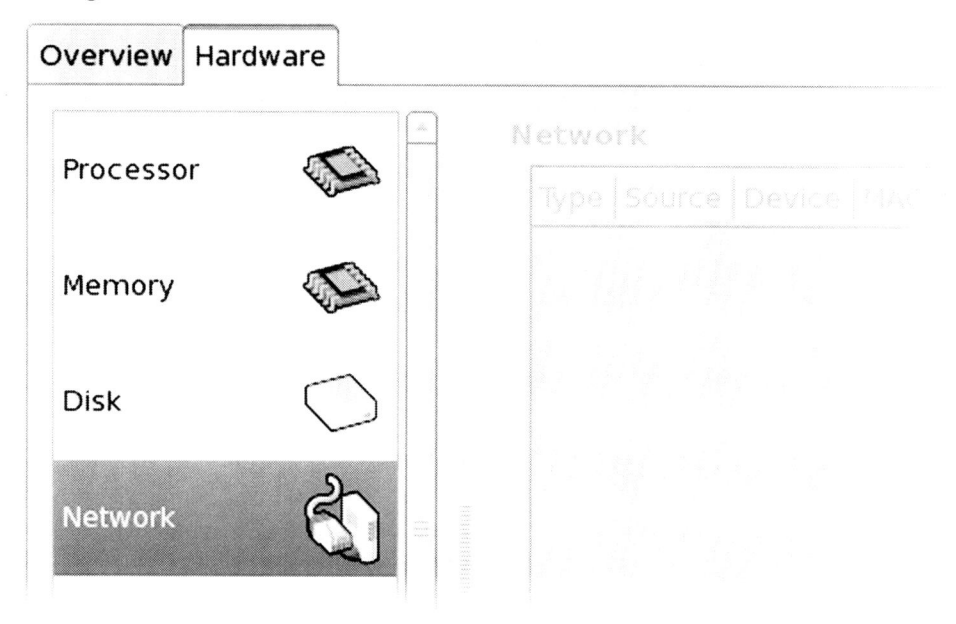

Figure 16.15. Displaying network configuration

16.8. Status monitoring

You can use the Virtual Machine Manager to modify the virtual system Status monitoring.

To configure Status monitoring, and enable Consoles:

Virtualization Guide

1. From the Edit menu, select Preferences.

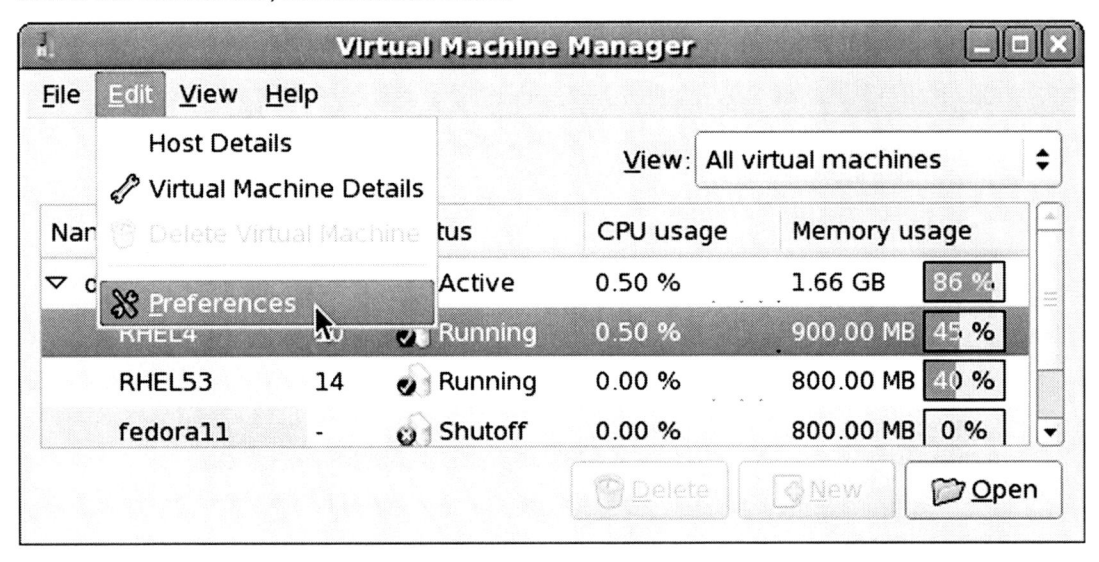

Figure 16.16. Modifying guest preferences

The Virtual Machine Manager Preferences window appears.

2. From the Status monitoring area selection box, specify the time (in seconds) that you want the system to update.

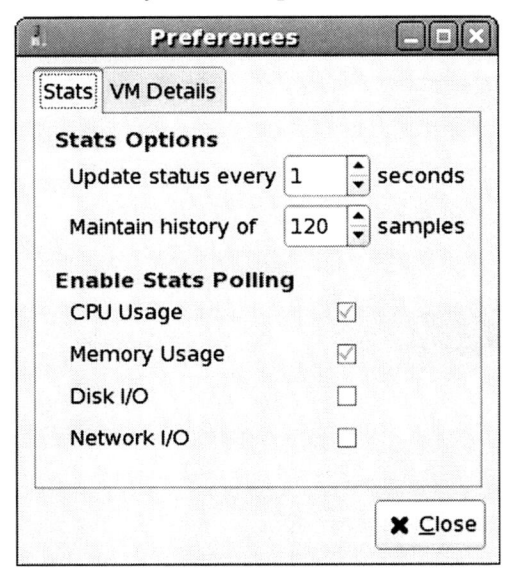

Figure 16.17. Configuring status monitoring

3. From the Consoles area, specify how to open a console and specify an input device.

199

16.9. Displaying guest identifiers

To view the guest IDs for all virtual machines on your system:

1. From the View menu, select the Domain ID check box.

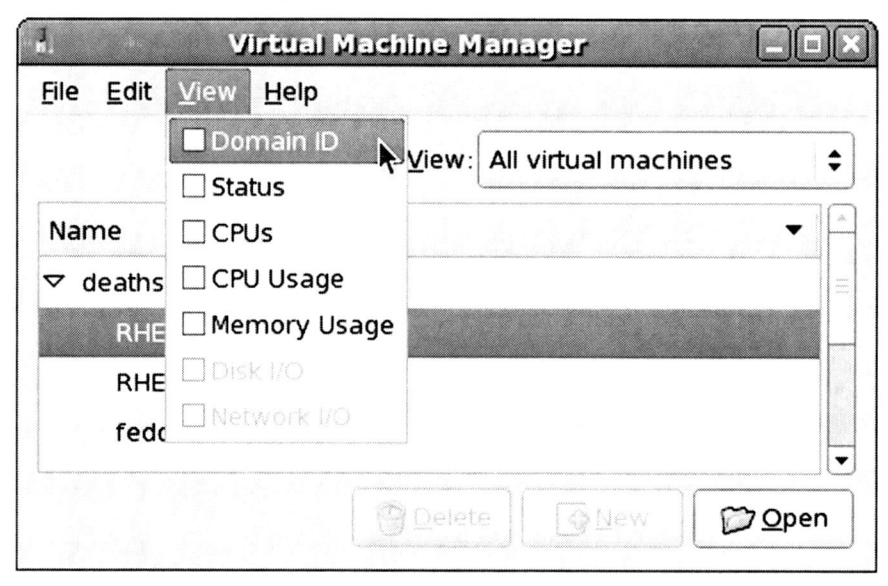

Figure 16.18. Viewing guest IDs

2. The Virtual Machine Manager lists the Domain IDs for all domains on your system.

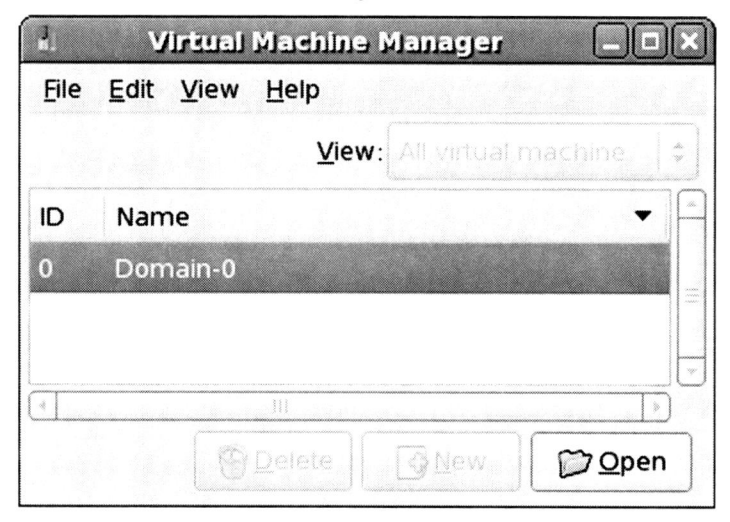

Figure 16.19. Displaying domain IDs

16.10. Displaying a guest's status

To view the status of all virtual machines on your system:

1. From the View menu, select the Status check box.

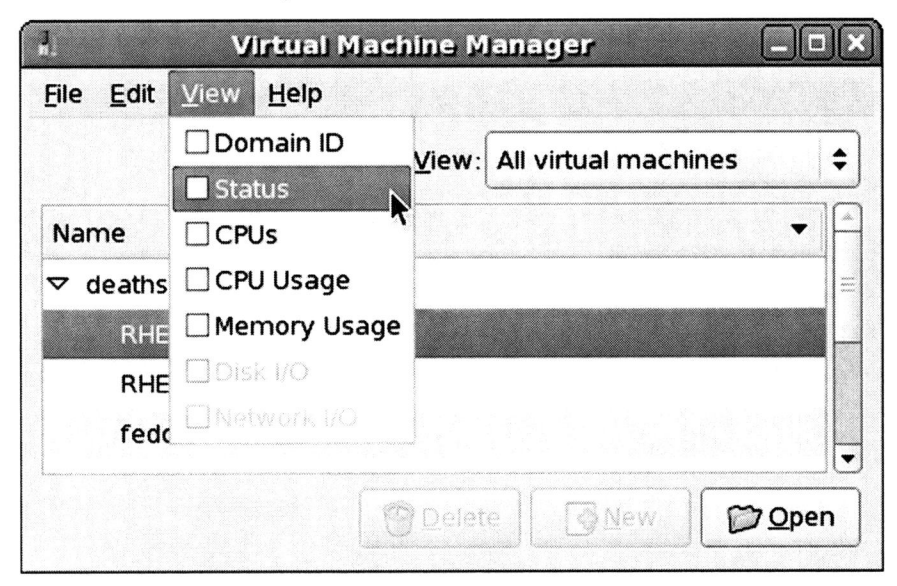

   Figure 16.20. Selecting a virtual machine's status

2. The Virtual Machine Manager lists the status of all virtual machines on your system.

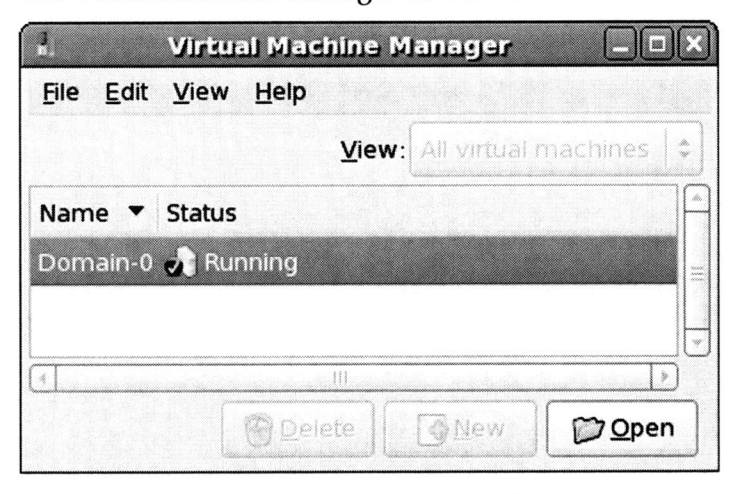

   Figure 16.21. Displaying a virtual machine's status

16.11. Displaying virtual CPUs

To view the amount of virtual CPUs for all virtual machines on your system:

1. From the View menu, select the Virtual CPUs check box.

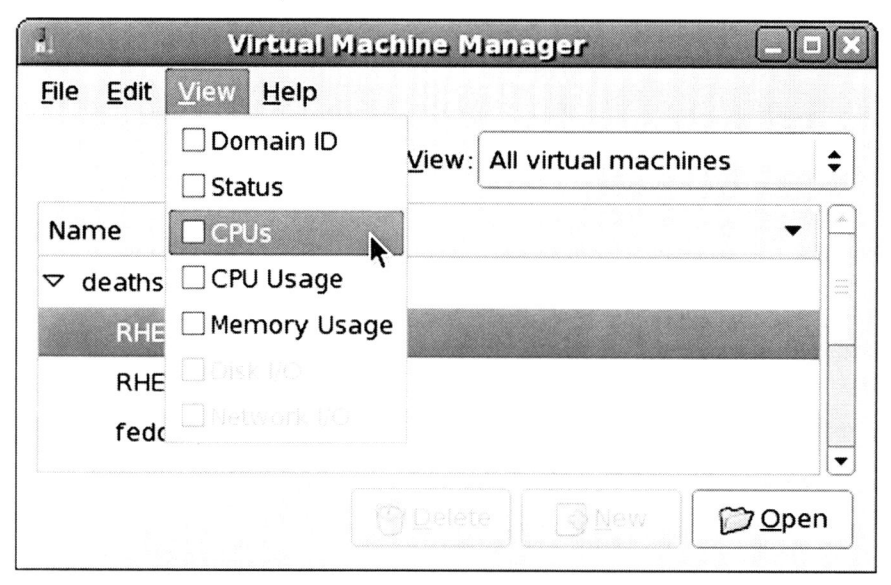

   Figure 16.22. Selecting the virtual CPUs option

2. The Virtual Machine Manager lists the Virtual CPUs for all virtual machines on your system.

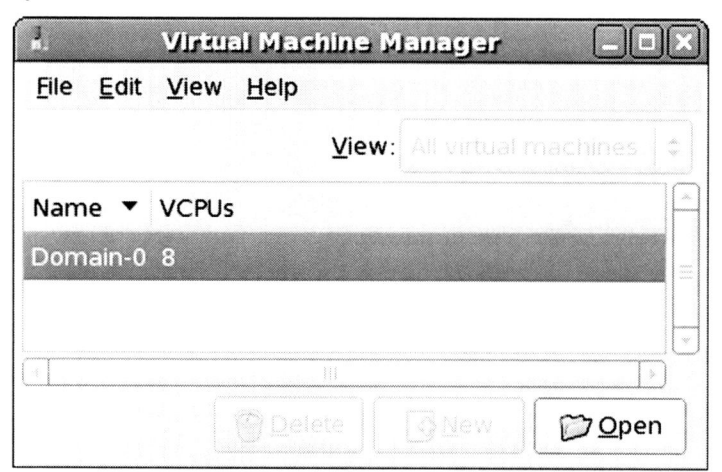

   Figure 16.23. Displaying Virtual CPUs

Virtualization Guide

16.12. Displaying CPU usage

To view the CPU usage for all virtual machines on your system:

1. From the View menu, select the CPU Usage check box.

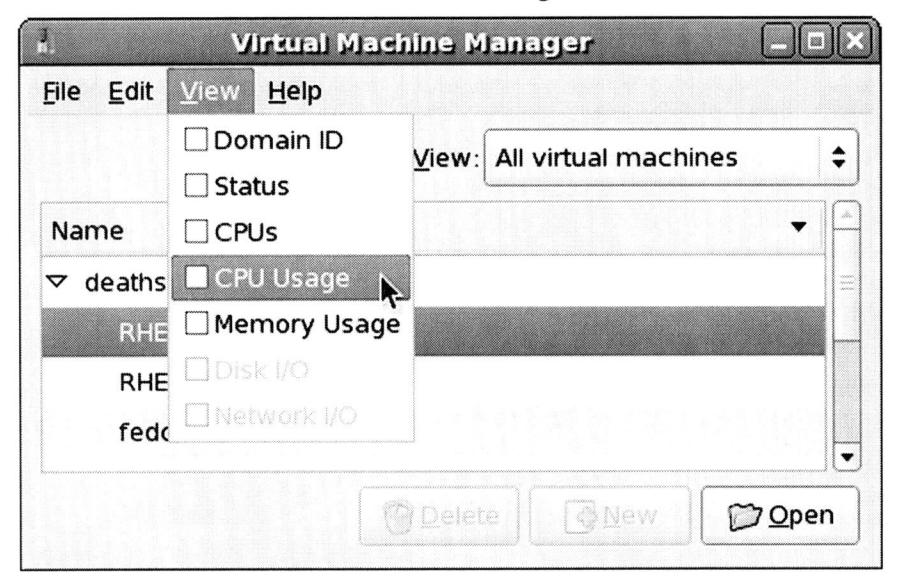

Figure 16.24. Selecting CPU usage

2. The Virtual Machine Manager lists the percentage of CPU in use for all virtual machines on your system.

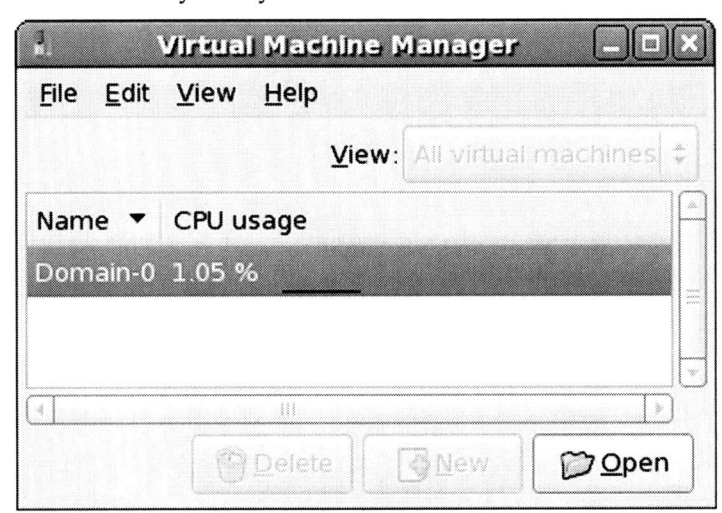

Figure 16.25. Displaying CPU usage

203

Fedora 12

16.13. Displaying memory usage

To view the memory usage for all virtual machines on your system:

1. From the View menu, select the Memory Usage check box.

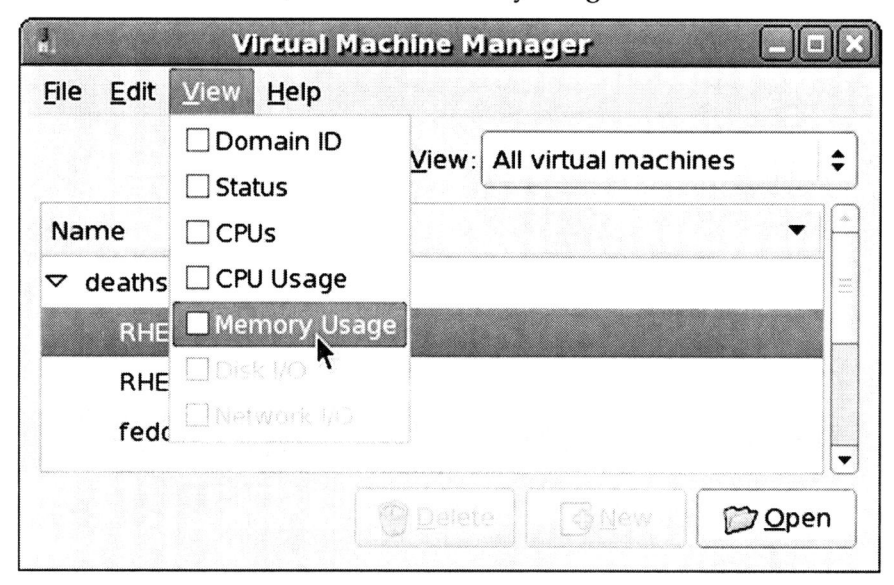

Figure 16.26. Selecting Memory Usage

2. The Virtual Machine Manager lists the percentage of memory in use (in megabytes) for all virtual machines on your system.

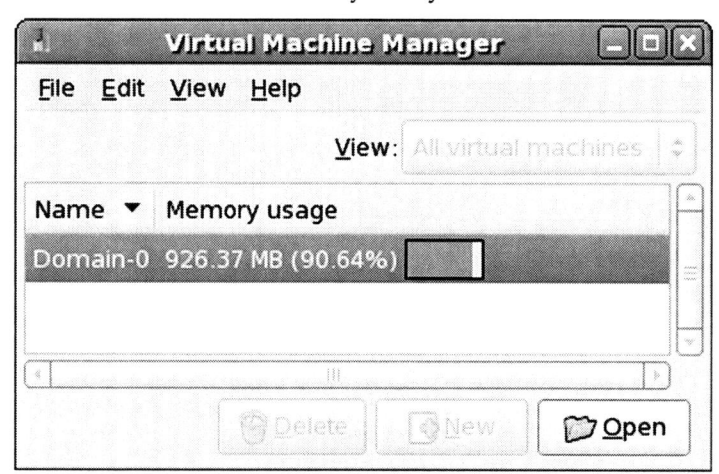

Figure 16.27. Displaying memory usage

204

16.14. Managing a virtual network

To configure a virtual network on your system:

1. From the Edit menu, select Host Details.

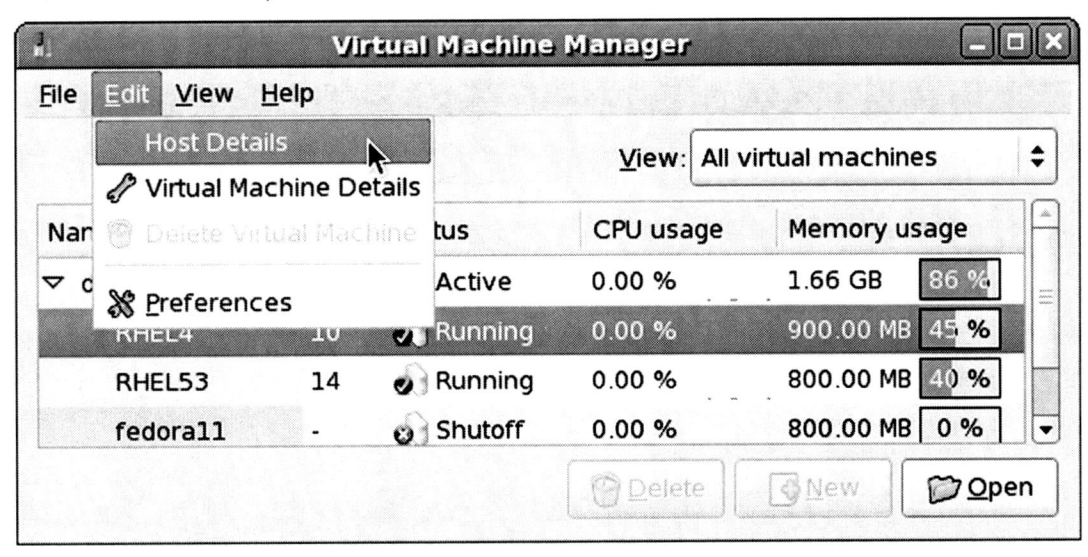

Figure 16.28. Selecting a host's details

Fedora 12

2. This will open the Host Details menu. Click the Virtual Networks tab.

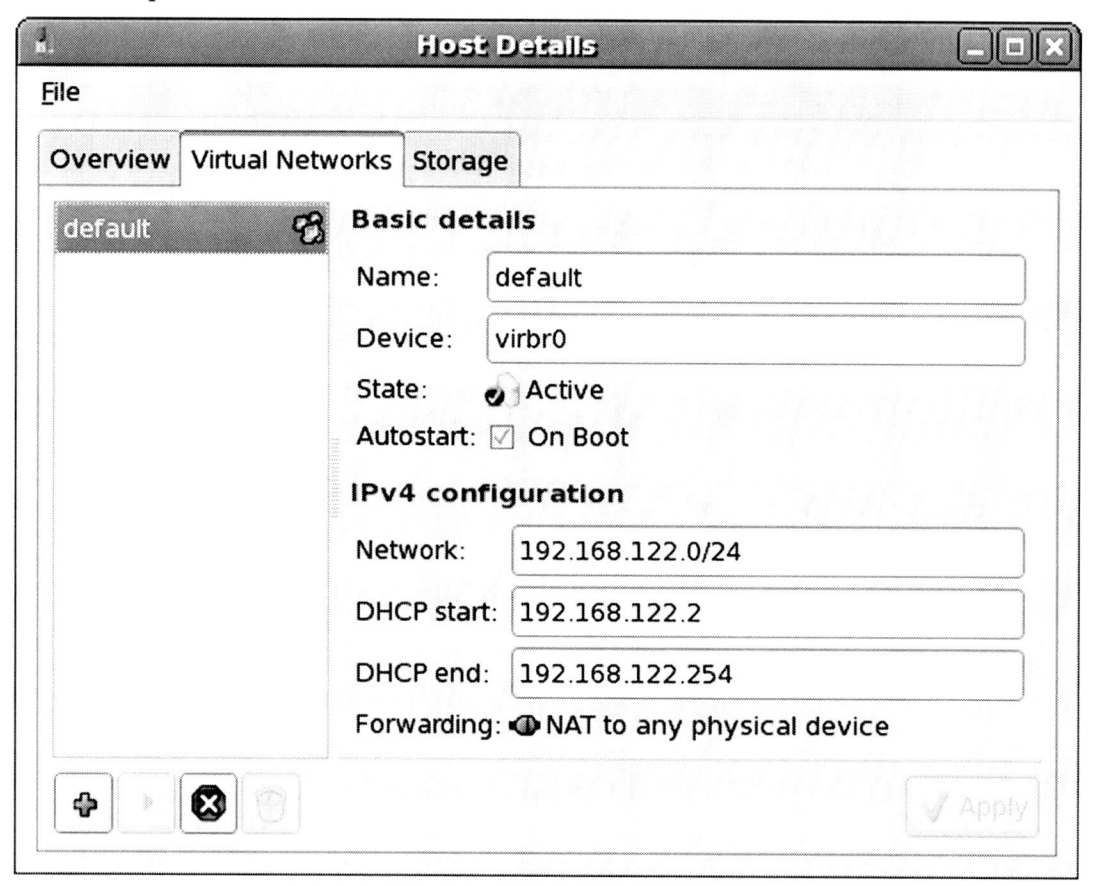

Figure 16.29. Virtual network configuration

3. All available virtual networks are listed on the left-hand box of the menu. You can edit the configuration of a virtual network by selecting it from this box and editing as you see fit.

16.15. Creating a virtual network

To create a virtual network on your system:

1. Open the Host Details menu (refer to Section 16.14, "Managing a virtual network") and click the Add button.

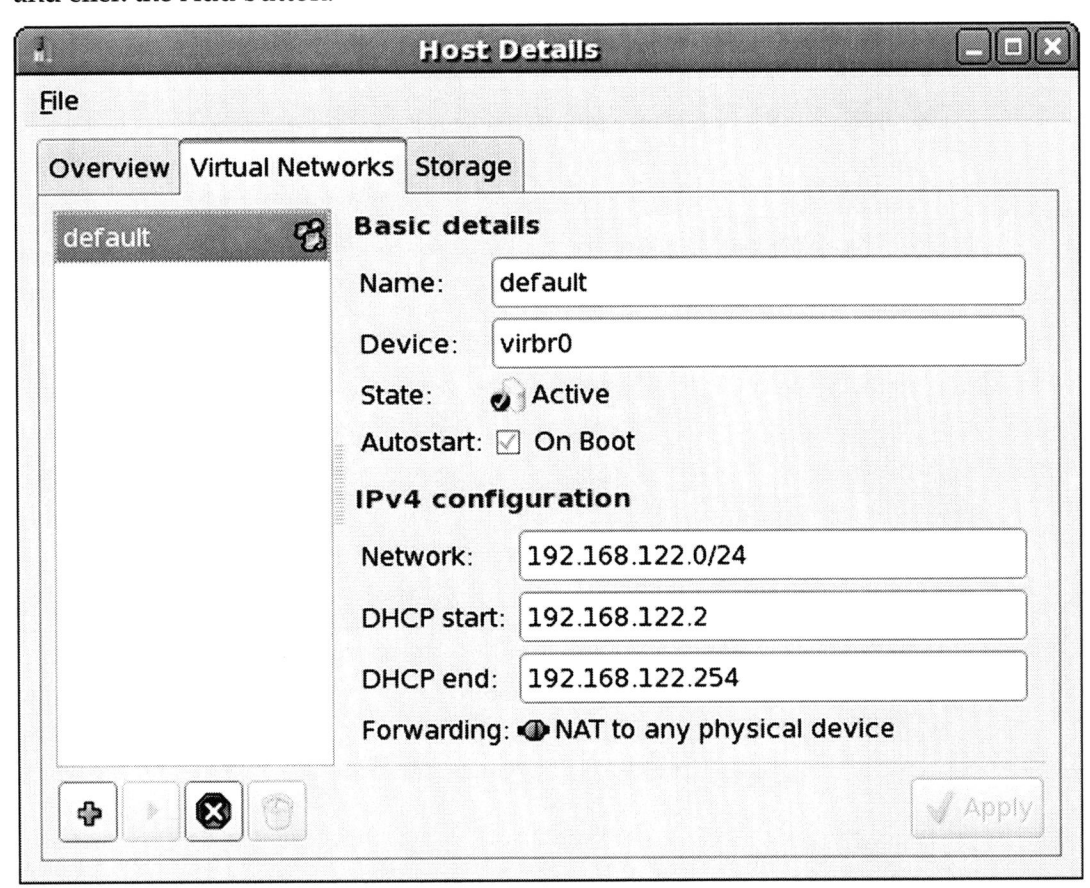

Figure 16.30. Virtual network configuration

Fedora 12

This will open the Create a new virtual network menu. Click Forward to continue.

Creating a new virtual network

This assistant will guide you through creating a new virtual network. You will be asked for some information about the virtual network you'd like to create, such as:

- A **name** for your new virtual network
- The IPv4 **address** and **netmask** to assign
- The **address range** from which the **DHCP** server will allocate addresses for virtual machines
- Whether to **forward** traffic to the physical network

[Cancel] [Back] [Forward]

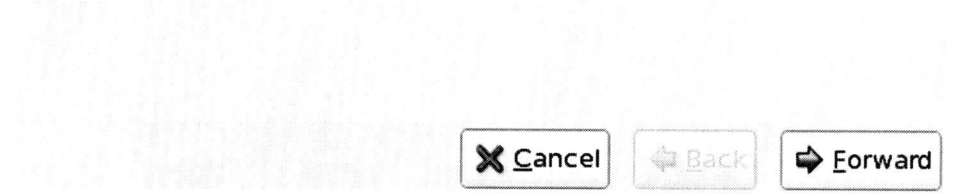

Figure 16.31. Creating a new virtual network

2. Enter an appropriate name for your virtual network and click Forward.

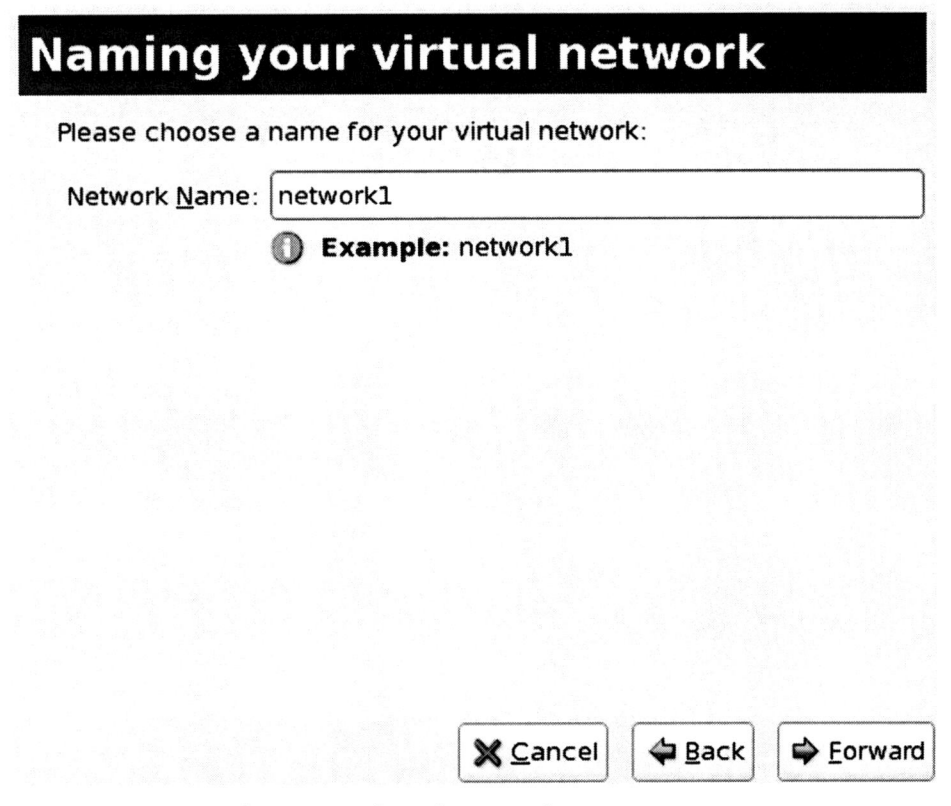

Figure 16.32. Naming your virtual network

Fedora 12

3. Enter an IPv4 address space for your virtual network and click Forward.

Choosing an IPv4 address space

You will need to choose an IPv4 address space for the virtual network:

Network: 192.168.100.0/24

Hint: The network should be choosen from one of the IPv4 private address ranges. eg 10.0.0.0/8, 172.16.0.0/12, or 192.168.0.0/16

Netmask: 255.255.255.0
Broadcast: 192.168.100.255
Gateway: 192.168.100.1
Size: 256 addresses
Type: Private

[✖ Cancel] [⬅ Back] [➡ Forward]

Figure 16.33. Choosing an IPv4 address space

Virtualization Guide

4. Define the DHCP range for your virtual network by specifying a Start and End range of IP addresses. Click Forward to continue.

Selecting the DHCP range

Please choose the range of addresses the DHCP server can use to allocate to guests attached to the virtual network

Start: 192.168.100.128

End: 192.168.100.254

Tip: Unless you wish to reserve some addresses to allow static network configuration in virtual machines, these parameters can be left with their default values.

[Cancel] [Back] [Forward]

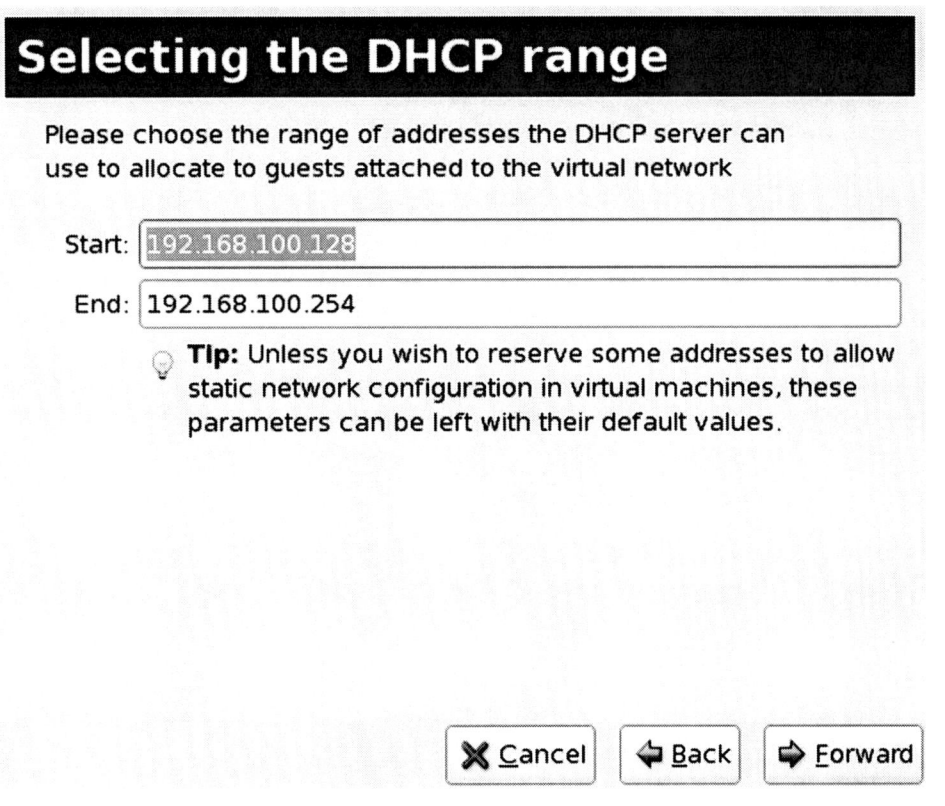

Figure 16.34. Selecting the DHCP range

5. Select how the virtual network should connect to the physical network.

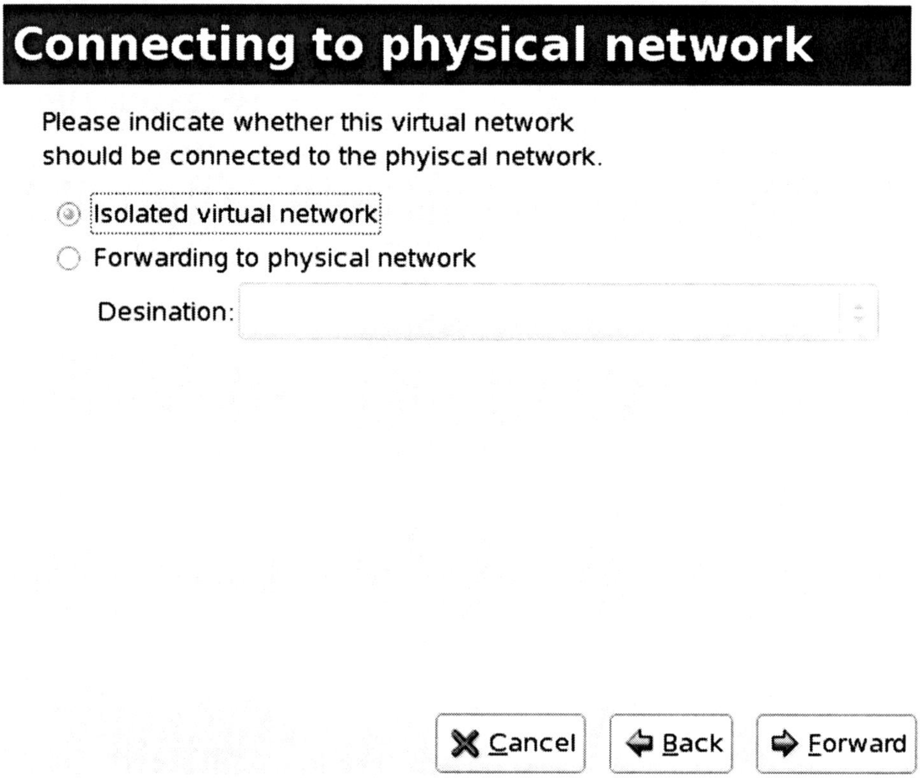

Figure 16.35. Connecting to physical network

If you select Forwarding to physical network, choose whether the Destination should be NAT to any physical device or NAT to physical device eth0.

Click Forward to continue.

6. You are now ready to create the network. Check the configuration of your network and click Finish.

Ready to create network

Summary

Network name: network1

IPv4 network

Network: 192.168.100.0/24
Gateway: 192.168.100.1
Netmask: 255.255.255.0

DHCP

Start address: 192.168.100.128
End address: 192.168.100.254

Forwarding

Connectivity: Isolated virtual network

[Cancel] [Back] [Finish]

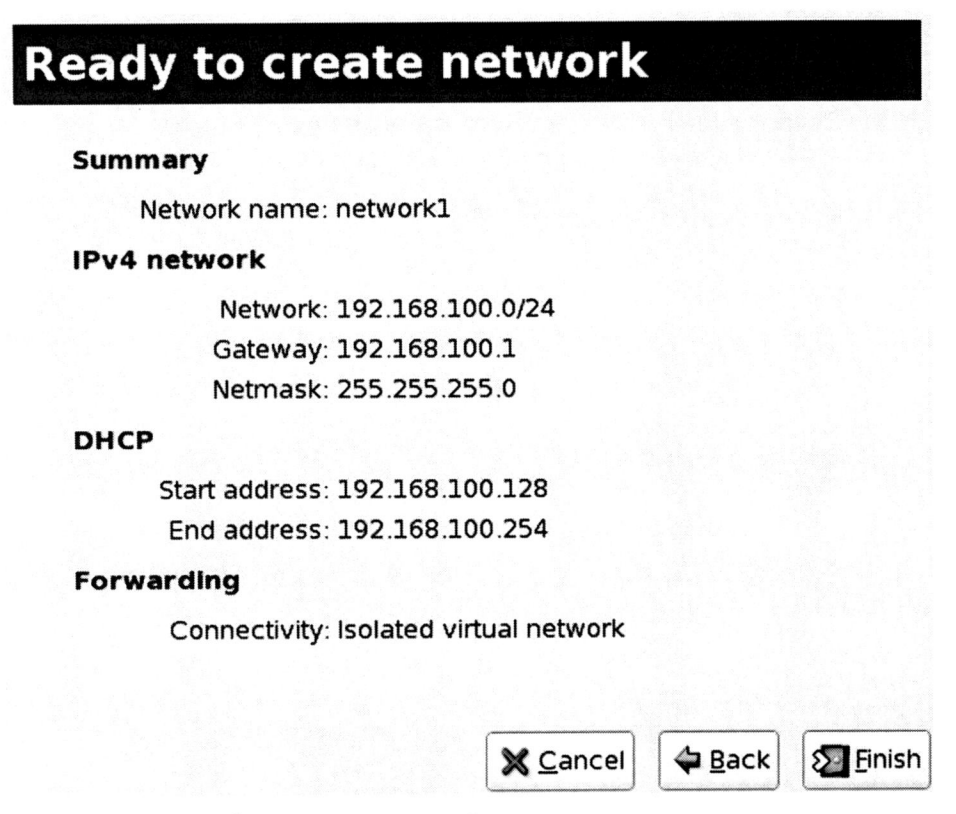

Figure 16.36. Ready to create network

Fedora 12

7. The new virtual network is now available in the Virtual Network tab of the Host Details menu.

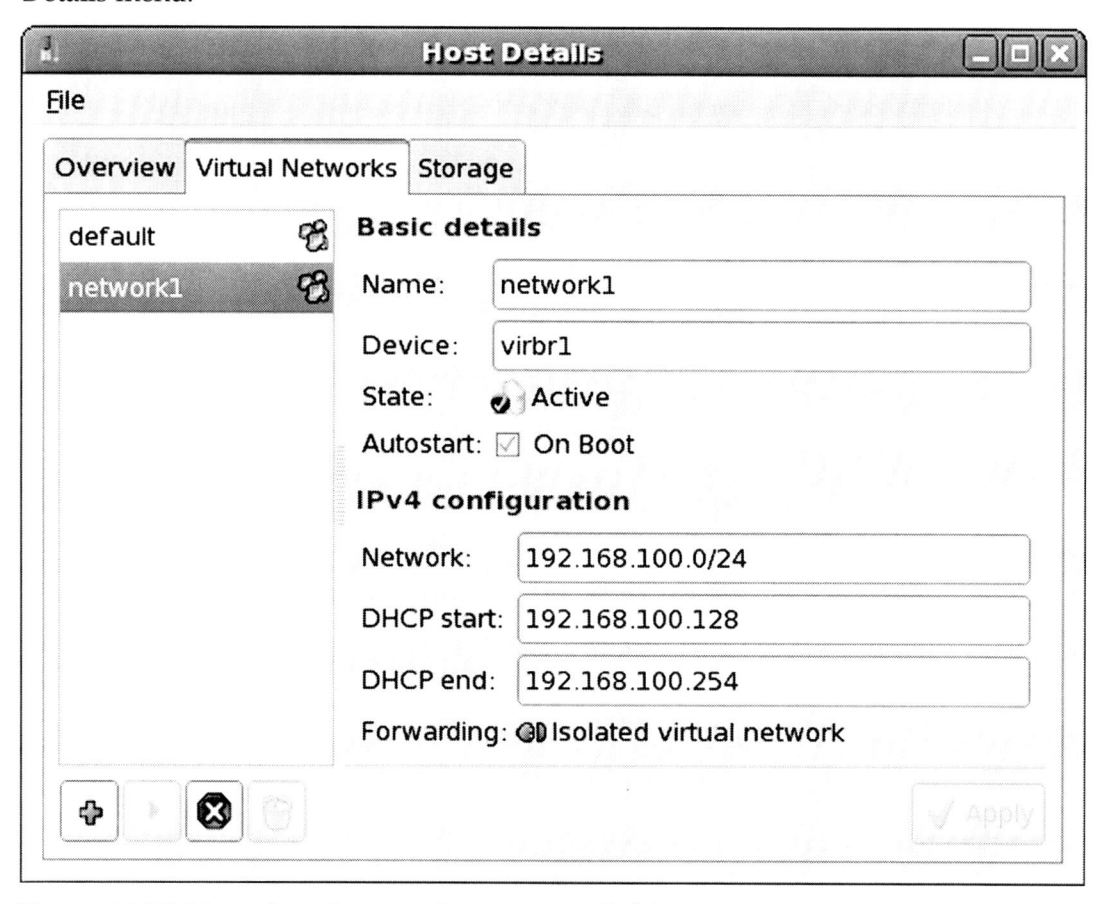

Figure 16.37. New virtual network is now available

Part V.
Tips and Tricks

Tips and Tricks to Enhance Productivity

These chapters contain useful hints and tips to improve virtualization performance, scale and stability.

Chapter 17.
Tips and tricks

17.1. Automatically starting guests

This section covers how to make virtualized guests start automatically during the host system's boot phase.

This example uses virsh to set a guest, *TestServer*, to automatically start when the host boots.

```
# virsh autostart TestServer
Domain TestServer marked as autostarted
```

The guest now automatically starts with the host.

To stop a guest automatically booting use the *--disable* parameter

```
# virsh autostart --disable TestServer
Domain TestServer unmarked as autostarted
```

The guest no longer automatically starts with the host.

17.2. Changing between the KVM and Xen hypervisors

This section covers changing between the KVM and Xen hypervisors.

Fedora only supports one active hypervisor at a time.

> **Migrating virtualized guests between hypervisors**
>
> Presently, there is no application for switching Xen-based guests to KVM or KVM-based guests to Xen. Guests can only be used on the hypervisor type that they were created on.

17.2.1. Xen to KVM

The following procedure covers changing from the Xen hypervisor to the KVM hypervisor. This procedure assumes the kernel-xen package is installed and enabled.

1. Install the KVM package

    Install the kvm package if you have not already done so.

    ```
    # yum install kvm
    ```

Virtualization Guide

2. Verify which kernel is in use

   The kernel-xen package may be installed. Use the uname command to determine which kernel is running:

   ```
   $ uname -r
   2.6.23.14-107.fc8xen
   ```

   The "2.6.23.14-107.fc8xen" kernel is running on the system. If the default kernel, "2.6.23.14-107.fc8", is running you can skip the substep.

   1. Changing the Xen kernel to the default kernel

      The grub.conf file determines which kernel is booted. To change the default kernel edit the /boot/grub/grub.conf file as shown below.

      ```
      default=1
      timeout=5
      splashimage=(hd0,0)/grub/splash.xpm.gz
      hiddenmenu
      title Fedora (2.6.23.14-107.fc8)
              root (hd0,0)
              kernel /vmlinuz-2.6.23.14-107.fc8 ro
      root=/dev/VolGroup00/LogVol00 rhgb quiet
              initrd /initrd-2.6.23.14-107.fc8.img
      title Fedora (2.6.23.14-107.fc8xen)
              root (hd0,0)
              kernel /xen.gz-2.6.23.14-107.fc8
              module /vmlinuz-2.6.23.14-107.fc8xen ro
      root=/dev/VolGroup00/LogVol00 rhgb quiet
              module /initrd-2.6.23.14-107.fc8xen.img
      ```

      Notice the default=1 parameter. This is instructing the GRUB boot loader to boot the second entry, the Xen kernel. Change the default to 0 (or the number for the default kernel):

      ```
      default=0
      timeout=5
      splashimage=(hd0,0)/grub/splash.xpm.gz
      hiddenmenu
      title Fedora (2.6.23.14-107.fc8)
              root (hd0,0)
              kernel /vmlinuz-2.6.23.14-107.fc8 ro
      root=/dev/VolGroup00/LogVol00 rhgb quiet
              initrd /initrd-2.6.23.14-107.fc8.img
      title Fedora (2.6.23.14-107.fc8xen)
              root (hd0,0)
              kernel /xen.gz-2.6.23.14-107.fc8
              module /vmlinuz-2.6.23.14-107.fc8xen ro
      root=/dev/VolGroup00/LogVol00 rhgb quiet
              module /initrd-2.6.23.14-107.fc8xen.img
      ```

3. Reboot to load the new kernel

   Reboot the system. The computer will restart with the default kernel. The KVM module should be automatically loaded with the kernel. Verify KVM is running:

   ```
   $ lsmod | grep kvm
   kvm_intel              85992  1
   kvm                   222368  2 ksm,kvm_intel
   ```

   The kvm module and either the kvm_intel module or the kvm_amd module are present if everything worked.

17.2.2. KVM to Xen

The following procedure covers changing from the KVM hypervisor to the Xen hypervisor. This procedure assumes the kvm package is installed and enabled.

1. Install the Xen packages

   Install the kernel-xen and xen package if you have not already done so.

   ```
   # yum install kernel-xen xen
   ```

   The kernel-xen package may be installed but disabled.

2. Verify which kernel is in use

   Use the uname command to determine which kernel is running.

   ```
   $ uname -r
   2.6.23.14-107.fc8
   ```

   The "2.6.23.14-107.fc8" kernel is running on the system. This is the default kernel. If the kernel has xen on the end (for example, 2.6.23.14-107.fc8xen) then the Xen kernel is running and you can skip the substep.

   1. Changing the default kernel to the Xen kernel

      The grub.conf file determines which kernel is booted. To change the default kernel edit the /boot/grub/grub.conf file as shown below.

      ```
      default=0
      timeout=5
      splashimage=(hd0,0)/grub/splash.xpm.gz
      hiddenmenu
      title Fedora (2.6.23.14-107.fc8)
              root (hd0,0)
              kernel /vmlinuz-2.6.23.14-107.fc8 ro
      root=/dev/VolGroup00/LogVol00 rhgb quiet
              initrd /initrd-2.6.23.14-107.fc8.img
      title Fedora (2.6.23.14-107.fc8xen)
              root (hd0,0)
      ```

```
        kernel /xen.gz-2.6.23.14-107.fc8
        module /vmlinuz-2.6.23.14-107.fc8xen ro
root=/dev/VolGroup00/LogVol00 rhgb quiet
        module /initrd-2.6.23.14-107.fc8xen.img
```

Notice the default=0 parameter. This is instructing the GRUB boot loader to boot the first entry, the default kernel. Change the default to *1* (or the number for the Xen kernel):

```
default=1
timeout=5
splashimage=(hd0,0)/grub/splash.xpm.gz
hiddenmenu
title Fedora (2.6.23.14-107.fc8)
        root (hd0,0)
        kernel /vmlinuz-2.6.23.14-107.fc8 ro
root=/dev/VolGroup00/LogVol00 rhgb quiet
        initrd /initrd-2.6.23.14-107.fc82.6.23.14-107.fc8.img
title Fedora (2.6.23.14-107.fc8xen)
        root (hd0,0)
        kernel /xen.gz-2.6.23.14-107.fc8
        module /vmlinuz-2.6.23.14-107.fc8xen ro
root=/dev/VolGroup00/LogVol00 rhgb quiet
        module /initrd-2.6.23.14-107.fc8xen.img
```

3. Reboot to load the new kernel

   Reboot the system. The computer will restart with the Xen kernel. Verify with the uname command:

   ```
   $ uname -r
   2.6.23.14-107.fc8xen
   ```

   If the output has xen on the end the Xen kernel is running.

17.3. Using qemu-img

The qemu-img command line tool is used for formatting various file systems used by Xen and KVM. qemu-img should be used for formatting virtualized guest images, additional storage devices and network storage. qemu-img options and usages are listed below.

Formatting and creating new images or devices

Create the new disk image filename of size size and format format.

```
# qemu-img create [-6] [-e] [-b base_image] [-f format] filename [size]
```

If base_image is specified, then the image will record only the differences from base_image. No size needs to be specified in this case. base_image will never be modified unless you use the "commit" monitor command.

Convert an existing image to another format

The convert option is used for converting a recognized format to another image format.

Command format:

```
# qemu-img convert [-c] [-e] [-f format] filename [-O output_format]
output_filename
```

convert the disk image filename to disk image output_filename using format output_format. it can be optionally encrypted ("-e" option) or compressed ("-c" option).

only the format "qcow" supports encryption or compression. the compression is read-only. it means that if a compressed sector is rewritten, then it is rewritten as uncompressed data.

The encryption uses the AES format with very secure 128 bit keys. use a long password (16 characters) to get maximum protection.

image conversion is also useful to get smaller image when using a format which can grow, such as qcow or cow. The empty sectors are detected and suppressed from the destination image.

getting image information

the info parameter displays information about a disk image. the format for the info option is as follows:

```
# qemu-img info [-f format] filename
```

give information about the disk image filename. use it in particular to know the size reserved on disk which can be different from the displayed size. if vm snapshots are stored in the disk image, they are displayed too.

Supported formats

The format of an image is usually guessed automatically. The following formats are supported:

raw

> Raw disk image format (default). This format has the advantage of being simple and easily exportable to all other emulators. If your file system supports holes (for example in ext2 or ext3 on Linux or NTFS on Windows), then only the written sectors will reserve space. Use qemu-img info to know the real size used by the image or ls -ls on Unix/Linux.

qcow2

> QEMU image format, the most versatile format. Use it to have smaller images (useful if your file system does not supports holes, for example: on Windows), optional AES encryption, zlib based compression and support of multiple VM snapshots.

qcow

   Old QEMU image format. Only included for compatibility with older versions.

cow

   User Mode Linux Copy On Write image format. The cow format is included only for compatibility with previous versions. It does not work with Windows.

vmdk

   VMware 3 and 4 compatible image format.

cloop

   Linux Compressed Loop image, useful only to reuse directly compressed CD-ROM images present for example in the Knoppix CD-ROMs.

17.4. Overcommitting with KVM

The KVM hypervisor supports overcommitting CPUs and overcommitting memory. Overcommitting is allocating more virtualized CPUs or memory than there are physical resources on the system. With CPU overcommit, under-utilized virtualized servers or desktops can run on fewer servers which saves power and money.

> **Xen support**
>
> CPU overcommitting is not supported for the Xen hypervisor. Overcommitting CPUs with the Xen hypervisor may cause system instability and crashes of the host and virtualized guests.

Overcommitting memory

Most operating systems and applications do not use 100% of the available RAM all the time. This behavior can be exploited with KVM to use more memory for virtualized guests than what is physically available.

With KVM, virtual machines are Linux processes. Guests on the KVM hypervisor do not have blocks of physical RAM assigned to them instead they function as processes. Each process is allocated memory when it requests more memory. KVM uses this to allocate memory for guests when the guest operating system requests more or less memory. The guest only uses slightly more physical memory than the virtualized operating system appears to use.

When physical memory is nearly completely used or a process is inactive for some time, Linux moves the process's memory to swap. Swap is usually a partition on a hard disk drive or solid state drive which Linux uses to extend virtual memory. Swap is significantly slower than RAM.

Fedora 12

As KVM virtual machines are Linux processes, memory used by virtualized guests can be put into swap if the guest is idle or not in heavy use. Memory can be committed over the total size of the swap and physical RAM. This can cause issues if virtualized guests use their total RAM. Without sufficient swap space for the virtual machine processes to be swapped to the pdflush process starts. pdflush kills processes to free memory so the system does not crash. pdflush may destroy virtualized guests or other system processes which may cause file system errors and may leave virtualized guests unbootable.

> **Warning**
>
> If sufficient swap is not available guest operating systems will be forcibly shut down. This may leave guests inoperable. Avoid this by never overcommitting more memory than there is swap available.

The swap partition is used for swapping underused memory to the hard drive to speed up memory performance. The default size of the swap partition is calculated from amount of RAM and overcommit ratio. It is recommended to make your swap partition larger if you intend to overcommit memory with KVM. A recommended overcommit ratio is 50% (0.5). The formula used is:

```
(0.5 * RAM) + (overcommit ratio * RAM) = Recommended swap size
```

The Red Hat Knowledgebase has an article on safely and efficiently determining the size of the swap partition — refer to *Knowledgebase*[1].

It is possible to run with an overcommit ratio of ten times the number of virtualized guests over the amount of physical RAM in the system. This only works with certain application loads (for example desktop virtualization with under 100% usage). Setting overcommit ratios is not a hard formula, you must test and customize the ratio for your environment.

Overcommitting virtualized CPUs

The KVM hypervisor supports overcommitting virtualized CPUs. Virtualized CPUs can be overcommitted as far as load limits of virtualized guests allow. Use caution when overcommitting VCPUs as loads near 100% may cause dropped requests or unusable response times.

Virtualized CPUs are overcommitted best when each virtualized guest only has a single VCPU. The Linux scheduler is very efficient with this type of load. KVM should safely support guests with loads under 100% at a ratio of 5 VCPUs Overcommitting single VCPU virtualized guests is not an issue.

---

[1] *http://kbase.redhat.com/faq/docs/DOC-15252*

Virtualization Guide

You cannot overcommit symmetric multiprocessing guests on more than the physical number of processing cores. For example a guest with four VCPUs should not be run on a host with a dual core processor. Overcommitting symmetric multiprocessing guests in over the physical number of processing cores will cause significant performance degradation.

Assigning guests VCPUs up to the number of physical cores is appropriate and works as expected. For example, running virtualized guests with four VCPUs on a quad core host. Guests with less than 100% loads should function effectively in this setup.

> **Always test first**
>
> Do not overcommit memory or CPUs in a production environment without extensive testing. Applications which use 100% of memory or processing resources may become unstable in overcommitted environments. Test before deploying.

17.5. Modifying /etc/grub.conf

This section describes how to safely and correctly change your /etc/grub.conf file to use the virtualization kernel. You must use the xen kernel to use the Xen hypervisor. Copy your existing xen kernel entry make sure you copy all of the important lines or your system will panic upon boot (initrd will have a length of '0'). If you require xen hypervisor specific values you must append them to the xen line of your grub entry.

The output below is an example of a grub.conf entry from a system running the kernel-xen package. The grub.conf on your system may vary. The important part in the example below is the section from the title line to the next new line.

```
#boot=/dev/sda
default=0
timeout=15
#splashimage=(hd0,0)/grub/splash.xpm.gz hiddenmenu
serial --unit=0 --speed=115200 --word=8 --parity=no --stop=1
terminal --timeout=10 serial console

title Fedora (2.6.23.14-107.fc8xen)
    root (hd0,0)
    kernel /xen.gz-2.6.23.14-107.fc8 com1=115200,8n1
    module /vmlinuz-2.6.23.14-107.fc8xen ro root=/dev/VolGroup00/LogVol00
    module /initrd-2.6.23.14-107.fc8xen.img
```

> **An important point regarding editing grub.conf...**
>
> Your grub.conf could look very different if it has been manually edited before or copied from an example.

To set the amount of memory assigned to your host system at boot time to 256MB you need to append dom0_mem=256M to the xen line in your grub.conf. A modified version of the grub configuration file in the previous example:

Fedora 12

```
#boot=/dev/sda
default=0
timeout=15
#splashimage=(hd0,0)/grub/splash.xpm.gz
hiddenmenu
serial --unit=0 --speed=115200 --word=8 --parity=no --stop=1
terminal --timeout=10 serial console

title Fedora (2.6.23.14-107.fc8xen)
    root (hd0,0)
    kernel /xen.gz-2.6.23.14-107.fc8 com1=115200,8n1 dom0_mem=256MB
    module /vmlinuz-2.6.23.14-107.fc8xen ro
    root=/dev/VolGroup00/LogVol00
```

module /initrd-2.6.23.14-107.fc8xen.img

17.6. Verifying virtualization extensions

Use this section to determine whether your system has the hardware virtualization extensions. Virtualization extensions (Intel VT or AMD-V) are required for full virtualization.

> **Can I use virtualization without the virtualization extensions?**
>
> If hardware virtualization extensions are not present you can use Xen para-virtualization with the fedora kernel-xen package.

Run the following command to verify the CPU virtualization extensions are available:

```
$ grep -E 'svm|vmx' /proc/cpuinfo
```

The following output contains a vmx entry indicating an Intel processor with the Intel VT extensions:

```
flags   : fpu tsc msr pae mce cx8 apic mtrr mca cmov pat pse36 clflush
    dts acpi mmx fxsr sse sse2 ss ht  tm syscall lm constant_tsc pni monitor
ds_cpl
    vmx est tm2 cx16 xtpr lahf_lm
```

The following output contains an svm entry indicating an AMD processor with the AMD-V extensions:

```
flags   :   fpu tsc msr pae mce cx8 apic mtrr mca cmov pat pse36 clflush
    mmx fxsr sse sse2 ht syscall nx mmxext fxsr_opt lm 3dnowext 3dnow pni cx16
    lahf_lm cmp_legacy svm cr8legacy ts fid vid ttp tm stc
```

The "flags:" content may appear multiple times for each hyperthread, core or CPU on in the system.

The virtualization extensions may be disabled in the BIOS. If the extensions do not appear or full virtualization does not work refer to *Procedure 19.1, "Enabling virtualization extensions in BIOS"*.

Virtualization Guide

17.7. Identifying guest type and implementation

The script below can identify if the environment an application or script is running in is a para-virtualized, a fully virtualized guest or on the hypervisor.

```bash
#!/bin/bash
declare -i IS_HVM=0
declare -i IS_PARA=0
check_hvm()
{
    IS_X86HVM="$(strings /proc/acpi/dsdt | grep int-xen)"
      if [ x"${IS_X86HVM}" != x ]; then
        echo "Guest type is full-virt x86hvm"
        IS_HVM=1
    fi
}
check_para()
{
    if $(grep -q control_d /proc/xen/capabilities); then
        echo "Host is dom0"
        IS_PARA=1
    else
        echo "Guest is para-virt domU"
        IS_PARA=1
    fi
}
if [ -f /proc/acpi/dsdt ]; then
    check_hvm
fi

if [ ${IS_HVM} -eq 0 ]; then
    if [ -f /proc/xen/capabilities ] ; then
         check_para
    fi
      fi
if [ ${IS_HVM} -eq 0 -a ${IS_PARA} -eq 0 ]; then
    echo "Baremetal platform"
fi
```

> **Examining hosts**
>
> For examining hosts, use the virsh capabilites command.

17.8. Generating a new unique MAC address

In some case you will need to generate a new and unique *MAC address* (see page 243) for a guest. There is no command line tool available to generate a new MAC address at the time of writing. The script provided below can generate a new MAC address for your guests. Save the script to your guest as macgen.py. Now from that directory you can run the script using ./macgen.py . and it will generate a new MAC address. A sample output would look like the following:

225

```
$ ./macgen.py
00:16:3e:20:b0:11

#!/usr/bin/python
# macgen.py script to generate a MAC address for virtualized guests on Xen
#
import random
#
def randomMAC():
    mac = [ 0x00, 0x16, 0x3e,
            random.randint(0x00, 0x7f),
            random.randint(0x00, 0xff),
            random.randint(0x00, 0xff) ]
    return ':'.join(map(lambda x: "%02x" % x, mac))
#
print randomMAC()
```

Another method to generate a new MAC for your guest

You can also use the built-in modules of python-virtinst to generate a new MAC address and UUID for use in a guest configuration file:

```
# echo  'import virtinst.util ; print\
 virtinst.util.uuidToString(virtinst.util.randomUUID())' | python
# echo  'import virtinst.util ; print virtinst.util.randomMAC()' | python
```

The script above can also be implemented as a script file as seen below.

```
#!/usr/bin/env python
#  -*- mode: python; -*-
print ""
print "New UUID:"
import virtinst.util ; print
virtinst.util.uuidToString(virtinst.util.randomUUID())
print "New MAC:"
import virtinst.util ; print virtinst.util.randomMAC()
print ""
```

17.9. Very Secure ftpd

vsftpd can provide access to installation trees for para-virtualized guests or other data. If you have not installed vsftpd during the server installation you can grab the RPM package from your Server directory of your installation media and install it using the rpm -ivh vsftpd*.rpm (note that the RPM package must be in your current directory).

1. To configure vsftpd, edit /etc/passwd using vipw and change the ftp user's home directory to the directory where you are going to keep the installation trees for your para-virtualized guests. An example entry for the FTP user would look like the following:
   ```
   ftp:x:14:50:FTP User:/xen/pub:/sbin/nologin
   ```

2. to have vsftpd start automatically during system boot use the chkconfig utility to enable the automatic start up of vsftpd.

3. verify that vsftpd is not enabled using the chkconfig --list vsftpd:
```
$ chkconfig --list vsftpd
vsftpd          0:off   1:off   2:off   3:off   4:off   5:off   6:off
```

4. run the chkconfig --levels 345 vsftpd on to start vsftpd automatically for run levels 3, 4 and 5.

5. use the chkconfig --list vsftpd command to verify vsftdp has been enabled to start during system boot:
```
$ chkconfig --list vsftpd
vsftpd          0:off   1:off   2:off   3:on    4:on    5:on    6:off
```

6. use the service vsftpd start vsftpd to start the vsftpd service:
```
$service vsftpd start vsftpd
Starting vsftpd for vsftpd:                                [  OK  ]
```

17.10. Configuring LUN Persistence

This section covers how to implement *LUN* persistence in guests and on the host machine with and without multipath.

Implementing LUN persistence without multipath

If your system is not using multipath, you can use udev to implement LUN persistence. Before implementing LUN persistence in your system, ensure that you acquire the proper UUIDs. Once you acquire these, you can configure LUN persistence by editing the scsi_id file that resides in the /etc directory. Once you have this file open in a text editor, you must comment out this line:

```
# options=-b
```

Then replace it with this parameter:

```
# options=-g
```

This tells udev to monitor all system SCSI devices for returning UUIDs. To determine the system UUIDs, use the scsi_id command:

```
# scsi_id -g -s /block/sdc
*3600a0b80001327510000015427b625e*
```

The long string of characters in the output is the UUID. The UUID does not change when you add a new device to your system. Acquire the UUID for each the device in order to create rules for the devices. To create new device rules, edit the 20-names.rules file in the /etc/udev/rules.d directory. The device naming rules follow this format:

```
# KERNEL="sd*", BUS="scsi", PROGRAM="sbin/scsi_id", RESULT="UUID", NAME="devicename"
```

Replace your existing *UUID* and *devicename* with the above UUID retrieved entry. The rule should resemble the following:

```
KERNEL="sd*",   BUS="scsi",   PROGRAM="sbin/scsi_id",
RESULT="3600a0b80001327510000015427b625e", NAME="mydevicename"
```

This enables all devices that match the /dev/sd* pattern to inspect the given UUID. When it finds a matching device, it creates a device node called */dev/devicename*. For this example, the device node is */dev/mydevice* . Finally, append the /etc/rc.local file with this line:

```
/sbin/start_udev
```

Implementing LUN persistence with multipath

To implement LUN persistence in a multipath environment, you must define the alias names for the multipath devices. For this example, you must define four device aliases by editing the multipath.conf file that resides in the /etc/ directory:

```
multipath  {
        wwid       3600a0b80001327510000015427b625e
        alias      oramp1
}
multipath  {
        wwid       3600a0b80001327510000015427b6
        alias      oramp2
}
multipath  {
        wwid       3600a0b80001327510000015427b625e
        alias      oramp3
}
multipath  {
        wwid       3600a0b80001327510000015427b625e
        alias      oramp4
}
```

This defines 4 LUNs: /dev/mpath/oramp1, /dev/mpath/oramp2, /dev/mpath/oramp3, and dev/mpath/oramp4. The devices will reside in the /dev/mpath directory. These LUN names are persistent over reboots as it creates the alias names on the wwid of the LUNs.

17.11. Disable SMART disk monitoring for guests

SMART disk monitoring can be disabled as we are running on virtual disks and the physical storage is managed by the host.

```
/sbin/service smartd stop
/sbin/chkconfig --del smartd
```

17.12. Cloning guest configuration files

You can copy an existing configuration file to create an all new guest. You must modify the name parameter of the guests' configuration file. The new, unique name then appears in the hypervisor and is viewable by the management utilities. You must generate an all new UUID as well by using the uuidgen command. Then for the vif entries you must define a unique MAC address for each guest (if you are copying a guest configuration from an existing guest, you can create a script to handle it). For the xen bridge information, if you move an existing guest configuration file to a new host, you must update the xenbr entry to match your local networking configuration. For the Device entries, you must modify the entries in the 'disk=' section to point to the correct guest image.

You must also modify these system configuration settings on your guest. You must modify the HOSTNAME entry of the /etc/sysconfig/network file to match the new guest's hostname.

You must modify the HWADDR address of the /etc/sysconfig/network-scripts/ifcfg-eth0 file to match the output from ifconfig eth0 file and if you use static IP addresses, you must modify the IPADDR entry.

17.13. Duplicating an existing guest and its configuration file

This section outlines copying an existing configuration file to create a new guest. There are key parameters in your guest's configuration file you must be aware of, and modify, to successfully duplicate a guest.

name

> The name of your guest as it is known to the hypervisor and displayed in the management utilities. This entry should be unique on your system.

uuid

> A unique handle for the guest, a new UUID can be regenerated using the uuidgen command. A sample UUID output:
> ```
> $ uuidgen
> a984a14f-4191-4d14-868e-329906b211e5
> ```

vif

> - The *MAC address* must define a unique MAC address for each guest. This is automatically done if the standard tools are used. If you are copying a guest configuration from an existing guest you can use the script *Section 17.8, "Generating a new unique MAC address"*.
> - If you are moving or duplicating an existing guest configuration file to a new host you have to make sure you adjust the xenbr entry to correspond with your local networking configuration (you can obtain the bridge information using the command brctl show command).
> - Device entries, make sure you adjust the entries in the disk= section to point to the correct guest image.

Fedora 12

Now, adjust the system configuration settings on your guest:

/etc/sysconfig/network

Modify the HOSTNAME entry to the guest's new hostname.

/etc/sysconfig/network-scripts/ifcfg-eth0

- Modify the HWADDR address to the output from ifconfig eth0
- Modify the IPADDR entry if a static IP address is used.

Chapter 18.
Creating custom libvirt scripts

This section provides some information which may be useful to programmers and system administrators intending to write custom scripts to make their lives easier by using libvirt.

Chapter 17, Tips and tricks is recommended reading for programmers thinking of writing new applications which use libvirt.

18.1. Using XML configuration files with virsh

virsh can handle XML configuration files. You may want to use this to your advantage for scripting large deployments with special options. You can add devices defined in an XML file to a running para-virtualized guest. For example, to add a ISO file as hdc to a running guest create an XML file:

```
# cat satelliteiso.xml
<disk type="file" device="disk">
    <driver name="file"/>
    <source file="/var/lib/libvirt/images/rhn-satellite-5.0.1-11-redhat-linux-as-i386-4-embedded-oracle.iso"/>
    <target dev="hdc"/>
    <readonly/>
</disk>
```

Run virsh attach-device to attach the ISO as hdc to a guest called "satellite" :

```
# virsh attach-device satellite satelliteiso.xml
```

Part VI.
Troubleshooting

Introduction to Troubleshooting and Problem Solving

The following chapters provide information to assist you in troubleshooting issues you may encounter using virtualization.

> **Important note on virtualization issues**
>
> Your particular problem may not appear in this book due to ongoing development which creates and fixes bugs. For the most up to date list of known bugs, issues and bug fixes read the Fedora Release Notes for your version and hardware architecture. The Release Notes can be found in the documentation section of the Fedora website, *http://docs.fedoraproject.org*.

Chapter 19.
Troubleshooting

This chapter covers common problems and solutions with Fedora virtualization.

19.1. Loop device errors

If file based guest images are used you may have to increase the number of configured loop devices. The default configuration allows up to 8 active loop devices. If more than 8 file based guests or loop devices are needed the number of loop devices configured can be adjusted in /etc/modprobe.conf. Edit /etc/modprobe.conf and add the following line to it:

```
options loop max_loop=64
```

This example uses 64 but you can specify another number to set the maximum loop value. You may also have to implement loop device backed guests on your system. To employ loop device backed guests for a para-virtualized guest, use the phy: block device or tap:aio commands. To employ loop device backed guests for a full virtualized system, use the phy: device or file: file commands.

19.2. Enabling Intel VT and AMD-V virtualization hardware extensions in BIOS

This section describes how to identify hardware virtualization extensions and enable them in your BIOS if they are disabled.

The Intel VT extensions can be disabled in the BIOS. Certain laptop vendors have disabled the Intel VT extensions by default in their CPUs.

The virtualization extensions can not be disabled in the BIOS for AMD-V (capable processors installed in a Rev 2 socket.

The virtualization extensions are sometimes disabled in BIOS, usually by laptop manufacturers. Refer to *Section 19.2, "Enabling Intel VT and AMD-V virtualization hardware extensions in BIOS"* for instructions on enabling disabled virtualization extensions.

Verify the virtualization extensions are enabled in BIOS. The BIOS settings for *Intel®*[1] VT or AMD-V are usually in the Chipset or Processor menus. The menu names may vary from this

---

[1] *http://www.intel.com*

Fedora 12

guide, the virtualization extension settings may be found in Security Settings or other non standard menu names.

Procedure 19.1. Enabling virtualization extensions in BIOS

1. Reboot the computer and open the system's BIOS menu. This can usually be done by pressing delete or Alt + F4.

2. Select Restore Defaults, and then select Save & Exit.

3. Power off the machine and disconnect the power supply.

4. Power on the machine and open the BIOS Setup Utility. Open the Processor section and enable Intel®Virtualization Technology or AMD-V. The values may also be called Virtualization Extensions on some machines. Select Save & Exit.

5. Power off the machine and disconnect the power supply.

6. Run cat /proc/cpuinfo | grep vmx svm. If the command outputs, the virtualization extensions are now enabled. If there is no output your system may not have the virtualization extensions or the correct BIOS setting enabled.

Appendix A.
Additional resources

To learn more about virtualization and Linux, refer to the following resources.

A.1. Online resources

- *http://www.cl.cam.ac.uk/research/srg/netos/xen/* The project website of the *Xen*™ para-virtualization machine manager from which the Fedora kernel-xen package is derived. The site maintains the upstream xen project binaries and source code and also contains information, architecture overviews, documentation, and related links regarding xen and its associated technologies.
- The Xen Community website: *http://www.xen.org/*
- *http://www.libvirt.org/* is the official website for the libvirt virtualization API.
- *http://virt-manager.et.redhat.com/* is the project website for the Virtual Machine Manager (virt-manager), the graphical application for managing virtual machines.
- Open Virtualization Center: *http://www.openvirtualization.com*
- Fedora Documentation: *http://docs.fedoraproject.org*
- Virtualization technologies overview: *http://virt.kernelnewbies.org*
- Red Hat Emerging Technologies group: *http://et.redhat.com*

A.2. Installed documentation

- /usr/share/doc/xen-<*version-number*>/ is the directory which contains information about the Xen para-virtualization hypervisor and associated management tools, including various example configurations, hardware-specific information, and the current Xen upstream user documentation.
- man virsh and /usr/share/doc/libvirt-<*version-number*> — Contains sub commands and options for the virsh virtual machine management utility as well as comprehensive information about the libvirt virtualization library API.
- /usr/share/doc/gnome-applet-vm-<*version-number*> — Documentation for the GNOME graphical panel applet that monitors and manages locally-running virtual machines.

- /usr/share/doc/libvirt-python-<*version-number*> — Provides details on the Python bindings for the libvirt library. The libvirt-python package allows python developers to create programs that interface with the libvirt virtualization management library.
- /usr/share/doc/python-virtinst-<*version-number*> — Provides documentation on the virt-install command that helps in starting installations of Fedora and Linux related distributions inside of virtual machines.
- /usr/share/doc/virt-manager-<*version-number*> — Provides documentation on the Virtual Machine Manager, which provides a graphical tool for administering virtual machines.

Appendix B.
Revision History

Revision History	Data	Author
Revision 12.1.3 Split from Red Hat Enterprise Linux 5.4 Virtualization Guide version 5.4-61.	Mon Oct 12 2009	Christopher Curran

Colophon

This manual was written in the DocBook XML v4.3 format.

This book is based on the work of Jan Mark Holzer and Chris Curran.

Other writing credits go to:

- Don Dutile contributed technical editing for the para-virtualized drivers section.
- Barry Donahue contributed technical editing for the para-virtualized drivers section.
- Rick Ring contributed technical editing for the Virtual Machine Manager Section.
- Michael Kearey contributed technical editing for the sections on using XML configuration files with virsh and virtualized floppy drives.
- Marco Grigull contributed technical editing for the software compatibility and performance section.
- Eugene Teo contributed technical editing for the Managing Guests with virsh section.

Publican, the publishing tool which produced this book, was written by Jeffrey Fearn.

The Red Hat Localization Team consists of the following people:

East Asian Languages

- Simplified Chinese
  - Leah Wei Liu
- Traditional Chinese
  - Chester Cheng
  - Terry Chuang
- Japanese
  - Junko Ito
- Korean
  - Eun-ju Kim

Latin Languages
- French
  - Sam Friedmann
- German
  - Hedda Peters
- Italian
  - Francesco Valente
- Brazilian Portuguese
  - Glaucia de Freitas
  - Leticia de Lima
- Spanish
  - Angela Garcia
  - Gladys Guerrero
- Russian
  - Yuliya Poyarkova

Glossary

This glossary is intended to define the terms used in this Installation Guide.

Bare-metal

> The term bare-metal refers to the underlying physical architecture of a computer. Running an operating system on bare-metal is another way of referring to running an unmodified version of the operating system on the physical hardware. Examples of operating systems running on bare metal are *dom0* or a normally installed operating system.

dom0

> Also known as the *Host* or host operating system.
>
> dom0 refers to the host instance of Linux running the Hypervisor which facilitates virtualization of guest operating systems. Dom0 runs on and manages the physical hardware and resource allocation for itself and the guest operating systems.

Domains

> *domU* and *Domains* are both domains. Domains run on the *Hypervisor*. The term domains has a similar meaning to *Virtual machines* and the two are technically interchangeable. A domain is a Virtual Machine.

domU

> domU refers to the guest operating system which run on the host system (*Domains*).

Full virtualization

> Xen and KVM can use full virtualization. Full virtualization uses hardware features of the processor to provide total abstraction of the underlying physical system (*Bare-metal*) and create a new virtual system in which the guest operating systems can run. No modifications are needed in the guest operating system. The guest operating system and any applications on the guest are not aware of the virtualized environment and run normally. Para-virtualization requires a modified version of the Linux operating system.

Fully virtualized

> See *Full virtualization*.

Guest system
: Also known as guests, virtual machines or *domU*.

Hardware Virtual Machine
: See *Full virtualization*

Hypervisor
: The hypervisor is the software layer that abstracts the hardware from the operating system permitting multiple operating systems to run on the same hardware. The hypervisor runs on a host operating system allowing other virtualized operating systems to run on the host's hardware.

Host
: The host operating system, also known as *dom0*.

 The host operating system environment runs the virtualization software for *Fully virtualized* and *Para-virtualized* guest systems.

I/O
: Short for input/output (pronounced "eye-oh"). The term I/O describes any program, operation or device that transfers data to or from a computer and to or from a peripheral device. Every transfer is an output from one device and an input into another. Devices such as keyboards and mouses are input-only devices while devices such as printers are output-only. A writable CD-ROM is both an input and an output device.

Kernel-based Virtual Machine
: KVM (Kernel-based Virtual Machine) is a *Full virtualization* solution for Linux on AMD64 and Intel 64 hardware. VM is a Linux kernel module built for the standard Linux kernel. KVM can run multiple, unmodified virtualized guest Windows and Linux operating systems. KVM is a hypervisor which uses the libvirt virtualization tools (virt-manager and virsh).

 KVM is a set of Linux kernel modules which manage devices, memory and management APIs for the Hypervisor module itself. Virtualized guests are run as Linux processes and threads which are controlled by these modules.

LUN
: A Logical Unit Number (LUN) is a number assigned to a logical unit (a SCSI protocol entity).

Migration

Migration is name for the process of moving a virtualized guest from one host to another. Migration can be conducted offline (where the guest is suspended and then moved) or live (where a guest is moved without suspending). Xen fully virtualized guests, Xen para-virtualized guest and KVM fully virtualized guests can all be migrated.

Migration is a key feature of virtualization as software is completely separated from hardware. Migration is useful for:

- Load balancing - guests can be moved to hosts with lower usage when a host becomes overloaded.
- Hardware failover - when hardware devices on the host start to fail, guests can be safely relocated so the host can be powered down and repaired.
- Energy saving - guests can be redistributed to other hosts and host systems powered off to save energy and cut costs in low usage periods.
- Geographic migration - guests can be moved to another location for lower latency or in serious circumstances.

Shared, networked storage is used for storing guest images. Without shared storage migration is not possible.

An offline migration suspends the guest then moves an image of the guests memory to the destination host. The guest is resumed on the destination host and the memory the guest used on the source host is freed.

The time an offline migration takes depends network bandwidth and latency. A guest with 2GB of memory should take several seconds on a 1 Gbit Ethernet link.

A live migration keeps the guest running on the source host and begins moving the memory without stopping the guest. All modified memory pages are tracked and sent to the destination after the image is sent. The memory is updated with the changed pages. The process continues until it reaches some heuristic; either it successfully copied all the pages over, or the source is changing too fast and the destination host cannot make progress. If the heuristic is met the guest is briefly paused on the source host and the registers and buffers are sent. The registers are loaded on the new host and the guest is then resumed on the destination host. If the guest cannot be merged (which happens when guests are under extreme loads) the guest is paused and then an offline migration is started instead.

The time an offline migration takes depends network bandwidth and latency as well as activity on the guest. If the guest is using significant I/O or CPU the migration will take much longer.

MAC Addresses

> The Media Access Control Address is the hardware address for a Network Interface Controller. In the context of virtualization MAC addresses must be generated for virtual network interfaces with each MAC on your local domain being unique.

Para-virtualization

> Para-virtualization uses a special kernel, sometimes referred to as the Xen kernel or the kernel-xen package. Para-virtualized guest kernels are run concurrently on the host while using the host's libraries and devices. A para-virtualized installation can have complete access to all devices on the system which can be limited with security settings (SELinux and file controls). Para-virtualization is faster than full virtualization. Para-virtualization can effectively be used for load balancing, provisioning, security and consolidation advantages.
>
> As of Fedora 9 a special kernel will no longer be needed. Once this patch is accepted into the main Linux tree all Linux kernels after that version will have para-virtualization enabled or available.

Para-virtualized

> See *Para-virtualization*,

Para-virtualized drivers

> Para-virtualized drivers are device drivers that operate on fully virtualized Linux guests. These drivers greatly increase performance of network and block device I/O for fully virtualized guests.

Security Enhanced Linux

> Short for Security Enhanced Linux, SELinux uses Linux Security Modules (LSM) in the Linux kernel to provide a range of minimum privilege required security policies.

Universally Unique Identifier

> A Universally Unique Identifier (UUID) is a standardized numbering method for devices, systems and certain software objects in distributed computing environments. Types of UUIDs in virtualization include: ext2 and ext3 file system identifiers, RAID device identifiers, iSCSI and LUN device identifiers, MAC addresses and virtual machine identifiers.

Virtualization

> Virtualization is a board computing term for running software, usually operating systems, concurrently and isolated from other programs on one system. Most existing implementations of virtualization use a hypervisor, a software layer on top

of an operating system, to abstract hardware. The hypervisor allows multiple operating systems to run on the same physical system by giving the guest operating system virtualized hardware. There are various methods for virtualizing operating systems:

- Hardware-assisted virtualization is the technique used for full virtualization with Xen and KVM (definition: *Full virtualization*)
- Para-virtualization is a technique used by Xen to run Linux guests (definition: *Para-virtualization*)
- Software virtualization or emulation. Software virtualization uses binary translation and other emulation techniques to run unmodified operating systems. Software virtualization is significantly slower than hardware-assisted virtualization or para-virtualization.

Virtualized CPU

A system has a number of virtual CPUs (VCPUs) relative to the number of physical processor cores. The number of virtual CPUs is finite and represents the total number of virtual CPUs that can be assigned to guest virtual machines.

Virtual machines

A virtual machine is a software implementation of a physical machine or programming language (for example the Java Runtime Environment or LISP). Virtual machines in the context of virtualization are operating systems running on virtualized hardware.

Xen

Fedora supports the Xen hypervisor and the KVM hypervisor (refer to Kernel-based Virtual Machine). Both hypervisors have different architectures and development approaches. The Xen hypervisor runs underneath a Linux operating system which acts as a host managing system resources and virtualization APIs. The host is sometimes referred to as as *dom0* or Domain0.

Xen Full Virtualization Architecture
With the para-virtualized drivers

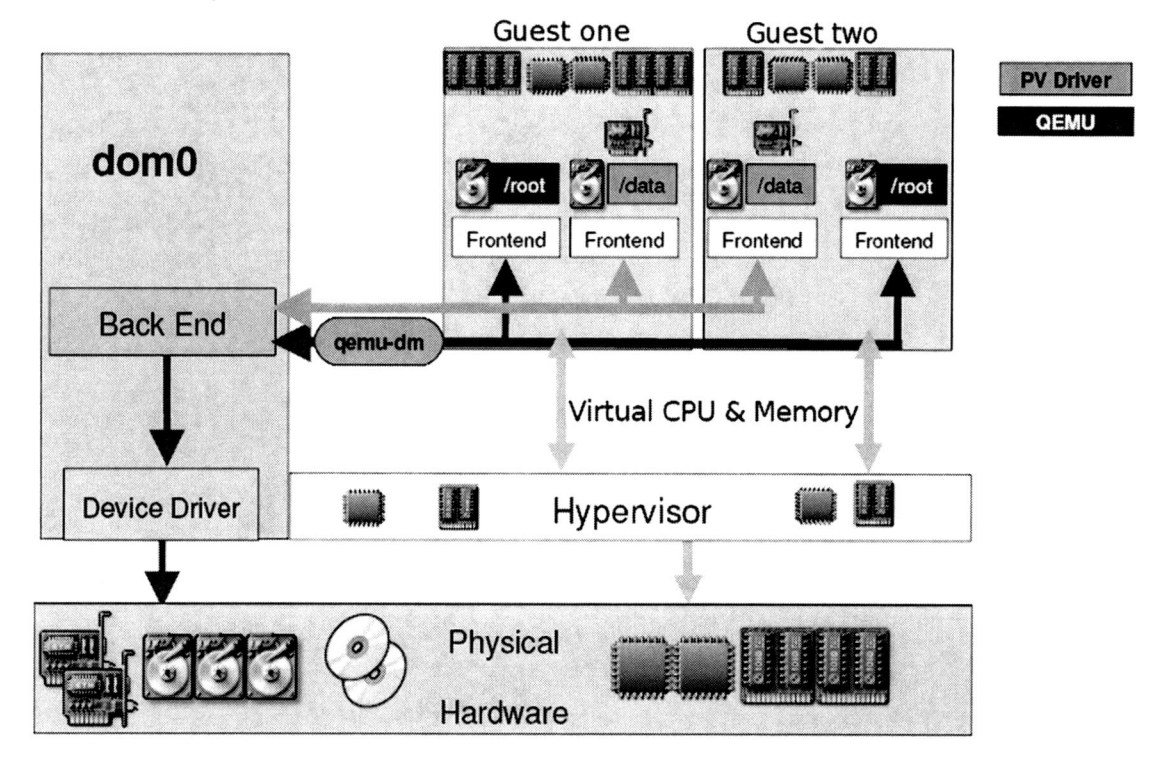

Xen Para-virtualization Architecture

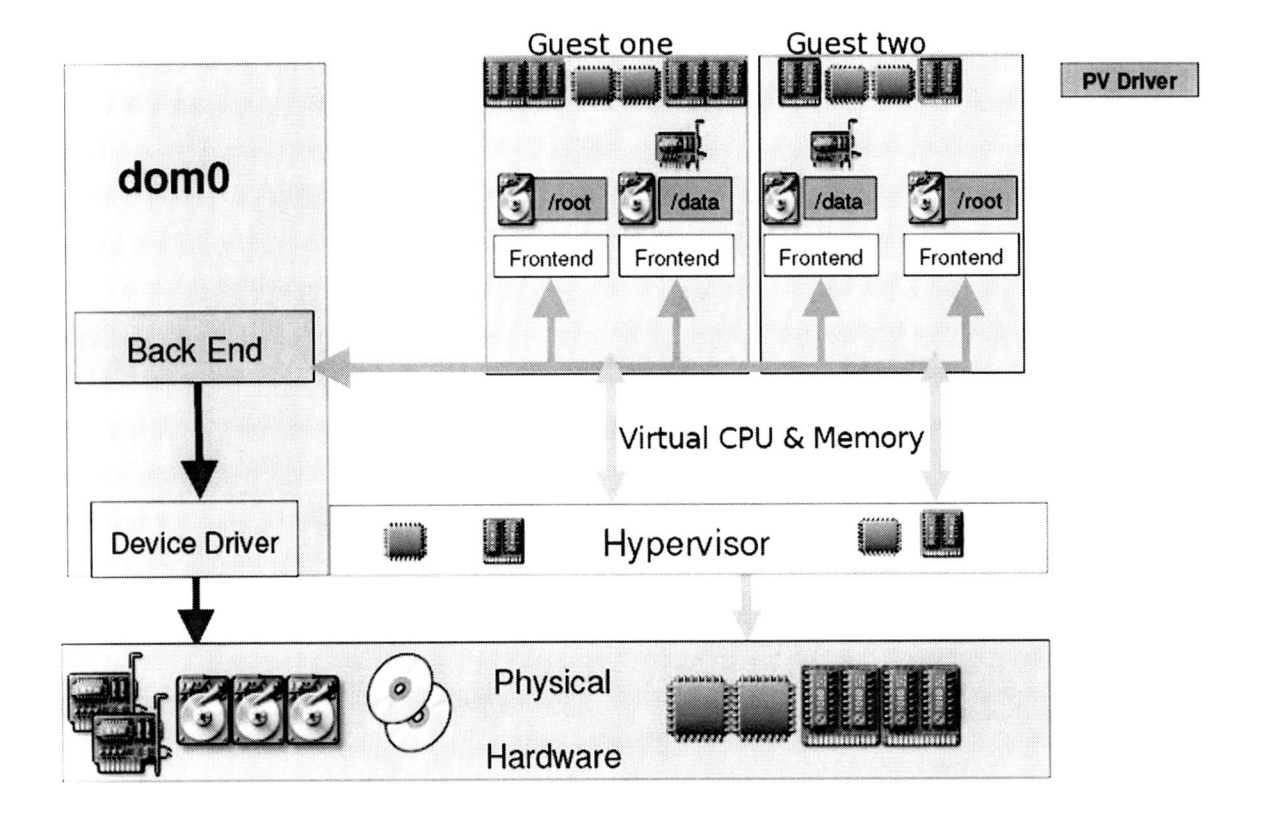

Fedora 12
Official Documentation Collection

Title	Author	Edition	ISBN-10	ISBN-13
Fedora 12 Installation Guide	Fedora Documentation Project	paperback	1-59682-179-5	978-1-59682-179-8
		eBook (pdf)	1-59682-184-1	978-1-59682-184-2
Fedora 12 User Guide	Fedora Documentation Project	paperback	1-59682-180-9	978-1-59682-180-4
		eBook (pdf)	1-59682-185-X	978-1-59682-185-9
Fedora 12 Security Guide	Fedora Documentation Project	paperback	1-59682-181-7	978-1-59682-181-1
		eBook (pdf)	1-59682-186-8	978-1-59682-186-6
Fedora 12 SE Linux User Guide	Fedora Documentation Project	paperback	1-59682-182-5	978-1-59682-182-8
		eBook (pdf)	1-59682-187-6	978-1-59682-187-3
Fedora 12 Virtualization Guide	Fedora Documentation Project	paperback	1-59682-183-3	978-1-59682-183-5
		eBook (pdf)	1-59682-188-4	978-1-59682-188-0
http://www.linbrary.com					

CPSIA information can be obtained at www.ICGtesting.com
Printed in the USA
LVOW110745030812

292487LV00003B/312/P